## Praise for *100 Places in Italy Every Woman Should Go*

"This book makes me want to pack my bag with the lightest of clothing and follow Susan Van Allen's alluring suggestions for traveling in Italy. Her knowledge reveals an intimacy with the country and a honed sense of adventure. Andiamo!"

—Frances Mayes, author of *Under the Tuscan Sun*

"Susan Van Allen might be the best girlfriend you never met...a virtual passport to a girl-friendly ride up and down the boot."

—*Pittsburgh Tribune*

"A wonderful gift for any woman traveling to Italy. With Susan's advice you won't be overwhelmed and you'll discover how nurturing it is to travel in a country that has honored us since we all descended from Venus."

—Marybeth Bond, author, *Gutsy Women* and
*Best Girlfriend Getaways Worldwide*

"One of the most innovative and fascinating travel guides dedicated to Italy...It fills a gap on the shelves at the right time. No ordinary directory of addresses, *100 Places in Italy Every Woman Should Go* is an authentic portrait of Italy from the charmed perspective of a woman, a writer and an experienced traveler."

—*Select Italy*

"I knew that Italy was the land of *la dolce vita* and *far niente*, but this is the first book to present an organized way to find your way through her earthly and soulful wonders. I want all my girlfriends to have a copy of *100 Places*."

—Camille Cusumano, editor of *Italy, a Love Story*

"Susan Van Allen's writing makes the magic of Italy jump off the page. She has a knack for capturing the charms, quirks and authenticity of this magnificent land. Don't go to Italy without reading this!"

—Kathy McCabe, editor and publisher,
*Dream of Italy Travel Newsletter*

"No matter how many times you've been to Italy and think you know it, reading Susan Van Allen's book almost guarantees a return trip...a delightful book you'll only put down long enough to check the flights to that fascinating country."

—Carol Coviello-Malzone, author of
*Flavors of Rome: How, What & Where to Eat in the Eternal City*

## Males Weigh In:

"Part guidebook, part history, and part manual to the good life in the land of La Dolce Vita, Susan Van Allen's magnum opus on all things Italian is essential reading for women (and men) who either want to get the most out of their next trip or want to be spirited back to their last."

—David Farley, author of *An Irreverent Curiosity*

"That old Freudian chestnut—'What do women really want?!' has been answered once again. Susan Van Allen has romped through Italy and picked the very best, mixing dreamy delights with drops of dainty decadence. She suggests readers: "treat this book like a cookbook...and make a full meal of it." ...you could—and you should."

—David Yeadon, author of *Seasons in Basilicata*

# 100 Places in Italy Every Woman Should Go

### Third Edition

SUSAN VAN ALLEN

TRAVELERS' TALES
AN IMPRINT OF SOLAS HOUSE, INC.
PALO ALTO

Travelers' Tales and Solas House are trademarks of Solas House, Inc., 2320 Bowdoin Street, Palo Alto, CA 94306. www.travelerstales.com

Cover Design: Kimberly Nelson Coombs
Author Photograph: Johanna Jacobson
Interior Design and Page Layout: Howie Severson/Fortuitous
Production Director: Susan Brady

**Library of Congress Cataloging-in-Publication Data**

Names: Van Allen, Susan, author.
Title: 100 places in Italy every woman should go / Susan Van Allen.
Other titles: One hundred places in Italy every woman should go | Hundred places in Italy every woman should go
Description: Third edition. | Palo Alto : Travelers' Tales, an imprint of Solas House, Inc., 2016.
Identifiers: LCCN 2016021830 (print) | LCCN 2016023100 (ebook) | ISBN 9781609521219 (paperback) | ISBN 9781609521226 (epub)
Subjects: LCSH: Italy--Guidebooks. | Women--Travel--Italy--Guidebooks. | Women travelers--Italy--Guidebooks. | BISAC: TRAVEL / Europe / Italy.
Classification: LCC DG416 .V36 2016 (print) | LCC DG416 (ebook) | DDC 914.504/9312--dc23
LC record available at https://lccn.loc.gov/2016021830

Third Edition
Printed in the United States
10 9 8 7 6 5 4 3 2 1

*To my mother*
*who opened the door to Italy*
*and always told me:*
*"Do what you love!"*

*Whenever I go anywhere but Italy for a vacation,*
*I always feel as if I have made a mistake.*
—ERICA JONG

# Table of Contents

*Introduction to the Third Edition*                                 xv

*Preface*                                                          xvii

SECTION I
THE DIVINE: GODDESSES, SAINTS, AND
THE BLESSED VIRGIN MARY                                             I

  1. The Campidoglio, Roman Forum, and Palatine Hill      7
  2. The Pietà, Saint Peter's Basilica—Rome               12
  3. Santa Maria Churches—Rome                            15
  4. Churches Dedicated to Female Saints—Rome             21
  5. Bernini's Beautiful Broads and the Galleria
    Borghese—Rome                                27
  6. Venuses, Madonnas, and Judith at the Uffizi—
    Florence                                      31
  7. Santa Maria Novella—Florence                         37
  8. Annunciations—Florence                               42
  9. Mary's Sacred Girdle and Salome Dancing—Prato,
    Tuscany                                       45
 10. Museum of the Madonna del Parto—Monterchi,
    Tuscany                                       49
 11. City of Saint Catherine—Siena, Tuscany                    52
 12. Town of Saint Margaret—Cortona, Tuscany                   56
 13. Santa Maria Churches—Venice                               59

14. Madonnas by Titian, Bellini, and Tintoretto–Venice     63
15. The Scrovegni Chapel–Padua, Veneto                     66
16. Venus of the Beautiful Buttocks and Other Museo
    Archeologico Nazionale Treasures–Naples               69
17. Cloister of Santa Chiara–Naples                        73
18. Cave of the Cumaean Sibyl–Cumae, Campania              76
19. Goddesses and Madonnas–Palermo                        79
20. Nymphs, Goddesses, and Santa Lucias–
    Ortygia, Sicily                                        83
21. Temple of Segesta–Sicily                               86

## Section II
### Ville, Palazzi, and an Apartment

                                                           89

22. Palazzo Barberini–Rome                                 93
23. Villa Farnesina–Rome                                   96
24. The Costume Gallery at the Pitti Palace–Florence       99
25. Casa Guidi–Florence                                   102
26. The Peggy Guggenheim Collection–Venice                106
27. Palazzo Fortuny–Venice                                110
28. Villa Valmarana Ai Nani–Vicenza, Veneto               113
29. Palazzo Ducale–Mantua, Lombardy                       117
30. The Royal Apartments in Palazzo Reale–Turin,
    Piedmont                                              120
31. Oplontis–Torre Annunziata, Campania                   124
32. Villa Romana del Casale–Sicily                        127

## Section III
### Gardens

                                                          131

33. Villa d'Este–Tivoli, Lazio                            135
34. The Park of the Monsters–Bomarzo, Lazio               138
35. Gardens Outside Florence–Tuscany                      141
36. The Tarot Garden–Capalbio, Tuscany                    146

37. Villa Cimbrone–Ravello, Campania 150
38. Parchi di Nervi–Liguria 153
39. Gardens of the Isole Borromee–Piedmont 156
40. Giardino della Minerva–Salerno, Campania 160

SECTION SECTION IV
BEACHES 163

41. Sperlonga, Lazio 167
42. Forte dei Marmi–Tuscany 169
43. Sirolo–Marche 171
44. Positano–Amalfi Coast 173
45. Parghelia–Calabria 175
46. Santa Teresa di Gallura–Sardinia 177
47. Scopello–Sicily 179

SECTION V
BEAUTY TREATMENTS AND SPAS 181

48. Hair Salons and Spas 185
49. Spas–Viterbo, Lazio 188
50. Spas–Tuscany 191
51. Grand Hotel Abano Terme–Veneto 195
52. Spas–Ischia, Campania 198
53. Masseria Torre Maizza–Puglia 202
54. Hammam–Palermo, Sicily 205

SECTION VI
INDULGE YOUR TASTEBUDS 207

55. Caffès 211
56. Gelato 216
57. Chocolate 219
58. Wine Bars 224

59. Women-Owned Wineries                                    228

SECTION VII
SHOPPING                                                    235

60. Shoes                                                   239
61. Leather                                                 243
62. Ceramics                                                247
63. Jewelry                                                 252
64. Fragrances                                              257
65. Lingerie                                                261
66. Embroidery and Lace                                     264
67. Paper                                                   268
68. Milan                                                   271
69. Antique Markets                                         275

SECTION VIII
ACTIVE ADVENTURES                                           279

70. Biking                                                  283
71. Hiking                                                  286
72. Skiing                                                  290
73. Boating                                                 293
74. Yoga                                                    297

SECTION IX
COOKING CLASSES                                             301

75. Cooking in Rome                                         305
76. Morning at the Market—Florence                          308
77. Cooking with Chef Patrizia—Venice                       311
78. Cook in Milano                                          314
79. Tuscan Women Cook—Montefollonico, Tuscany               316
80. Mamma Agata Cooking School—Ravello                      319
81. Cooking in Tropea—Calabria                              322

SECTION X
LEARN ITALIAN CRAFTS AND CULTURE                      325

  82. Mosaics at Cassio Workshop—Rome            329
  83. Florentine Crafts                          332
  84. Maskmaking at Tragicomica—Venice           336
  85. International School of Ceramic Art—Deruta,
      Umbria                                  339
  86. Landscape Painting—Buonconvento, Tuscany   342
  87. Giuditta Brozzetti Weaving and Embroidery
      Workshop—Perugia, Umbria                345
  88. Art Restoration Workshop—Puglia            348
  89. Italian Language Classes                   351


SECTION XI
BE ENTERTAINED                                        355

  90. Opera                                      359
  91. Classical Music                            363
  92. Jazz                                       366
  93. Puppet Shows                               370


SECTION XII
ADVICE FROM WRITERS                                   373

  94. Frances Mayes                              377
  95. Sarah Dunant                               380
  96. Marcella Hazan                             383
  97. Mary Taylor Simeti                         385


SECTION XIII
LA FAMIGLIA EXPERIENCES                               389

  98. Places for Children                        393

99.  An Italian Wedding                                      397
100.  Go Find Your Mammas                                    400


*Appendix 1: Tips for Italian Travel*                        403

*Appendix 2: Budget Travel Tips*                             407

*Appendix 3: Packing*                                        412

*Favorite Restaurants*                                       415

*Calendar of Madonna Holidays and Female Saints' Feast Days* 417

*Online Resources*                                           419

*Index*                                                      423

*Acknowledgments*                                            438

*About the Author*                                           441

# Introduction to the Third Edition

Wonderful surprises have come since the first edition of *100 Places in Italy Every Woman Should Go* hit the bookshelves in 2009. My world has been brightened by hearing from travelers far and wide that this book brought them new discoveries and added fun to their vacations. I've met women who've handed me their dog-eared copies with ecstatic reports: *"The Tarot Garden was amazing!" "Look at the necklace I bought at Angela Caputi's in Florence!" "My daughters and I went to all your chick churches in Rome!"*

The response for femme-focused travel in Italy has inspired me to custom design and host Golden Weeks, For Women Only Tours. It's been thrilling to introduce groups of wonderful women to special places and people I love, to share the pleasures of art, cooking classes, and spas, and to see friendships form over our long dinners, that flourish beyond our times together in Bell'Italia.

Going back in to refresh and embellish each of my original 100 entries has been a pleasure. As I continue my travels, my experience expands, so I'm happy to add more tips for my chosen sites, more immersion experiences—such as learning to row Venetian style and an Art Restoration Workshop in Puglia. What a joy it is to continue my research of artisan shops and spas, which thickened up my coverage of the fabulous *terme* in Tuscany and on the island of Ischia. And since I'm always asked for restaurant advice, in this edition I've slipped in a short list of favorites—places where delicious, memorable meals await.

As the beautiful journey continues, let's keep in touch through www.susanvanallen.com and the ever-expanding channels our world of social media brings us.

With heartfelt gratitude to all you readers and travelers, I send you all my best wishes for your adventures in Italy.

—SUSAN VAN ALLEN

# Preface

I fell in love with Italy at a dining room table in Newark, New Jersey. It was Nana and Papa's dining room, my maternal grandparents—immigrants from Southern Italy. The walls were painted in a pale-rose stenciled pattern, the table spread with an ivory-colored lace cloth. On the mahogany sideboard sat a soccer-ball-sized jar of wild cherries marinating in syrup, next to a Capodimonte lamp, with porcelain figures of fancy ladies in flouncy dresses fanning themselves under the shade. A soprano on the hi-fi sang "*Un Bel Di Vedremo*"—"One Beautiful Day We'll See Each Other."

Nana, with her apron tied up under her marshmallow-baggie arms, lit the candles. My mother and aunts carried in platters heavy with mozzarella, roasted peppers, shiny black olives, steaming bowls of macaroni. I sat propped up on a telephone book, clinking my tumbler of half-red wine/half-water along with the grown-ups toasting, "*Salute!*" By the time the feasts were finished, the candles had burnt to their bottoms, dripping onto the lace cloth. Papa poured Strega, a golden liqueur, into curvy glasses, and sliced a dome-shaped, slathered-with-whipped-cream rum cake.

This was my first Italy: a big, delicious, loving heart.

Every August Papa would get on a ship to visit his sisters who still lived near Naples. He'd send back postcards of statues and churches. He'd return after Labor Day with beads from Venice, rosaries blessed by the Pope, rocks from Mount Vesuvius.

Italy became magical and mysterious, beckoning me—a billowy cartoon finger wafting out of a pot of bubbling tomato sauce.

When I got there for the first time in 1976, I arrived in Roma Termini with a pack on my back and a bursting anticipation. The trip was a sweltering August blur of standing awestruck in the Sistine Chapel, tasting my first gelato, getting my bottom pinched. Naturally there was romance: on the train I'd met a *bel ragazzo* named Luciano who'd sat across from me in the compartment. We fell madly in love for forty-eight hours and rendezvoused in the Forum: moonlight, a Chianti bottle with a straw-covered bottom, two nineteen-year-olds singing Beatles songs to each other.

Feeling transformed into a woman of the world, I headed to my Roman cousins where I was embraced with smothering-lovering and seated at their dining room table, coming full circle to my childhood Italy.

The spell was cast. Italy grabbed hold of my heart forever. Over these many years it's drawn me back, again and again.

Tonight as I'm sitting here in an apartment on Rome's Piazza Paradiso, way past bedtime, even for Italy, I'm realizing there's been absolutely no logic to my times here. The trips started off with visits to the major sights in the big cities, but then out went the plans, and instinct flung me to such spots as a classroom near Rome's Colosseum where I struggled to tackle the subjunctive, a quiet farm road in Puglia surrounded by old olive trees, dancing at the Excelsior in Florence with my husband one New Year's Eve.

I became the "girlfriend with the lists"—scribbling down places I'd loved visiting and passing them along to my traveling pals. If I was back in the States counting the days till my next trip, I lived in Italy vicariously—knowing that Babs was in Rome seeing all those provocative Bernini sculptures with my notes in hand, Sheila at a glove shop in Florence, Louise drinking wine at my favorite *bacaro* in Venice.

When the opportunity to write this book came along, so did elation, gratitude, and then a freezing panic. How could I choose 100 out of the infinite pleasures I'd experienced in Bell'Italia? So let's just get the most obvious fact out of the way: there are more places than any one book could hold. I've even left out some of the most obvious—such as the Sistine Chapel, Pisa, and Michelangelo's *David*—things well covered in other guidebooks.

In these pages, I'm sharing with you some places from my list of favorites, along with those my savvy Italian and American friends have raved to me about. I've put a spotlight on goddesses, the Madonna, female saints, beauties who've inspired masterpieces, women who've taken power. After all, isn't the fact that women have been worshipped here for thousands of years one of the reasons we love Italy so much? Though in modern times females haven't yet triumphed as far as business and political realms go, as Luigi Barzini in *The Italians* says: "Men run the country, but women run men." Here where *la famiglia* is the power source, women are at the core of it.

What about your male traveling partners? They're likely to enjoy a lot of these places, too, whether it's a museum, beach, or spots for adventure and learning. Okay, the guys probably won't be into buying lace in Rapallo, but they'll certainly enjoy Venus of the Beautiful Buttocks in Naples!

Italy seduces both sexes, with irresistibly feminine appeals. Shaped like a boot we'd love to strut around in, she transforms herself as she transforms travelers. She's the nurturing mama, the drop-dead-gorgeous vixen, the compassionate spirit. She's even the unreliable girlfriend who exasperates you with travel snafus, but you forgive her because she's so darn charming. She's constantly coaxing, "Come on, lighten up and enjoy my beauties and flavors."

Treat this book like a cookbook. What do you want a taste of? Botticelli's *Birth of Venus*? The best chocolate in Rome? A ceramic painting class in Deruta? A wine therapy spa treatment in the Veneto? Allow your mood to be your guide, savoring the experience Italian style, letting it unfold with an unhurried Old World pace.

To make a full meal of it, I've included suggestions for "Golden Days"—matching a place to a nearby restaurant, just like I do when I send out lists to girlfriends. These are only suggestions, because each of us has our own deeply personal experience of encountering Italy.

But as unique as each encounter is, I'm amazed at always hearing, even from travelers without a drop of Italian blood in them, the same words: "It felt like home." Home, in the sweeping sense of a place that brings peace and comfort, a place that stirs the soul.

For me, Italy brings back that childhood dining room table feeling. It sneaks up on me now, looking out the window of this apartment in late-night Rome. There's a light shining on a little Madonna altar across the way, her robe the same rose as those dining room walls. Out of the shadows, from a nearby restaurant, comes a dark-haired *signorina*, walking as if she absolutely knows she's a descendant of Venus, with her Adonis—a *bel ragazzo* in a leather jacket—linked to her side. They stop for a smooch under the Madonna, pressing up against each other as if this was their last night on earth.

Italy, once again, playing an endless beautiful song.

My wish for you is to enjoy her many places of pleasure, wherever your desires lead you to go.

—SUSAN VAN ALLEN
ROME

Valle d'Aosta

Trentino-Alto Adige

Lombardia

Veneto

Friuli-Venezia Giulia

Piemonte

Emilia-Romagna

Liguria

Toscano

Marche

Umbria

Abruzzo

Lazio

Molise

Puglia

Campania

Sardegna

Basilicata

Calabria

THE TWENTY
REGIONS
OF ITALY

Sicilia

# I

The Divine:
Goddesses, Saints,
and the Blessed
Virgin Mary

Italy begins with **Venus—Goddess of Love, Beauty, Fertility, and Sexual Healing**. She's that gorgeous divine gal you'll see posed naked all over the country.

The Ancient Romans believed they were her chosen descendants. It was Venus who seduced a Greek mortal and thus became the great grandmother of Romulus and Remus, those twins suckled by a she-wolf on Rome's Palatine Hill who founded the Eternal City.

Her presence is eternal. If you have doubts, watch Italian women striding down the *via*, knowing that spark of Venus lives inside them.

Moving from Pagan to Christian times, churches honoring the **Blessed Virgin Mary (aka the BVM)** were built smack over Venus's temples. Mary is everywhere: dangling off taxicab mirrors, popping out of alleyway altars, wowing you in masterpieces.

*Madonna Mia!* Two divine females embody the essential spirit of Italy.

* Italy is Venus: Country of beauty, freedom, mercurial passions, surprising possibilities.
* Italy is Mary: Country of motherly love, compassion, serenity.

With those two adored beauties and many more goddesses and saints surrounding you, go and have a divine time exploring...

## Mythology 101

You'll be seeing goddesses all over Italy, so here are clues to identify Who's Who.

**Venus** (Goddess of Love and Beauty), is easiest to recognize, as she's usually nude or scantily draped.

Other goddesses that made up Ancient Rome's Big Six (Worshipped **equally** alongside six major gods) are:

**Juno** (Jupiter's Queen and Goddess of Marriage) dressed like a soldier for her job of protecting the finances of the Romans.

**Minerva** (Virgin Goddess of Rome, Wisdom, and War) with her helmet and spear.

**Ceres** (Goddess of Agriculture, Motherhood, and Patron of Sicily) holding a cornucopia of wheat.

**Diana** (Virgin Goddess of the Hunt and the Moon) carrying bows and arrows, with a moon crowning her.

**Vesta** (Goddess of Hearth and Home) veiled, surrounded by her perpetual flame.

## Mary's Rites of Passage 101

Italian artists wore down paintbrushes and chisels to express the divine human nature of the Blessed Virgin Mary (BVM). In their masterpieces, they created scenes from this heroine's journey to show experiences that could mirror our life experiences. Some scenes are familiar, others may be less so:

**Presentation in The Temple:** She accepts her fate. Three-year-old Mary, brought to the temple by her parents, dances up the steps.

**Annunciation:** She receives the announcement that the Divine is within her. Angel Gabriel swoops in to tell the virgin she's pregnant with the Son of God.

**Visitation:** She shares the miraculous news. Pregnant Mary visits her cousin Elizabeth, who was way beyond childbearing years, but pregnant with John the Baptist.

**Nativity:** She becomes the loving mother.

**Assumption:** She triumphs. Mary dies and rises body and soul to be crowned queen of heaven.

# 1 The Campidoglio, Roman Forum, and Palatine Hill

YOU'LL NEVER FORGET YOUR FIRST TIME. You'll be walking along or speeding in a cab from the airport and then will appear...the Colosseum...the Arco di Tito...the whole glorious spread of jaw-dropping triumph and ruin.

It's a place to let your imagination run wild. Picture women rattling tambourines in torch-lit processions, chariots carrying tanned muscular men in togas to the baths.

Goddesses' temples, Empresses' tombs, and churches dedicated to the Virgin Mary are all to be discovered in the thousand-plus years of history that surrounds you. It's impossible to absorb it all in one shot. Hiring a good guide is best since hardly any of the sculptures and ruins are marked. Or just stroll around and surrender to your fantasies.

Here are some places where women take center stage:

## The Campidoglio

The Michelangelo-designed piazza is a perfect place to begin, where Minerva (just behind Marcus Aurelius) sits on a throne holding her mighty spear. To either side of her are the Capitoline Museums, packed with sculptures of characters who once roamed the area surrounding you.

In the Palazzo Nuovo (museum to the left of Minerva) head to the first-floor hallway to see The Capitoline Venus. She's featured in a sunlit niche, posed as Venus *Pudica* (modest Venus), with one hand over her breast, the other covering her Cupid's cloister. Yes, she's modest, but also teasing, as if to say: "Look what I'm hiding…"

Venus was the deity who flitted from passion to passion. She was married to Vulcan, God of Fire, but even the best couple's counselor couldn't have kept this beauty tied to that angry, crippled god. Venus had hot affairs with Mars (God of War), the devastatingly handsome Adonis, and disguised herself as a mortal for trysts with men she found attractive. Every year she bathed herself in the sea from which she was born to renew her virginity.

In the same hallway, you'll see a statue of a **Roman Woman Dressed As Venus** (hardly dressed), proving how closely Romans associated themselves with the Goddess. The Roman woman breaks out of the Modest Venus pose, standing proud and naked with one hand on her hip. For a laugh further down the hall, check out the **Drunken Old Woman**, who's crouched, laughing, and guzzling a jug of wine.

## The Roman Forum

Here in the ongoing archaeological excavation, is the **Temple of the Vestal Virgins**, now rows of pillars with remains of female statues.

The Cult of Vesta, Goddess of Hearth and Home, was the oldest of the ancient world. Some say this cult still exists in modern Italy, where *la famiglia* remains the country's core.

The Vestals were young girls (between the ages of six and ten), who were put in charge of guarding and leading the worship at Vesta's temple. The upside for the virgins, in a time when women didn't have that much freedom, was that they could come and go as they pleased and got perks all over town, like special seats at games and festivals. The downside was gruesome: if they let Vesta's flame go out they'd be flogged and if they had sex with anyone they'd be buried alive.

## The Palatine Hill

Walking up from the Forum, you come to this pretty and serene place, where Romulus (great grandson of Venus) chose to begin the city. It went on to become the Beverly Hills of Ancient Rome, where noble palaces were built. In the sixteenth century the Farnese family created gardens here, so you can wander through rows of boxwood shrubs, cypress trees, laurel and rose bushes, and enjoy lovely views of the sights below.

As for the palaces, the **House of Augustus** and **Casa di Livia** (Livia's House) are open to the public with special reservations. In Livia's house, you'll be treated to a vast arched space with frescos of vibrant garlands, symbols of Augustus's victories. The Palatine is a great place to fantasize about the grand days of Livia and Augustus, who ruled Rome for forty-five years, bringing the city into its Golden Age.

Back in 39 B.C., just after Julius Caesar's assassination, Livia was a beautiful nineteen-year-old, married to the much older Tiberius Claudius Nero, and pregnant with their sec-ond child. Along came Octavius, a rising star on the military scene, married with a pregnant wife. Octavius fell in love with Livia, divorced his wife the day she gave birth, and married the pregnant Livia. Livia's old husband gave her away at the ceremony, even throwing in a dowry. It turned out to be a good political move for all involved and in those days the citizenry didn't even blink over it.

Octavius became Emperor Caesar Augustus and ruled Rome with his perfect mate Livia, who took charge of all the biz at home when he set off to conquer distant lands. Livia was an exemplary Roman wife. She was famously chaste, "worked wool" (made her husband's togas), and never showed off with fancy jewelry or dress. The couple lived simply here throughout their fifty-one years of marriage, with Livia putting up with philandering Augustus, who was known for his S&M exploits. Together they revived Rome, restoring monuments in the Forum and building new ones throughout the city.

Livia's become famous in fiction, particularly through Robert Graves' *I Claudius*, where she's portrayed as a conniving woman who poisoned potential heirs to make sure her family line would inherit the throne. Whatever version of the story you believe; Livia's descendants did end up ruling Rome. She died at the ripe old age of eighty-six and was honored as Diva Augusta. Her image was revered in the streets that surround you, carried in celebrations by elephant-drawn carriages.

To get a more vivid experience of Livia's lifestyle, head to the **Palazzo Massimo alle Terme**, near the Termini station. The entire garden room of her suburban villa has been moved to the top floor of this museum, so you can stand in the midst of amazing frescos that feature a harmonious, abundant landscape of trees, flowers, and birds.

**TIPS:** *Don't go to the Forum between 10 A.M. and 2 P.M., the heaviest tourist times. The museums, on the other hand, are rarely crowded, and in addition to the Palazzo Nuovo, the Palatine Museum, with its mosaics and sculptures, is a good choice. To avoid lines, you can make reservations in advance and also get tickets for the House of Augustus and Casa di Livia at www.coopculture.it*

**Capitoline Museums**: Tuesday through Sunday. 9:30-7:30 (www.turismoroma.it). **Roman Forum and Palatine Hill**: Daily 8:30 until one hour before sunset. Check the website for opening times of House of Augustus and Casa di Livia. (www.coopculture.it). **Palazzo**

**Massimo alle Terme**: Largo di Villa Peretti 1 (near Termini), Tuesday-Sunday 9-7:30, www.archeoromabeniculturali.it.

❧

**Golden Day**: Time your visit so you'll be on the **Palatine Hill** at sunset, then head to **Terre e Domus Enoteca della Provincia** for an *aperitivo*. This is an excellent restaurant and wine bar that features products of the Lazio region, facing Trajan's Column. (Via Foro Traiano 82, 066 994 0273, lunch and dinner reservations essential, open daily 9 A.M.-midnight).

### TOURS

For the best guided small group tours, contact **Context Travel** at www.contexttravel.com.

### RECOMMENDED READING

*A Traveler in Rome* by H. V. Morton

*SPQR, A History of Ancient Rome* by Mary Beard

# 2 The Pietà, Saint Peter's Basilica—Rome

YOU'LL FEEL THE PULL OF THE greatest sculpture ever made as soon as you enter the doors of Saint Peter's. It's over there, to your right. Where the cameras are flashing. Where tourists are posing. Where among the crowd there is at least one nun. Get close: the *Pietà*. *Pietà* means pity. And compassion.

Has compassion ever looked more beautiful? How did Michelangelo make marble flow? How did he capture such grace and serenity in Mary's face?

Michelangelo modeled the face of Mary after his mother: his mother who died when he was six.

He got all kinds of criticism for it. "Mary looks too young," people said. "If she has a thirty-three-year-old son, she's gotta be at least forty-five."

And Michelangelo said: "A woman so pure of body and soul is eternally young."

He was twenty-two, in 1498, when French Cardinal Jean de Bilheres, thinking ahead, commissioned Michelangelo to sculpt it for his tomb. The Cardinal gave him 450 papal ducats. Not that Michelangelo cared much about money. He slept in his clothes in his studio; got his nose broken in drunken street brawls.

After he signed the contract, Michelangelo took off to Carrara in Tuscany to pick out the best piece of marble for the *Pietà*. He believed "Every block of stone has a statue inside of it and it is the task of the sculptor to discover it, to free the form from the stone."

Michelangelo was supposed to have the ***Pietà*** done in 1500, for the Holy Year. But when the pilgrims came through, he was still working on it. They stood back and watched Michelangelo free the form from the stone. *Can you imagine?* They thought it was amazing— divine grace made flesh. They went back home spreading the word.

When it was finally unveiled, Michelangelo heard visitors saying he didn't sculpt it, that another artist, Gobbo di Milano did. He got so enraged he snuck in late at night and carved his name onto Mary's sash. It was the only work he ever signed. He always regretted it.

This is one of the many masterpieces in Italy that may hold a memory for you of the first time you saw it. Maybe it was on a post-card or a slide in art history class.

For me, each time I see it in Rome, I'm pulled back to 1964, when the *Pietà* came to New York for the World's Fair. I lined up with the crowd, my mother behind me. The Vatican Pavilion!

We stepped onto a moving walkway. I heard a chorus singing "Alleluia, Alleluia." I felt my mother's hands on my shoulder. The room was draped in blue velvet with a sparkling light over the *Pietà*.

We floated by. It was the first A-R-T that I ever saw. I was seven, the age of reason. I wondered: How could something sad be beautiful? I heard gasps. I took a long look and reasoned: Beautiful.

**Saint Peter's Basilica:** Daily 7-6:30, www.vaticanstate.va.

☙❧

**Golden Day:** See the *Pietà* and the rest of the awe-inspiring **Saint Peter's Basilica.** Have lunch at **Da Benito e Gilberto** (Via del Falco 19, 06 686 7769, reservations essential, closed Sunday and Monday), a cozy family-run place that serves great seafood. Or if a caffè or wine bar better suits your timing, head to **Sorpasso** (Via Properzio 31-33, 06 8902 4554).

**TIP**: *Best to go in the afternoon, when the lines where you are screened, ala airport security, are shorter. Avoid Wednesday mornings when there are Papal Audiences in the square...unless you want to join the crowds to see the Pope!*

## RECOMMENDED READING

*A Journey into Michelangelo's Rome* by Angela K. Nickerson

# 3

## *Santa Maria Churches—Rome*

CHRISTIANS BEGAN TO OFFICIALLY CALL MARY "Mother of God" after the Council of Ephesus in 43 B.C. That's when the devotion to her took hold in Rome, and goddesses temples were abandoned or replaced with churches. Today there are twenty-six churches in the Eternal City dedicated to Santa Maria, the Blessed Virgin Mary, aka BVM.

The grandest, largest, and oldest is the **Basilica Santa Maria Maggiore**, on the Esquiline Hill (near Termini). It was built over what was once a fertility temple, dedicated to Cybele, who Romans called *Magna Mater*—Great Mother. It's also called **The Madonna of the Snow**, because one summer night, on August 5, 359 A.D., Mary answered the prayer of Pope Liberius who had asked for a sign of where to build a church, by miraculously bringing a snowfall to this hill. Every year on August 5, white rose petals are released from the dome of the church to commemorate this event.

Inside the dazzling rectangular expanse, in the **Borghese Chapel**, is Rome's most important Marion icon: a Byzantine painting of the Virgin and Child, the *Salus Populi Romani*—Protectress of the Roman People—believed to have saved worshippers from the plague.

My favorite spot in the basilica is the ***Loggia delle Benedizioni***, which you can see by winding around past the gift shop to the museum and requesting a guide, who, (for a small fee), will lead you upstairs to view amazing thirteenth century mosaics that tell the

15

story of the Madonna of the Snow. Grand baroque angel statues adorn this loggia and the view from up here is stunning. Also, the guide is a member of the Vatican police—mine was a proud Pope's bodyguard—whose enthusiasm was exhilarating: "Look at this!" he said, taking me around the corner of the loggia to see a circular staircase. "Bernini built this when he was only sixteen! Imagine how many popes have touched this railing!"

**Basilica of Santa Maria Maggiore:** Daily 7-7.

Other favorite Santa Maria churches are:

❋ **Santa Maria and the Martyrs**
No one will know what you're talking about if you call it this, except maybe a priest. Everybody else knows it as the **Pantheon**, a fantastic monument built to honor all the Goddesses and Gods. It was consecrated in the seventh century as a church dedicated to Mary and the Martyrs.

The "Eye of God"—the humongous, uncovered circular opening at the top of the Pantheon's dome, frames the dramatic Roman sky, making the ever-changing city a part of this architectural wonder. It's fabulous near sunset. One winter I got there just before closing when a rosy cotton-candy-tinged-with-gold cloud floated across it, inspiring even one of the guards to throw his head back and sigh. It's even great in the rain, when water pours through and drains out the holes in its floor.

You also should take a moment to look at the plaque to the right of artist Raphael's tomb. On it is the name of the girl he was engaged to, Maria Bibbiena, his patron's niece. Raphael died at thirty-seven without ever marrying Maria. According to his biographer Vasari, he died from too much sex. Not with Maria, but with a baker's daughter who was his steady mistress.

**Pantheon, aka Santa Maria and the Martyrs:** Monday–Saturday 9–7:30, Sunday 9–6.

❈ **Santa Maria Sopra Minerva**

A zigzag away from the Pantheon takes you to this, Rome's only Gothic church. It's fronted by **Bernini's Elephant sculpture**; which Romans affectionately call *Pulcino* ("little chicken"). "Sopra" means "over," as the church was built over a place where there once was a temple complex devoted to Minerva and Isis (Egyptian Goddess of Fertility).

I love **Sopra Minerva's ceiling**—a vaulted expanse of dreamy blue and stars, outlined in burgundy. There's a Renaissance **Chapel of the Annunciation**, where a willowy Mary, against a gold background, is handing out dowries to young maidens, just as the Dominican friars of this church once did. The masterpiece here is the **Carafa Chapel**, painted by **Filipino Lippi**, where the BVM is surrounded by musical angels as she flies up to heaven. At the main altar is the **tomb of Saint Catherine of Siena**, a powerhouse of the fifteenth century who bravely fought to bring the Pope back to Rome from Avignon. And to the right of that main altar is **Michelangelo's *Christ Carrying the Cross***—the cover over Jesus's privates is from baroque days.

**Santa Maria Sopra Minerva:** Monday–Friday 7:30–7, Saturday–Sunday 7:30–12:30 and 3:30–7.

❈ **Santa Maria in Cosmedin**

This church, near the forum, wins for the best photo op, with the *Bocca della Verità* (Mouth of Truth) at its entrance, along with long lines of tourists unless you get there early or late in the day. The medieval legend of the big-faced disk says if a liar sticks his hand in its mouth, it'll get bitten off. Gregory Peck did a great job of faking his hand being eaten in *Roman Holiday*, and Audrey Hepburn's freaked-out yet charming reaction is a gem of a scene I replay on *You Tube* when I am Rome-sick.

**Santa Maria in Cosmedin:** Daily 9:30-6.

❋ **Santa Maria in Trastevere**
You cross the Tiber, head through a maze of narrow streets, arrive at the piazza and BAM: topping this church is a vibrant mosaic frieze of Mary nursing Jesus, surrounded by ten lamp-holding virgins.

This was built on a spot where it's believed oil spurted from the ground and flowed the entire day Jesus was born.

Over the inside altar, Mary's life story is told in Pietro Cavallini's thirteenth-century mosaics, culminating with her being crowned Queen of Heaven. It's best to get there on a sunny day, when the light bounces and sparkles off the gold background.

One of the most popular spots in the huge church is Saint Anthony's statue, surrounded by candles and covered with hand-scribbled notes, written to beg for miracles or help finding whatever's lost.

At night the piazza surrounding this Santa Maria church gets magical. The lit-up mosaic makes it seem like Mary's blessing the whole Fellini-esque scene of tourists and locals passing through or hanging around the fountain. I can never resist indulging in a caffè or Campari at the **di Marzio** to take it all in.

**Santa Maria in Trastevere:** Daily 7:30-9.

❋ **Santa Maria della Pace**
"Every moment is an opportunity for something wonderful to happen," was the baroque artists' philosophy. It's how I feel

when this church appears like a pearl tucked at the end of a cobblestoned street in one of Rome's most theatrical settings.

Maybe I love della Pace so much because its opening hours (see below) make it more elusive than the others—like an ultra-handsome guy who's hardly ever available. When your timing is right, you open the door to the small sanctuary and get a glorious blast of Raphael's frescos of four sibyls—prophetesses in flowing robes, beautifully blending grace and power.

Sibyls were brilliant older women of Greece, Italy, and Persia who studied the moon and the stars, predicting eclipses and creating the basis for astrology. Catholics adopted them, believing Cumae (the sibyl on the left) predicted the birth of Christ. In this painting, completed by Raphael's students after he died, sibyls listen to the words of swooping angels.

To the left of that fresco is a chapel designed by Michelangelo and throughout the church are paintings of events of Mary's life, from her birth to Assumption. Lots of female saints are honored here as well, including Bridget and Catherine who border Mary in the painting opposite Raphael's. Sculptures of Saints Cecilia, Agnes, and Chiara adorn the arches.

Even if Santa Maria della Pace isn't open, you'll find another treasure if you head left from the church's entrance: the **Bramante Cloister**. This was the first work Bramante did in Rome, right before he went to work on Saint Peter's Square, and shows on a smaller scale his genius for harmony.

If you take the stairs from the cloister, you can peek through the bookshop window into the church for a view of Raphael's masterpiece, which takes the edge off disappointment if the sanctuary is closed.

**Santa Maria della Pace:** Vicolo del Arco della Pace 5, Monday and Friday 10-4, Tuesday-Thursday 9-12, closed Saturday and Sunday.

※

**Golden Day**: Visit **Santa Maria Sopra Minerva** and then the **Pantheon** as the sun is setting. Have dinner at my favorite restaurant in Rome: **Armando al Pantheon** (Salita dei Crescenzi 31, 06 6880 3034, Closed Saturday night and Sunday, reservations essential, www.armandoalpantheon.it), a family-run Rome institution, that serves delicious traditional dishes—such as *Spaghetti Cacio e Pepe*, pasta with cheese and pepper, and *Abbacchio a Scottadito*, baby lamb chops.

**TIP**: *Roaming through the central areas of these churches during Mass times (Sunday mornings, Saturday evenings), is not permitted, so plan your visits accordingly.*

### RECOMMENDED READING

*A Catholic's Guide to Rome: Discovering the Soul of the Eternal City* by Frank J. Korn

# 4 Churches Dedicated to Female Saints—Rome

WOMEN OF STEADFAST CONVICTION, WHO STRUGGLED, suffered, and triumphed in Rome, were elevated to sainthood and are remembered in churches all over the Eternal City.

Some are honored in tombs, such as Saint Monica, Patron of Mothers, who spent most of her life worrying about her ne'er-do-well son, Augustine. She lived to see him change his ways and is enshrined in the church named after him, Sant' Agostino.

Some of my favorite churches dedicated to female saints are:

* **Saint Cecilia in Trastevere: Patron Saint of Singers, Composers, and Musicians**

   A quiet Trastevere *via* opens to a large landscaped courtyard, which fronts this Basilica that was built over the home where Cecilia lived and died. The courtyard is a lovely neighborhood playground—where you're bound to see mammas circling strollers around the central Roman urn and nuns chatting away after mass.

   In third century Rome, Cecilia was known as the girl who heard angelic harmonies—she could play any instrument or sing any song. She secretly swore to be a chaste Christian, but went through with a marriage her parents arranged anyway. On the wedding night, she broke the news to her husband Valerian, telling him the only way he could touch her was to become a Christian, so he ran off to get baptized. When he returned, he found their bridal chamber transformed—full of flowers and Cecilia wearing a crown of lilies and roses. This miracle swept Valerian into the faith. He made it his mission to help the poor and bury Christian martyrs, and was beheaded for his belief.

Then Cecilia was tortured for her faith, forced into a tub of boiling water in her own bathtub. She sang all through the trial and miraculously survived, so a soldier was sent in to behead her. The three slashes of his sword didn't kill her immediately; but three days later, still singing, Cecilia died.

A marble sculpture of Cecilia in her death pose, with those three slashes on her neck, is set at the church's central altar. It was sculpted by Stefano Maderno, when her tomb was opened in 1595, and her body discovered in her death pose, miraculously not decomposed after 1,200 years.

Have a seat to admire the ninth-century mosaics above the altar, where Cecilia and husband Valerian are featured on the right of Christ, in regal Byzantine style. Downstairs there's an excavation, where you can see what's believed to be Cecilia's home, and if you're lucky, you may get into the nineteenth-century glittering Neo-Byzantine mosaic crypt, where Saint Agatha and Saint Agnes are honored along with Cecilia—otherwise peek at it through the grating on the right of the main altar.

The most impressive attraction here is a thirteenth-century fresco of *The Universal Judgement* by Pietro Cavallini. It's behind the nun's choir loft, and the process of seeing it is a mini-adventure. From the outside of the church, you ring a buzzer to the left of the main entrance, and are admitted into the Benedictine nun's convent. When I visited, I was met by the elderly, stooped Sister Cecilia, (she of the wire rimmed glasses and white hairs sprouting from her chin), who shuffled ahead of me into an elevator, escorted me to the loft, and then sat murmuring Ave Marias over her plastic rosary beads, as I had the joy of experiencing the fresco all to myself.

Cavallini's masterpiece had been covered by paneling, and rediscovered in the early 1900s. It's a glorious example of Roman naturalism, that broke stiff Middle Ages form, beautifully expressing the profound emotions of Christ and the apostles, flanked by angels, elaborately winged, in shades of gold, rose, and sage. Art historians believe this was a major influence on Giotto, who went on to fresco the Scrovegni Chapel in Padua.

**Santa Cecilia in Trastevere:** Piazza Santa Cecilia, open daily 9:15-12:45, 4-6. Vespers daily at 7:15 P.M.

**TIP:** *The Cavallini fresco in Saint Cecilia's can be viewed weekday mornings from 10 A.M.-12:30 P.M, for 2.50 euro. There's a gift shop in the convent, where you can buy nun-made fruit jams and lavender sachets.*

## ❂ Saint Agnes in Agone: Patron Saint of Virgins and Girl Scouts

Don't let the word "Agone" make you think of "agony" and keep you away from this glorious Borromini-designed structure that graces the Piazza Navona with its splendid curves and towers. "Agone" comes from the Latin "Campus Agonis," meaning "the site of competitions," which is what this piazza was in the Middle Ages, when it was filled with water for boat races.

Soft baroque music pipes through the ornate, dripping-with-gold church sanctuary. To the right of the altar is a statue of Saint Agnes, set against a pale blue background, with her arms outstretched and flames lapping at her feet. It was sculpted by a pupil of Bernini, and features Agnes in a breathtaking, transcendent moment.

Back in 304, men all over Rome were hot for beautiful thirteen-year-old Agnes, but she turned them away with her sweet smile, saying she was engaged to Jesus. "Let's strip her naked and

have her walk to a whorehouse, that'll show her!" was the governor's idea to solve the problem. But miraculously, right where this church was built, Agnes' golden hair grew down to her knees to cover her up, Lady Godiva style. Totally flummoxed by the cheerful virgin, the governor had her head cut off. A chapel to the left of the altar holds Agnes's shrunken head, in an ornate silver case.

The church is the perfect place to escape the Piazza Navona hubbub and one of the few left in Rome where you can light real candles.

**Saint Agnes in Agone:** Piazza Navona, open Tuesday-Friday 9:30-12:30, 3:30-7. Sundays and Holidays: 9-1, 4-8 (www. santagneseinagone.org).

### ❀ Church of Santa Brigida a Campo de' Fiori: Patron of Scholars and Sweden

If you get to this jewel-box between four and five in the afternoon, you'll hear nuns singing vespers in sweet harmonies. They're Brigittines, the best-dressed sisters in Rome, with long gray habits and tight headpieces accented by a white band and shining red studs. They belong to an order founded by Saint Bridget of Sweden in the fourteenth century.

Bridget's famous mystical visions started coming to her when she was just a girl. She married when she was fourteen and had eight children. When her husband died, Bridget was forty-two, and she decided to follow her childhood visions by founding an order of nuns. The monastery she built became a Swedish literary center (thus her scholarly patron side), because she allowed her holy assistants to have as many books as they wanted.

Bridget came to Rome in 1349 for two reasons. One, she wanted the Pope to approve her order, and two, she'd had a vision that he'd die soon so she thought she should tell him. She met the Pope, he approved the Brigittines and then (true to Bridget's prophecy), he died four months later. Bridget stayed in Rome, living near what is now her church, and died there at the age of seventy-one.

Bridget's convent, around the corner from her church, is now the **Casa di Santa Brigida guesthouse**, run by her nuns. The downstairs rooms where the saint lived are furnished with antiques and elegant draperies, and the rooftop terrace has amazing views.

The roof of Saint Bridget's church is graced with baroque statues of Bridget and her daughter, Saint Catherine. Inside it's prettily done up in rust-colored marble and gold moldings, with frescos telling Bridget's life story. It's located right on the Michelangelo-designed **Piazza Farnese**, which features fountains made from tubs taken from the Baths of Caracalla, the harmonious façade of the Palazzo Farnese, and handsome priests passing by on their way to Vatican City.

**Golden Day**: Get to **Saint Bridget's** between 4 and 5 to hear vespers. Have a caffè or *aperitivo* right outside the door at the **Caffè Farnese**, and reserve a table for dinner at nearby **Roscioli** (Via dei Giubbonari 21/22, 06 687 5287, www.salumeriaroscioli.com, closed Sunday), for refined Roman classics.

## RECOMMENDED READING

*Saints Preserve Us!* by Sean Kelly and Rosemary Rogers

*The Pilgrim's Italy: A Travel Guide to the Saints* by James and
   Colleen Heater

# 5 Bernini's Beautiful Broads and the Galleria Borghese–Rome

YOU'D THINK THE ARTIST WHO SCULPTED the Fountain of the Four Rivers in Piazza Navona, the Triton in the Piazza Barberini, and Saint Peter's flamboyant altar would have been a wild man. But actually Gian Lorenzo Bernini took on his masterpiece work like a monk, sculpting seven hours a day, up until his death at eighty-one. He poured all his passion into his creations—sculptures of figures caught in theatrical moments that absolutely define baroque Rome.

Bernini did have one enticing affair, with Constanza Bonarelli, the wife of one of his assistants. Things heated up when Constanza started to fool around with Bernini's younger brother. Bernini flew into a violent rage, threatening to throw acid on Constanza's face and beating up that younger brother, until the Pope stepped in to put a stop to the whole deal. Bernini's *Constanza* bust is in the Bargello in Florence. With her lips slightly parted and blouse unbuttoned, it seems as though she was sculpted just before she and Bernini were going to have a good time in bed.

Bernini calmed down after Constanza, married at forty-one, and fathered eleven kids. His daily routine was morning mass at the Gesu, work-work-work, and then back to church where he prayed with the Jesuits.

Unlike Michelangelo's sculptures (such as the *Pieta* and *David*) that have a powerful meditative style, Bernini's creations seem to be formed in wax. Their robes flow, they laugh, scream, sigh, and pulse with vitality.

On the **Ponte Sant'Angelo** you'll be surrounded by the dramatic angels he designed. And in these sculptures, you'll see how Bernini captures women in climactic moments...literally:

* *Ecstasy of Saint Teresa,* **1647-1652** (Santa Maria della Vittoria, Via XX Settembre 17)

  It looks like the Carmelite Spanish nun Bernini placed in a stage-set altar is having quite an "ecstasy" as an angel pierces her with a golden shaft.

  Saint Teresa had loads of mystical visions, and wrote that this piercing left her "on fire with the love of God" and "The pain was so great that it made me moan; and yet so surpassing was the sweetness of this excessive pain that I could not wish to be rid of it." Clearly, Bernini's genius took Teresa's account and ran with it.

* *Beata Ludovica Albertoni,* **1671-1674** (San Francesco a Ripa, Piazza San Francesco d'Assisi 88)

  Here the mystic Ludovica is sprawled out in bed with her head thrown back as she clutches her breast. Some say she's in her death throes, but since she has her shoes on, others believe Bernini caught her in a private, earth-shattering, "seeing the Divine" pose. It's best to visit the church in the morning when sunlight streams over Ludovica from the cupola above.

Make reservations to visit the splendid **Galleria Borghese,** where you'll find these Bernini masterpieces:

* *Daphne and Apollo,* **1622-1625 (Room III)**

  The virgin water nymph manages a fantastic escape from Apollo by transforming into a laurel tree before your eyes. Her hair and fingertips become leaves, her feet and ankles the tree trunk.

## ❊ *Pluto and Proserpina,* 1621-1622 (Room IV)

A teardrop runs down Proserpina's face as she smushes her hand into Pluto's chin, fighting him off with a heaven-help-me look. Pluto scoops her up and gets a firm grab on her thigh. The three-headed barking dog adds to the drama.

This is Bernini's version of the Greek myth that told how Pluto, God of the Underworld, got wowed by the beautiful Goddess of Vegetation he saw picking flowers in a field, and swooped up to kidnap her.

Other fabulous women in the Borghese are:

## ❊ *Venus Victrix,* 1805-1808 (Room I)

Here's Pauline Bonaparte (Napoleon's sister), posed regally on a chaise as the nude goddess. Pauline came to Rome as a ravish-

ing twenty-three-year-old widow, won the heart of Prince Borghese, married him, and became mistress of the Villa. Though it caused quite a scandal when Pauline stripped to model for the sculptor Canova, and her husband kept this statue hidden away while he was alive, Pauline's only comment on the affair was, "The room was well heated." Famously vain woman that she was, Pauline was also known to have used her servants as footstools and liked to have, in her words, "a large Negro" carry her to her bath.

## ❊ *Sacred and Profane Love,* 1805-1808 (Room XX)

Painted by Titian when he was just twenty-five for a Venetian nobleman's marriage, the Venuses here are named differently than what you'd expect. The Profane Venus is in proper

Renaissance dress, drawing a pot of gold to her side, signifying "fleeting earthly happiness." The Sacred Venus is naked, holding an eternal flame, meaning "eternal happiness in heaven." She wears only her magic girdle, which gave her the power to attract her many lovers.

**Galleria Borghese:** 8:30-7:30, closed Monday, 06 32810, www.galleriaborghese.it.

**TIP:** *Reservations for the Borghese are a must and you can make them easily by phone or online. This turns out to be a good thing, because you get to browse without crowds.*

**Golden Day:** Plan a picnic in the **Borghese Gardens** before or after your visit to the **Galleria Borghese.** You can gather goodies at an *alimentary* (deli)—there are good places around the Campo dei Fiori, such as **Roscioli** (Via dei Chiavari 34, www.rosciolifinefood .com)—and stash them in a locker at the museum. Or you can have it all done for you at **GiNa** (Via San Sebastianello 7/A, 06 678 0251, www.ginaroma.com), near the Spanish Steps, where they'll rent you a picnic basket with plates and cutlery and you can pick up panini and salads to go.

## RECOMMENDED READING

*Bernini's Beloved: A Portrait of Constanza Piccolomini* by Sarah McPhee

# 6
## Venuses, Madonnas, and Judith at the Uffizi—Florence

FLORENCE IS THE HOT SPOT WHERE the Renaissance burst forth, with artists creating masterpieces that revered the female form. In the city's major museum, the **Uffizi**, you'll see women adored in such paintings as:

❀ *The Birth of Venus*, **1484**, by Sandro Botticelli

Describing a woman as a Botticelli automatically brings up this famous image of a naked, curvy Venus stepping off a seashell to the shore. But Botticelli actually translates to "little barrel." It was the artist's nickname, because in truth he was a roly-poly guy.

A better description of a beautiful woman would be to call her a Simonetta Vespucci, the name of the model for this paint-

ing. Simonetta was Botticelli's muse, the most adored woman in Florence, and his neighbor's wife.

She came to Florence from Genoa as the fifteen-year-old bride of Marco Vespucci, whose cousin was the famous Italian explorer Amerigo. Her fans called her *La Bella Simonetta* and liked to say she was born in the Ligurian coastal town of Portovenere, where the Romans believed Venus arose from the sea.

Though these days she'd be ordered to do Pilates to tighten
her abs, in 1469 Simonetta's pear shape was ideal. Only poor
starving gals were skinny back then, and Renaissance guys adored
chicks with childbearing hips. In Florence, artists clamored to
have Simonetta pose for them, writers sent her love poems, and
she was showered with gifts from admirers.

The brothers Lorenzo and Giuliano de Medici, the family who ran Florence at the time, introduced Simonetta to
Botticelli, an artist on the rise. Lorenzo, who was involved with
being Magnificent and his banking and philosophy biz, ordered
a painting of Simonetta for his bed chamber, which some say
became Botticelli's *Venus*.

Giuliano, a sporty type, starred in a jousting tournament to
be held in honor of this glamor puss who had quickly become
the Marilyn Monroe of Florence. Botticelli painted Giuliano's
joust banner with the words "The Unparalleled One" under
Simonetta's image. Giuliano won and Simonetta was declared
"Queen of Beauty." Since she was married, there's no record
of nooky between Simonetta and Giuliano, though the locals
imagined their steamy affair as fervently as the tabloid romances
of our times.

A year after the joust, twenty-two-year-old Simonetta died
of consumption. Her funeral was an Italian day of mourning.
Thousands came to Florence to join in her casket procession,
weeping and tossing flowers.

Botticelli had started painting *The Birth of Venus* before
Simonetta died. It took him nine years to finish it, perhaps
because the thought of his nude muse being gone from him was
too tragic to bear.

As you look around the room, you'll see how Botticelli used
Simonetta's inspiration again and again—from *Primavera* to *The
Annunciation*. He never married, in fact said the idea of marriage

was a nightmare. And there were reports of him "liking boys," followed by charges of sodomy, that were dropped.

When he died, thirty-four years after *La Bella Simonetta,* Botticelli asked to be buried at her feet. In the Church of Ognissanti, which was Simonetta's family parish, you can see his wish was granted.

## ✦ *Venus of Urbino,* 1538, by Titian

Here's the most erotic painting in the museum. Titian probably used a Venetian prostitute for his model, as there were around 10,000 in Venice during the time he did this painting and they traditionally took on the extra work.

Venus stretches out on a couch *au naturale* in elegant surroundings, with a confident look and roses in one hand that symbolize Venus. The most attention goes to her other hand, with her curled fingers between her legs.

The painting was commissioned by the Duke of Urbino, probably as a hint for his young bride. They married when the girl was only ten years old, but things couldn't be consummated—which meant the Duke couldn't have heirs—until she became a woman at fourteen. The medical belief in those days was that conception could only occur if both man and woman had orgasms, so Titian's Venus is teaching the Duke's bride how to do her wifely duty.

## ✦ *Madonna with Child and Two Angels,* 1505-1506, by Filippo Lippi

In this totally enchanting painting, the Friar Lippi probably used the novice Lucrezia Buti as his model. The two had a scandalous love affair that lead to her getting pregnant. The baby here is probably their child, who grew up to be the painter Filippino Lippi.

❋ *Annunciation,* **1472-1475, by Leonardo da Vinci**
It's amazing to think of Leonardo painting this when he was only twenty-one. Here Mary gracefully accepts her calling, looking up from her book, while the angel holds out a lily, the symbol of Florence.

❋ *Holy Family, aka Doni Tondo,* **1506-1508, by Michelangelo**
The master who sculpted the *David* and *Pieta* always claimed he wasn't good at painting. But he shows his genius here with vibrant color and his sculptural sense of dimension. I see it as a great example of shared parenting, with Mary passing her son off to father Joseph, who seems to be able to handle it.

It was commissioned by the Doni family when their second child was born, as their first child had died in infancy. At first the Donis didn't appreciate Michelangelo's background nudes, but then accepted it as symbolic of the passing of pagan times.

❋ *Madonna of the Goldfinch,* **1505, by Raphael**
Mary, who symbolizes "The Seat of Wisdom," gets interrupted from reading, by her son and his cousin, John the Baptist, at her feet. (It's my sister's favorite—as the mother of two, she relates.) The goldfinch John the Baptist hands to Jesus is a symbol of his future violent death.

It was a wedding gift to Raphael's friend, was destroyed in an earthquake, breaking into seventeen pieces, and has undergone many meticulous restorations.

❋ *Judith Beheading Holofernes,* **1614-1620, by Artemisia Gentileschi**
Finally, a painting by a woman! It's displayed on the lower floors along with some awesome Caravaggios, and was done by the great Renaissance artist Artemisia Gentileschi.

Gentileschi began painting in her father's workshop, showing her talent early on. She was raped by a painter her father teamed her up with, Agostino Tassi. To ensure she was telling the truth during the trial, she was tortured. Horribly tortured, with a gynecological examination and wrapping and tightening of leather thongs around her fingers to the point of excruciating pain. It was believed if she could tell the same horrendous rape story under torture as the one she'd told as an accusation, it had to be true. Paintings such as this one, which tells the story of the Jewish heroine Judith cutting off the head of an enemy's general, have been interpreted as Gentileschi's revenge against that gruesome treatment.

Gentileschi's life story is ultimately inspiring. She went on to have a successful career and six children and was highly respected by her contemporaries, even though it was very unusual for a woman to be among them. Since she was passed over for the high altar commissions the men around her were getting, she moved around to find work—from Florence to Rome to Venice, and finally settled in Naples.

Feminists have always taken an interest in her life, and playwright Wendy Wasserstein used her in *The Heidi Chronicles*, in scenes of the main character lecturing about female painters.

**Uffizi:** Open 8:15-6:50, closed Monday, 055 294 883, www.firenzemusei.it.

**TIPS:** *(1) Be sure to make a reservation for the Uffizi Gallery to avoid long lines. (2) Afternoons are less crowded. (3) Only backpacks and umbrellas can be checked, so leave your shopping bags at your hotel to avoid having to lug them around the museum.*

శ్కు

**Golden Day:** Visit the **Uffizi** in the late afternoon when crowds are less, and save time for a break at the rooftop café. Then have dinner at **La Sostanza** (Via Porcellana 25r, 055 212 692, reservations essential, closed Saturday and Sunday), a fantastic old school trattoria that serves wonderful *bistecca* and chicken. Be sure to leave room for the meringue cake dessert.

RECOMMENDED READING

*Uffizi Art History Guide* by Alexandra Korey

# 7 Santa Maria Novella-Florence

ONE OF THE GREAT JOYS OF ITALIAN TRAVEL is arriving by train to Florence, emerging from the *stazione*, and winding around to stand before the **Church of the New Saint Mary: Santa Maria Novella**. It's a dazzle of emerald and ivory marble, blending Gothic and Renaissance styles, dedicated to the Madonna of the Assumption, and packed with art inspired by the BVM.

This was the first great Florentine Basilica. Dominican friars, famous for their passionate preaching, began the project in 1279, to make room for their many followers. At the time, Florence was just a collection of humble huts, and Santa Maria Novella brought in a new architecture that the Dominican friars had seen while studying in Bologna, Paris, and Cologne. The grandiose building kicked off the city's rise to glamorous fame and was further adorned in the fifteenth and sixteenth centuries.

Breakthrough art appears inside, which showcases the beginnings of the Renaissance. The most stunning examples are **Giotto's crucifix**, hanging in the center of the church, and **Massacio's 3D *Trinity*** that astounded viewers with its masterful use of perspective.

Here are some female highlights:

* **Cappella Tornabuoni**
  Behind the central altar you'll discover this chapel, dedicated to the Madonna of the Assumption, covered with masterpiece

frescos by Renaissance artist **Ghirlandaio** and his workshop. Among his students was fourteen-year-old **Michelangelo**, who Ghirlandaio threw off the project when the young artist boldly began to redraw his designs.

**Giovanni Tornabuoni**, a big shot in the Medici banking world, commissioned this late fifteenth-century chapel. While today we associate Tornabuoni with the famous *Via*—Florence's fanciest shopping street—back then these frescoes are what shouted out the greatness of the Tornabuoni family. Giovanni probably chose Ghirlandaio for the job because the artist had a talent for portrait painting, and slipped in figures of family members throughout the biblical scenes. It's a great way to see how Florentines were dressing in those days (1486-1490), and Ghirlandaio's warm, clear style brings a deep humanity to every frame.

Focusing on the center of the chapel, in a lower panel, you'll see Giovanni kneeling, opposite his wife **Francesca Pitti**, who died in childbirth in 1477.

- **The Life of the Virgin** is told in the left fresco cycle. Starting at the bottom you'll see her birth, presentation in the temple, annunciation, marriage, the birth of Christ, and her assumption into heaven. Curved above the window is her triumphant coronation.

- On the right, the story continues with the **Life of John the Baptist**, aka **Giovanni the Baptist**, which donor Giovanni Tornabuouni probably also appreciated. Here you'll see the Visitation, where Mary greets Elizabeth, who at an advanced age finds out she's pregnant with John the Baptist.

Focusing on **Tornabuoni ladies...**

❋ **Giovanna degli Albizi** can be seen in the Visitation, in sharp profile on the right, wearing a golden brocade gown with her hair done up in a lovely braided up-do. She was from a noble family that held power before the Medici, and her beauty was legendary, not only in Florence, but all over Europe. She married Lorenzo Tornabuoni in an extravagant 1486 celebration, gave birth to a son, and then tragically in 1488, at the age of tweny, died in childbirth with her second pregnancy. This portrait is an homage to her, and Ghirlandaio included an inscription—a line from a Roman poet, that translates to: *Art, if only you could portray mores and spirit, there would be no more beautiful picture on earth.*

❋ **Dianora Tornabuoni,** the Patron's sister, also appears in the Visitation, as the veiled woman dressed in black to the right of Giovanna, in the days when wives wore veils.

❋ **Lucrezia Tornabuoni,** another sister of Giovanni, appears in the Birth of John the Baptist—she's the older woman wearing blue shoes. Lucrezia was the wife of Piero de Medici, mother of Lorenzo the Magnificent—a noble, artsy woman who wrote sonnets.

❋ **Ludovica Tornabuoni,** Giovanni's only daughter, is painted in the fresco on the lower left: the Birth of Mary. Ludovica stands in profile, with her hair in a long braid, wearing a dress similar to the beautiful Giovanna degli Albizi. Since Ludovica was only about fourteen at the time of the painting, it must have been quite flattering to her (and her donor father) to be associated with the glamorous Giovanna.

## Rucellai Chapel

On the right side of the main altar, you'll find this chapel dedicated to **Saint Catherine of Alexander**, the fourth-century martyr. She was a virgin beauty, devoted to Christ, who was condemned to death on a spiked wheel by the Emperor Maxentius. Miraculously, the wheel broke, so she was then beheaded. The painting is credited to Bugiardini, and many experts believe Michelangelo helped him out.

## Spanish Chapel

Don't miss the amazing fourteenth-century frescos in this chapel adjoining the Green Cloister, featuring jewel-toned images by Andrea di Boniauto, which illustrate the complex philosophy of the Dominicans. It was renamed the Spanish Chapel in the sixteenth century, when it was given to Eleonora Toledo, who came from Spain to marry Cosimo de Medici and brought her Spanish entourage with her. (Read more about Eleonora in Chapter 24, focusing on the Costume Gallery at the Pitti Palace.)

Check out the women in the right wall fresco: *The Church Militant, Church Triumphant*. My eye is always drawn to those dancing beauties in the middle of it. According to the Dominicans, these women symbolize the perils of seductive pleasures—such as Lust, symbolized by the woman in the red dress with the monkey on her lap.

On the lower left there's legendary woman gathered to the side of the Duomo, including stars of beloved poets: Dante's Beatrice, Boccaccio's Fiammetta, and Petrarch's Laura.

In the main altar fresco, the Triumph of the Catholic Doctrine, fourteen maidens are lined up on thrones, symbolizing good things, according to the Dominicans: the Sacred Sciences and the Liberal Arts—aspects of the intellect, which Dominicans believed should be perfected to reach God's salvation.

**Santa Maria Novella:** Piazza Santa Maria Novella, Open Monday-Thursday 9–5:30, Friday 11–5:30, Saturday 9–5, Sunday (after morning mass) 12–5, www.chiesasantamarianovella.it.

**Golden Day:** Allow yourself an hour or more to visit the Basilica and cloisters. Depending upon the time of day, you may want to head for a delicious Tuscan lunch at cozy **Osteria Belle Donne** (Via delle Belle Donne 16, 055 238 2609, reservations recommended). Or if you're more in the mood for a chic cocktail experience, slip into the **Hotel Brunelleschi's Tower Bar** (Piazza Sant'Elisabetta 3, 055 27370).

**TIP:** *There are two entrances to the complex: One from Piazza Santa Maria Novella and one from the Piazza della Stazione, just opposite the train station, next to the Tourist Information office. I've found the entrance from Piazza della Stazione to often be less crowded, and this is also the entrance that Florence Card holders must use.*

### RECOMMENDED READING

*Domenico Ghirlandaio: 95 Masterpieces* by Maria Tsaneva

# 8 Annunciations–Florence

FLORENTINES ARE SO WILD ABOUT MARY they've always celebrated their New Year on her Annunciation, March 25.

These days there's partying to celebrate the event in the Piazza of the **Church of the Most Holy Annunciation (Santissima Annunziata)**, where a thirteenth-century miracle is believed to have taken place. An artist (some say Pietro Cavallini) was painting a fresco of the Annunciation, and felt so overwhelmed when he got to the face, he stepped away and fell into a deep sleep. When he woke up, the painting was finished. (There's a universal dream of every artist if I've ever heard one.) The Annunciation fresco is to the left of the church entrance in an ornate tabernacle and Florentine brides traditionally visit it to drop off their bouquets.

Besides the Chiesa Santissima Annunziata, Florence is chock-a-block with Annunciations. Renaissance painters loved interpreting the action-packed scene and the variations you'll see all over the city go from austere to absolutely flirty. I'm partial to Pontormo's Mannerist one in **Santa Felicitá**, where Mary's a willowy figure with a rose robe swirling about her, like a runway model.

The most famous Annunciation painting can be found in **Museo San Marco**. The Dominican Friars of this fifteenth-century monastery were very lucky to have a talented painter in their gang, Guido di Pietro. He was such a great guy, they named him Fra Angelico, which means Brother Angel. This Fra Angelico is not to be confused with the monk from northern Piedmont, for whom the hazelnut liqueur is named.

This Fra Angelico (now called Beato Angelico) spent eight years with his assistants frescoing San Marco's hallways and monks' cells, with images to support them in their meditation and prayer. He was so spiritually on fire, he prayed every time he picked up a brush, never changed what he'd done (thinking it would insult the Divine who gave him  inspiration), and wept every time he painted a crucifixion. The frescos here, painted over gold backgrounds downstairs and in muted jewel tones upstairs, clearly reflect his deep faith and humility.

On your way up the stairs to the cells, you'll turn on a landing and get hit with the sight of his most well-known Annunciation, which has been called the most beloved painting of the Renaissance. It's been reproduced so many times you'll get that weird brain readjustment that happens when suddenly you're in front of the real thing. Stay on that landing, with the stairs ahead of you to get the viewpoint Fra Angelico intended.

Peaceful power! Mary is timid, leaning forward with her hands crossed over her heart in acceptance. In its soft, luminous style, the moment of her transformation is striking. Taking in the whole image, you'll realize Fra Angelico's message. He included the beams of the house, to ground the event in reality. At the same time the figures are totally out of proportion—as tall as the pillars and doors that surround them, so the expansive nature of the moment is palpable.

In Cell Number 3, believed to be Fra Angelico's, is a simpler Annunciation. There Saint Dominic, the monks' patron, stands in a corner. It's as if the painter, through the saint, was teaching the monks to contemplate this image of humility.

In 1982, Pope John Paul officially beatified Fra Angelico, praising the divine beauty he painted, and putting him on the path to become the Patron Saint of Artists.

Also in the Museo are beautiful paintings of Madonnas and female saints by other Fras. Two very memorable ones of the Virgin and Child by Fra Bartolomeo have been placed in one of the cells that belonged to Savonarola, the fanatic friar who inspired masterpieces to be burned in the famous 1497 Bonfire of the Vanities. Go figure.

**Museo San Marco**: Piazza San Marco, weekdays 8:15-1:50, weekends 8:15-4:15. Closed 1st, 3rd, and 5th Sunday, and 2nd and 4th Monday of month, www.polomuseale.firenze.it.

❧

**Golden Day**: Visit **San Marco** in the early morning, when the light is best for viewing the frescos. Enjoy shopping nearby at the outdoor stalls of the San Lorenzo market, and have lunch at **Trattoria Mario** (Via Rosina 2r, closed Sunday, no reservations), a classic, folksy place.

---

### RECOMMENDED READING

*Fra Angelico: San Marco, Florence,* by M. Jane McIntosh

# 9 Mary's Sacred Girdle and Salome Dancing— Prato, Tuscany

SALOME, THE BIBLE'S VIRGIN FLOOZY, fantastically frescoed by Fra Filippo Lippi, is the logo for the town of Prato, and it's well worth it to take the half-hour train ride from Florence to see it. This town first got on the tourist map back in medieval days when Mary's sacred girdle ended up here. In a classic example of Italians combining such concepts, both the Virgin Mother's Girdle and the Virgin Floozy can be found in Prato's Romanesque Duomo.

Mary's girdle, kept locked in a sacred chapel, is nothing like the "this girdle is killing me" kind of my mother's day. It's a green belt that Mary untied when she ascended into heaven and threw to doubting Saint Thomas to prove that yes, it was she whooshing away.

The girdle was passed down to Thomas' disciples, and then to a Jerusalem priest who was married (A.O.K. back in those days) and had a gorgeous daughter. The priest disapproved of a merchant named Michael who fell in love with his daughter, but the girl's sympathetic mother helped the couple elope and threw in Mary's girdle as a dowry. Michael and his bride sailed from Jerusalem to Prato, where Michael slept with the girdle under his mattress to protect it, until on his deathbed he handed it over to a Prato priest. The Chapel of the Sacred Girdle is decorated with frescos that tell that whole story.

Five times a year, with much pomp and incense, Mary's girdle is taken from the chapel and shown to thousands. Because the event attracts more than the Duomo can hold, master Renaissance sculptor Donatello created a pulpit attached to the outside of the church, adorned with flying *putti*. There's a copy of the original pulpit up there now, but you can see Donatello's original in the attached museum.

The Duomo's main attraction, on the center altar, is Fra Filippo Lippi's cycle of *The Life of John the Baptist*, especially *The Feast of Herod*, featuring Salome.

As the Bible story goes, Salome danced so fabulously for her stepfather, King Herod, that he "was pleased" and told her he'd do anything for her. Young Salome didn't have an answer for Herod, so she asked her mother, Herodias, for advice. "Bring me John the Baptist's head on a platter," was her mother's demand.

Herod didn't want to have John's head cut off, but since he'd made that promise to Salome in front of everyone at his birthday party, he couldn't back down. He'd put John in prison because the holy man had called him and Herodias adulterers. Yes, it was true they'd had a wild affair when they were married to others, got divorced, and then became husband and wife. Herod didn't really want to kill John, as the holy man had so many followers. But his wife Herodias held quite the grudge for that adultery accusation.

I blame Herodias for Salome going down in history as a bloodthirsty whore, when actually she was just a naïve Shirley Temple-like ten-year-old, who didn't have an answer to "your wish is my command." Over the years Oscar Wilde and Hollywood screenwriters have taken Salome's story and spiced it up, so now her name brings visions of "The Dance of the Seven Veils," and it's assumed Herod's "being pleased" meant she dirty-danced for him.

In Lippi's image that follows Salome dancing, she's shown holding out the head of John the Baptist to her unfazed mother Herodias, while others look on shocked. Only Salome and Herod look straight out at the viewer, as if Lippi was guiding us to have compassion for these two.

It took Lippi thirteen years to finish these frescos, because he had major *amore* distractions from his work. While fresco-ing and friar-ing, he became smitten with Lucrezia Buti, a beautiful novice, and asked the nun's permission to use her for a model. Sparks flew in Lippi's studio, and during one of the Feasts of the Sacred Girdle when the whole town was partying, the two ran off together. Lucrezia got pregnant and gave birth to Filippino, who would also grow up to be a great painter. Because Lippi was so talented, and his patrons wanted to end the scandal, the Pope stepped in and gave Lippi and Lucrezia dispensation from their vows so they could marry. Lucrezia was Lippi's model for most of his masterpieces, which inspired Botticelli and Michelangelo.

A visit to this Duomo is not only a chance to enjoy Lippi's frescos; Prato is also a leisurely place to wander around with the locals, taste their famous *biscotti di Mattonella*, and get a break from the tourist crowds of Florence.

**Duomo Fresco:** Monday-Saturday 10-7, Sunday 1-7.

**Museo dell'Opera dell Duomo:** Monday-Saturday 10-1, 2-7, Sunday 2-7, Closed Tuesday, www.diocesiprato.it.

**NOTE:** If you're there September 8, you'll hit the town's biggest Sacred Girdle party of the year, with parades and festivities all over Prato. Other Sacred Girdle showings are Christmas, Easter, May 1, and August 15.

**TIP:** *You can get to Prato's Duomo easily by train from Santa Maria Novella station in Florence to the* **Prato Porta al Serraglio Station** *(1/2 hour ride), then walk a few blocks to the Duomo.*

ॐ

**Golden Day:** Visit the Prato Duomo, then have lunch at **La Vecchia Cucina di Soldano**, a cozy budget place, typically packed with locals, that serves excellent Tuscan classics (Via Pomeria 23, 0574 34665, www.trattoriasoldano.it).

# 10 *Museum of the Madonna del Parto— Monterchi, Tuscany*

THIS MAY BE THE ONLY MUSEUM ON EARTH where pregnant women get in free. There's only one painting displayed here, the striking *Madonna del Parto*, that shows Mary in her ninth month of pregnancy.

It's a fifteenth-century masterpiece by Piero della Francesca, who dedicated it to his mother who was born in Monterchi. Mary stands in a pale blue robe, her hand over her full middle, flanked by boy angels who draw back curtains of a regal tent. It's dramatic and serene—capturing Mary in a meditative moment, completely involved with the life growing inside her.

Francesca was a mathematician and in all his paintings there's an arresting symmetry of precise lines and lighting, combined with a gentle spirit of compassion. He created the *Madonna del Parto* for a Monterchi church that was built on a Cult of Fertility site. Back in pagan days pregnant women traditionally went to this site to bathe in a hilltop spring and pray for protection and abundant breastmilk. The church

built over it, called the Momentana, was actually a cemetery chapel, so ceremonies for both birth and death took place there for centuries.

The Momentana became severely damaged over the years, and Francesca's fresco barely survived. Even though the only way to save the *Madonna del Parto* was to move it, the local women were so attached to it being in the cemetery chapel that they put up a fight, and ultimately lost.

It's been expertly restored and is displayed under glass in a sterile modern room in this museum that was once an elementary school. You've got to use your imagination to picture it in its original place, when all those Monterchi women would be kneeling in prayer before it. Now there's a bench in the room with the painting (handy for pregnant women), so you can settle in and absorb. In other rooms of the museum there's a theater where you can watch a movie about Piero della Francesca, displays about the *Madonna del Parto's* restoration, and a gift shop with books and prints.

Outside the museum, the tiny medieval village of Monterchi is a dreamy place to circle up cobblestoned streets and enjoy hilltop views of the valley. When I stopped by, I felt part of a classic Sunday afternoon, with two elderly town couples sitting next to me at a caffè, drinking beer and playing cards.

Nearby is Arezzo, where you'll find Piero della Francesca's most famous fresco, *The Legend of the True Cross*, in the Basilica di San Francesco. As for female images, a wonderful Annunciation and scene featuring the Queen of Sheba meeting Solomon are a part of that masterpiece.

**Museum of the Madonna del Parto:** Open Daily, 9-1, 2-5. Closed Tuesdays, www.madonnadelparto.it. Pregnant women and children under fourteen get in free.

⊰⊱

**Golden Day:** Visit **Monterchi** (a half-hour drive from Arezzo), see *The Madonna del Parto* and have lunch at **Al Travato** (Piazza Umberto 1, 0575 70111), an old-style *enoteca*. For luxury accommodations, and a great base to explore Tuscany and Umbria, stay at the **Castello di Procopio** (www.santaeurasia.it), an eight-room seventeenth-century palazzo that also has a fantastic spa and pool.

## RECOMMENDED READING

*Travelers' Tales Italy* edited by Anne Calcagno, introduction by Jan Morris

*30 Days in Italy* edited by James O'Reilly, Larry Habegger, and Sean O'Reilly

*Travelers' Tales Tuscany*, edited by James O'Reilly, Tara Austen Weaver, Ann Calcagno

# 11 City of Saint Catherine–Siena, Tuscany

THE EVENING SKY IN SIENA IS A DIVINE WONDER to behold. Get a seat in the Piazza del Campo as the sun sets and you're in for a show. Colors change from blue-pink-golden to a rich navy. Then out pop the stars. Whoever is doing the lighting here is brilliant.

Any time of day, Siena is one of the most pleasant cities to stroll around. You'll be awed by the Gothic **Duomo** outside and in. There's Duccio's *Maestà* (Majesty) in the **Museo dell'Opera Metropolitana,** where the BVM sits enthroned, holding a rose-robed baby Jesus, surrounded by twenty angels and nineteen saints. When this masterpiece was unveiled in 1311, the whole town came out with candles to *ooh* and *aah* over it as church bells rang.

All over Siena, Saint Catherine, the most important woman of the Middle Ages, is honored with statues, paintings, and altars. The beloved *Mystic of Politics* was born here in 1347, in the area called Contrada dell' Oca, or Neighborhood of the Goose.

Pilgrims flock to the church she went to while growing up, which is now the **San Domenico Basilica.** There you'll find the richly decorated Santa Caterina Chapel, with frescos by Sodoma, who was a student of Leonardo da Vinci. In the center of it all is Catherine's head. Compared to a lot of other relics I've seen, it looks more like a mask, in amazing shape. Her thumb is nearby under a bell jar.

A short walk away is the **Santuario e Casa di Santa Caterina,** where the saint was born and grew up. It doesn't look as it probably did in her day, as it's been transformed to a shrine with Renaissance paintings that tell stories from her life. But still, as you walk through what was her kitchen and go upstairs to her bedroom you get a feel for the strong spirit of this brilliant woman. Get a load of the stone pillow she used—just one example of how she denounced creature comforts to feel closer to God.

Catherine was the twenty-fourth of twenty-five children, whose twin sister died in childbirth. She shocked her parents when she was seven and announced, "I've had a vision! I'm devoting my life to Christ!" Her mother tried to pull her away from her incessant praying and marry her off when she was twelve, but Catherine chopped off her hair and put up a fight. Her parents finally relented, and allowed her to join the Dominican nuns as a "tertiary," a lay person associated with the clergy.

Catherine devoted herself to nursing the sick, but even the devout around her were concerned about her religious zeal, as she'd only eat communion wafers. These days, psychologists who've examined the lives of female saints focus on Catherine. They say she had survivor's guilt because of the death of her twin, and it manifested as holy anorexia nervosa.

Despite her diet, Catherine became a powerful, influential woman. She had a vision that set her on a path to change the world through letter-writing. This was amazing, because she was illiterate. She dictated letters to her followers, and sent them off to the Pope in Avignon, encouraging him to come back to Rome. Those fourteenth-century times were a mess with divisions in the papacy and Italy. Dante and Petrarch had written to Pope Gregory XI to try to get him to come back to Italy, but it was Catherine's outright begging, addressing the Pope as "Sweet Babbo" (Sweet Daddy), and demanding "Up father, like a man!" that got him to think about budging.

For the ultimate push, Catherine went on horseback to Avignon and had a one-on-one meeting that got the Pope to pull up stakes. He died shortly after, and Catherine joined the new Pope in Rome, continuing to fight to unite the church through her writing. She died in Rome at thirty-three, of a paralytic stroke.

Catherine was canonized in 1461 as the Patron of Nurses and Fire Prevention. In 1939 she was named Co-Patron Saint of Italy (along with Saint Francis), in 1970 a Doctor of the Church, and in 1999, the Patron of Europe.

The Romans treasured her and have her body enshrined in the **Santa Maria Sopra Minerva** church, which coincidentally has a frescoed ceiling that to me resembles the Siena sky.

Her head is in Siena, because, according to legend, it was stolen by Sienese. When Roman guards caught the thieves on their way out of the Eternal City and asked them to open their sack, it appeared to be full of rose petals. But when they got it back to Siena, the head reappeared. Catherine's foot is now enshrined in Venice, at Santi Giovanni e Paolo. Everybody wanted a piece of this amazing woman. But you'll feel her presence living on most powerfully in Siena.

**Getting there:** Buses leave regularly from Florence and take about an hour and a half. When driving check out www.discovertuscany. com for info on parking lots outside the town walls, as the historic center is mostly pedestrian only.

⁂

**Golden Day:** Enjoy **Siena** and **Saint Catherine** sights. Treat yourself at **Nannini**, (Via Banchi di Sopra 24), a famous pasticerria where the *ricciarelli* (almond cookies) are divine. Get to the **Campo** for sunset. If you don't want to splurge at the obvious caffès, head to **Key Largo,** where you can walk up a narrow stairway (more like a hole in the ceiling) with your glass of wine and wind up on a narrow wooden balcony to take in the whole scene. Eat at **Ristorante Guidoriccio** (Via Giovanni Dupre 2, 0577 44350, closed Sunday). Stay at **Palazzo Ravizza** (www.palazzoravizza.it), a restored Renaissance palace.

**Siena Tourist Info:** www.discovertuscany.com

## RECOMMENDED READING

*Saint Catherine of Siena as Seen in Her Letters* edited by Vida Scudder
*Holy Anorexia* by Rudolph M. Bell

# 12 Town of Saint Margaret–Cortona, Tuscany

THIS PLACE HAS EVERYTHING ON THE CHECKLIST to fulfill the Tuscan hill town dream. Walls built by the Etruscans, which is where the name Tuscany comes from. A masterpiece *Annunciation* by Fra Angelico, in the **Museo Diocesano**. And a patron saint with a twisted story.

A steep, *very* steep, uphill walk from the Cortona historic center will take you to the place Saint Margaret once lived, where she's buried and honored: the **Chiesa di Santa Margherita**. It's a place that is worth the climb.

This is Saint Margaret's story:

Once upon a time in the thirteenth century, there lived a beautiful, high-spirited farmer's daughter named Margaret. Her mother died when she was young and Margaret's father remarried some shrew who had an automatic hate-on for Margaret. Meanwhile beautiful Margaret kept her spirits up by enjoying the attention from all the young lads in her little town. But no matter how hard she tried to enjoy her lot, she had the gnawing "there's gotta be something better than this" feeling. Lo and behold, along came a knight from Montepulciano who asked Margaret to come live with him...and work as his maid. Not insulted in the least, Margaret, then seventeen, jumped at the chance to get away from her evil stepmother. She moved into the knight's castle and surprise, surprise, he couldn't keep his hands off her. Before you know it, she got pregnant and gave birth to a son.

"Now will you marry me?" Margaret asked her knight. "Uh... umm...uh...no," was his reply.

Margaret decided not to push it, looked on the bright side, and was grateful for her good fortune. She went out every day to help the poor, even though the townsfolk would come by and call her a tramp. "Ha-ha, someday I'll be a saint," was her reply.

Then one day her knight went off for a trip and didn't come home as planned. But his dog did, and ala Lassie, led Margaret into the woods. There she came upon a horrifying site: her knight murdered and rotting. Margaret had a suspicion that she was the cause of it. She knew other men wanted her, and they probably whacked her knight, thinking they could take his place. "It's all my fault!" Margaret said. "If I weren't so beautiful none of this would have happened!"

She decided to repent big time. She gave all the riches she'd gotten from the knight back to his family. She went home to her father and stepmother, all ready to confess that her whole life had been wrong up to this day. Her stepmother threw her out: "Wanton woman!"

In despair, she ran to Cortona, through a gate that's now called the **Porta Margherita**. Huffing and puffing, she arrived at the Franciscan Friars. "Please let me in, I want to repent!" They weren't going to make it so easy for her. To prove her faith, she put on a hair shirt. She fasted. She took out a knife and was all set to cut her beautiful nose off.

That's when the Franciscan monk, Fra Giunta, stepped in and became her confessor. Many tongues began wagging: "They're lovers!" But Giunta convinced his brothers that Margaret had suffered long enough, and after three years of penance they let her join their order.

Soon a miracle occurred. As Margaret was praying below a crucifix, Jesus himself leaned forward and whispered, "Poverella..." That began a whole bunch of conversation and ecstasies for Margaret.

Inspired, she went back to what she'd been doing in the first place when everyone called her a tramp: helping the poor. This time it was the poor of Cortona, and she really put muscle into it. She started an order of nuns she called "le Poverelle," founded a hospital for the poor and sick, and a charity organization—The Confraternity of Our Lady of Mercy—to support the hospital.

As she got older, Margaret wanted peace and quiet. So she moved up the hill to the Church of Saint Basil, and had it repaired. She died there in 1297. Immediately the people of Cortona forgot about Saint Basil, named the place Chiesa di Santa Margherita, and started rebuilding it. What you see up there now is mainly from the church's nineteenth century renovation.

Margaret's body is in an open tomb above the high altar. She was canonized in 1728, as the Patroness of Fallen Women.

The view from up there—the rolling hills of the Val di Chiana—is awesome.

❦

**Golden Day:** Visit the **Museo Diocesano** to see Fra Angelico's *Annunciation*, then walk to the **Chiesa di Santa Margherita**. Eat and stay near Cortona at **Il Falconiere** (www.ilfalconiere.com), a converted eighteenth-century country villa that's been elegantly turned into a Relais & Châteaux hotel.

**Tourist Info:** www.cortona.com

## RECOMMENDED READING

*Under the Tuscan Sun* by Frances Mayes

# 13 Santa Maria Churches—Venice

VENICE IS A SEXY PLACE. The curves of its Grand Canal and palazzos, mysterious passageways, and flowing tides make it magically seductive.

It's always been closely tied to Mary and was officially established as an Italian republic on the same day as her Annunciation (March 25). It also has a history of being a bustling port town, and along with sailors and wealthy single merchants went prostitutes and high-class courtesans, like the famous poet Veronica Franco.

The mix of these two female aspects of Venice is literally carved in stone on the Rialto Bridge. On one side there's a bas-relief of the Annunciation. On the other side, to the left, is a woman with her legs spread, sitting over flames. The story of this gal is that she was a prostitute who was around when the idea for building the Rialto Bridge was first proposed. "Impossible," she said. "If you build it, I'll burn my crotch!" And so the bridge was built and the bawdy woman remembered.

Back on the BVM side of Venice, you'll see in its museums and churches how architects, painters, and sculptors pay homage to Mary in Venetian Renaissance style, bringing out the passionate emotions of her story.

Here are two of my favorite Santa Maria churches:

❋ **Santa Maria della Salute (Dorsoduro)**

At the opening of the Grand Canal, *The Salute*, or what my husband calls "the giant white boob," welcomes visitors to Venice.

*Salute* means health and salvation, which is what the Venetians needed desperately in 1631. For two years, the plague had ravaged the city, causing 45,000 deaths, a loss of one third of their population. The doge ordered prayers to Mary, the plague stopped, and it was decided to build a church to thank her.

Baldassare Longhena, at thirty-two years old, won a contest to design the church and came up with a Mary-centric plan. The dome represents her crown, the round shape her womb, the octagonal interior, her eight-sided star. The center of the marble floor features thirty-two roses, symbolizing the beads of her Rosary.

It's refreshing to step into the airy expanse of this church, with loads of light flooding through its giant dome. A marble sculpture at the main altar tells the plague story. In the center of it is the Madonna and child, bordered on one side by a pretty *signorina* who represents Venezia. On the other side is the plague— an old hag running from an angel who holds out a torch.

Pay the extra couple euros to get into the sacristy and see such masterpieces as Tintoretto's folksy hit on the *Marriage at Cana*, where he got his friends to pose and women are in charge of pouring wine out of giant jugs. Titian's ceiling paintings here are also stunning, especially *The Sacrifice of Abraham*, where an angel swoops in to save Abraham's son Isaac, depicted as an adorable three-year-old with Titian-colored hair. Use the mirrors set on the side benches to get the best view.

In a corner are four simple Madonna portraits by Sassoferrato, a baroque painter who was influenced by Raphael. Though critics call them too sentimental, they win me over.

**Santa Maria della Salute**: Dorsoduro 1, Daily 9-noon, 3-5:30.

❋  **Church of Santa Maria dei Miracoli (Cannaregio)**
This tiny glowing marble treasure chest looks like it should be
kept under glass in a museum. If you catch it on a sunny day it
shimmers. It was built with marble left over from San Marco,
by Pietro Lombardo, who fitted pink, gray, and butter-yellow
stones together to dazzling effect inside and out.

The motivation to build this church came from a portrait
of the Madonna that back in the fifteenth century was kept in
a Cannaregio neighborhood yard. Venetians used to stop and
pray to it, and miraculously their prayers were answered. It
became so popular that people started to leave money in front
of the portrait—enough to fund the building of a church, which
became Santa Maria dei Miracoli. In fact, so much money was
given that a second story and a convent were added.

The miraculous Madonna portrait now sits at the altar, up
a flight of marble steps. The church's gilded ceiling is painted
with fifty portraits of saints and prophets, there are pillars
carved with mermaids, *putti*, and floral motifs. It all blends
seamlessly to create a romantic Renaissance masterpiece. It's no
wonder this is the first choice for brides around the world who
want to get married in Venice.

**Santa Maria dei Miracoli**: Campo dei Miracoli, Monday-
Saturday 10-5.

**TIP**: *Santa Maria dei Miracoli belongs to a group of fifteen Chorus churches that
charge admission to help pay for the upkeep and restoration of the treasures inside.
More info: www.chorusvenezia.org*

❧

**Golden Day**: Visit **dei Miracoli**, enjoy a caffè in the adjoining
*campo* to gawk some more at the church exterior. Have lunch at

**Fiaschetteria Toscana** (Salizada San Giovanni Grisostomo 5719, Cannareggio, 041 528 5281, www.fiaschettiratoscana.it), one of late cookbook author Marcella Hazan's favorite Venice restaurants. Closed all day Tuesday and Wednesday for lunch.

## RECOMMENDED READING

*The Honest Courtesan: Veronica Franco, Citizen and Writer in Sixteenth-Century Venice* by Margaret F. Rosenthal

# 14 Madonnas by Titian, Bellini, and Tintoretto—Venice

THE MOST SPECTACULAR PAINTING OF THE ASSUMPTION you'll ever see is in **The Frari**. It's an action-packed transcendent scene. You'll gasp. The first time I saw it, there was an organ rehearsal going on. May you be so lucky.

It appears in the center of this massive church's altar. Mary dances while flying up to golden heaven, her red robe swirling, arms open to the light, she's lifted on a cloud by twenty-two happy *putti*. Bearded God swoops down, like Batman; an angel by his side crown a-ready. The earthbound apostles fall all over each other in awe over the miraculous moment, as if a wondrous storm is sweeping through.

The painting caused quite a sensation, like the opening of *Star Wars*, when folks back in 1518 first saw what Titian painted specifically for this chapel. I imagine he was miffed when the Franciscan friars (whose church it was) gave him flak and waffled about paying him, because they thought his dancing Mary was way too provocative compared to the calm scenes of her levitating on a throne, which was the proper, traditional way to portray her. But soon everybody else declared it revolutionary, Titian became a superstar, and to this day the painting is praised as the best Assumption out there.

Also beautiful is Titian's *Madonna di Ca' Pesaro*. Here he broke the rules again, placing Mary at the side of the painting and putting the Doge who paid for it in the center. Jesus playfully squirms away, tugging at Mary's veil. She was modeled after Titian's wife, who died in childbirth not long after the painting was finished.

Titian's teacher, Giovanni Bellini, painted the delicate, bathed in golden light *Madonna* triptych in the sacristy. You can take a seat here to admire this stunning, serene image of Mary surrounded by serenading angels. And yes, the Bellini that you'll be drinking in Venice, that fabulous prosecco and peach juice mixture, was named in honor of this artist.

## Scuola San Rocco, Campo San Rocco, San Polo

Next door is another wonderful painting by Titian. It's an Annunciation, where a red-robed angel dances in to break the news to Mary. You'll find it upstairs in this Scuola, a place the artist Tintoretto covered with over fifty of his paintings, making it his lifelong project.

For a short time, Tintoretto was a student of Titian's, but the older artist kicked him out of his studio, some say because Titian was threatened by Tintoretto's talent. It looks to me more like their styles were so different, probably Titian couldn't stand to have this artist, nicknamed "Il Furioso" around.

Tintoretto's paintings have a folksy exuberance, with massive characters jammed together telling stories of dramatic biblical moments. The first painting of his you'll notice on the left as you enter the Scuola is the most bizarre Annunciation I've ever seen. Typically, Mary is in a sacred bedroom, with a lovely garden in the background. But here she's in a broken down home, dropping a cloth from her spinning wheel, bewildered and anxious, as a muscular Angel Gabriel bursts in through the brick wall with tumbling *putti* overhead. In the background, Mary's husband Joseph works in the yard, oblivious to the event. It's quintessential Tintoretto, mixing the Divine with the everyday.

The Great Hall upstairs features wall-to-ceiling Old and New Testament scenes. You can pick up mirrors on side carts to get a better look at all that drama above you.

Though the overall effect of Tintoretto's Scuola borders on too Vegas-like for my taste, it's well worth it to stop by here for those two completely different Annunciations.

**Basilica dei Frari**: San Polo 3072 (near San Toma vaporetto stop). Open Monday-Friday 9-6, Saturday-Sunday 1-6. Check their website for occasional concerts: www.basilicadeifrari.it.

**Scuola Grande di San Rocco**: Campo San Rocco, San Polo. Open daily 9:30-5:30, www.scuolagrandesanrocco.it.

☙

**Golden Day**: Visit the **Frari** and **Scuola San Rocco**, then have lunch at **Antiche Carampane** (Rio Tera delle Carampane, Rialto, near Ponte delle Tette, 041 524 0165, reservations well in advance essential, closed Sunday and Monday, www.antichecarampane. com) for extraordinary fish and pastas, in an atmosphere that perfectly blends warmth and elegance.

# 15 The Scrovegni Chapel— Padua, Veneto

IT'S TOUGH TO PULL AWAY FROM VENICE, but a half-hour train ride will bring you to this splendid fourteenth-century chapel, dedicated to Mary and frescoed by Giotto, who inspired all the Renaissance greats. It was built over ruins of a Roman arena, which is why its real name is the **Church of the Madonna dell'Arena**. But it's better known as the **Scrovegni Chapel,** because it was originally a part of their family villa.

The inspiration to call in Giotto to fresco this place came from Enrico Scrovegni, who was desperate to not burn in hell. His father, Reginaldo, was a scumbag money lender—the embodiment of the worst credit card company you can imagine, who charged ridiculously high interest rates and awful late fees. Reginaldo was so despised that the church denied him a burial. Dante put him in the Seventh Circle of Hell, where he was doomed to sit on hot sand with his head bent while Florentines shouted in his ears for eternity.

Enrico, a wealthy merchant and banker, wasn't so different from his father, so to atone for Reginaldo's sins, save his soul and his family's, he went overboard and called in the best painter of the day to work on the church adjoining his home.

You'll walk in to be wowed by the intense blue of Giotto's curved star-studded ceiling that tops thirty-eight frescos, all backed by that heavenly blue, which narrate the life of Mary and then Christ.

Giotto broke the mold of the stiff Middle Ages, bringing emotion to these figures, which in 1306 was as radical as adding special effects to a movie. There's an innocent beauty to every panel. Characters plead, embrace, conspire and lament as angels sweep in like comets.

Here, sort of like how Ron Howard took the *Da Vinci Code* and made it into a movie, Giotto took *The Golden Legend*, a bestselling book of his day, and made a medieval graphic novel with Mary in the lead. *The Golden Legend*, written by a friar, told imaginative stories of Christianity's major players. Folks back then loved relating to holy people in a contemporary way for the first time.

Since you probably haven't read the book, the images need some explanation. Giotto's scenes play out in three tiers, beginning at the top left corner to "establish the conflict," as Hollywood script analysts would say. Joachim, Mary's father, gets thrown out of the temple because after twenty years of marriage, he and his wife Ann are still childless. What follows is Joachim retreating to his fields in despair, sacrificing a goat to lift the barren curse. Meanwhile home-alone Ann receives the news from an angel that she's finally pregnant. The couple rejoices, Mary is born and taken at three years old to the temple.

In the eighth fresco you'll see men lined up with sticks in their hands, for the *Presentation of the Rods*. The story goes that when Mary was fourteen and marriage-ready, the high priest called in every bachelor in town to lay their rod on the altar, and whoever had a rod that flowered could marry Mary. The guy standing to the side with a beard is Joseph, who figured he was too old to marry a fourteen-year-old, so he doesn't even enter the rod contest. In the next shot, the high priest has convinced him to add his rod and all the men are huddled and waiting. What follows is *The Betrothal of Mary and Joseph*, with Joseph proudly holding a rod with a blossoming lily, the symbol of Mary. Joseph's miffed contenders stand to the side, one of them breaking a rod over his knee as if to say, "Drat! I wanted to marry Mary!"

On the wall opposite Mary's Annunciation is the *Last Judgment*, said to be painted by Giotto's assistants because it doesn't have the elegance of the master. Amidst the fires of hell is Reginaldo Scrovegni holding up a model of the chapel to the Madonna in a, "Please forgive me! Look at this pretty chapel I made for you!" gesture.

It's good to visit the chapel knowing these stories because you'll only have fifteen minutes inside to view the frescos. The place has been restored and a sterilized, climate-controlled environment created to preserve the frescos. Your visit begins in an antechamber where you view a fifteen-minute film about the chapel before you're escorted in for your limited time with the masterpiece.

**Scrovegni Chapel**: Piazza Eremitani 8, Daily 9-7. Reservations are a must, so book ahead through the website (www.cappelladegliscrovegni .it). That said, I did visit one November weekday without reserving, got a ticket for an hour later, and had pleasant waiting time strolling through the nearby Padua market.

**TIP**: *Check the website for periodic extended visiting hours in the evenings.*

**How to Get There**: Trains from Venice leave often, and the ride takes about a half an hour (www.trenitalia.it).

**Golden Day**: Visit to **Scrovegni Chapel**, lunch at **Isola di Caprera** (Via Marsilio di Padova 11/15, 049 8760244, closed Sunday) for great seafood, and caffè at the classic (since 1831) **Caffè Pedrocchi** (Via VIII Febbraio 15).

# 16 Venus of the Beautiful Buttocks and Other Museo Archeologico Nazionale Treasures—Naples

"Do you think all the men here know how good looking they are?" Sheila asked as we took in the view from our table at the Piazza Bellini in Naples. This is a place where you could O.D. on infinite variations of bedroom eyes. Top it off with *delizioso* pizza, *sfogliatelle*, and the spontaneous theater that bombards you as you wander through Naples' lively markets and you'll be won over by the vibrant soul of this city.

The idea of stepping out of such fun into a place called the **Museo Archeologico Nazionale** may sound like a buzz kill, but get over it. Even here, the Neapolitan ambience—a mix of classic beauty, deep sensuality, and naughty humor is inescapable. One memorable visit, the flirty guy at the ticket booth kept me waiting as he took bites of a huge chocolate torta, then held it out to me, insisting I have a taste. It was a perfect start for a couple of rich hours.

Here are just a few highlights of this amazing place:

❀ *Callipygian Venus (Venus of the Beautiful Buttocks)*
The classic stars of the museum's ground floor sculpture collection are *Hercules* and the *Farnese Bull,* but I'm always drawn to this enticing Venus. She's posed lifting up her robe and turning to peek at her rear end. The statue is a Roman copy of the Greek *Callipygian Aphrodite* (Venus to the Romans) that was found in Syracuse, Sicily.

There's a good story behind this behind.

Two Sicilian farm girl sisters were fighting over which one had the better rear. To settle the feud, they ran to the road, lifted their skirts, and asked a signor passing by to be the judge. He chose the older sister's rear, fell in love, and ran back home to tell his brother all about it. The brother decided to head out there and judge for himself—which he did, and chose the younger sister's behind. These guys were from a wealthy family, and their father tried to marry them off to rich girls, but they refused to give up on the sisters with the beautiful buttocks. And so those lucky farm girls ended up marrying money.

In gratitude they built a temple in Syracuse and dedicated it to Aphrodite Callipygos, because in Greek *calli* means beautiful and *pygos* means buttocks. A Sicilian cult grew around the temple, with many coming to worship at the statue, hoping that they would receive good fortune from those buttocks, just as those farm girls had.

The Callipygian Venus statue here in this museum was considered so pornographic in the nineteenth century only privileged men on the Grand Tour who paid were allowed to have a look at it. Notice how those beautiful buttocks got smudged by all the kisses they received from her admirers.

Upstairs you're going to love the mosaics and frescos from the villas of Pompeii, Herculaneum, and Stabia. Especially four small beautiful frescos from Stabia, where Medea, Flora, Leda, and Diana delicately float in pale blue and green backgrounds. There are also frescos from the Temple of Isis (the Egyptian mother goddess), whom the Romans worshipped, where a deep Pompeii red backs enchanting ornamental designs and dramatic figures.

And you definitely can't miss:

## ✤ The Secret Cabinet (Il Gabinetto Segreto)

Women weren't officially allowed to enter this room until the year 2000. Men's logic was that the weaker sex shouldn't see displays of what they labeled pornography, dug up from Pompeii and Herculaneum in the eighteenth century.

What did they think females would do if we saw such things as Pan screwing a she-goat or Zeus frolicking with a naked maiden? Was it all those penises in so many shapes and sizes that the fellas feared would make things dangerous?

Now even kids are allowed in to see the frescos and vases here that are painted with scenes that bring to mind the *Kama Sutra*, with a strong emphasis on doggie-style positions. When they were first discovered, it was believed these objects came from Pompeii whorehouses, as the town of 40,000 people was known to have 400 brothels. But eventually the racy scenes and objects were also found in the remains of noble villas, where the images must have added inspiration to the grand banquet-orgies of those days. Some are ancient jokes. Such as a fresco of Pan, that lusty God of Shepherds, lifting up the skirt of a maiden and discovering "she" has a penis!

As for the abundance of penises—made into wind chimes, oil lamps, and gigantic ones hanging off dwarves—they were fertility symbols used to bring luck, like our garden gnomes. It all started with Priapus, the Greek god of fertility, whom the Romans also worshipped. They put statues of him in front of their homes and a stroke of his penis as you walked by insured your good fortune.

Priapus was the son of Aphrodite (Goddess of Love and Beauty) and Dionysus (God of Wine and Sexual Ecstasy). Hera (Zeus' wife) cursed Priapus when he was in Aphrodite's womb, condemning him to ugliness and impotence. When Priapus was born looking like a freak with a huge erect penis, Aphrodite was horrified and threw him down to earth from Mount Olympus, where he was raised by shepherds.

Everywhere Priapus with the three-foot shlong went, animals started humping each other and plants sprouted up, which is why he became known as the God of Fertility. The irony was that he was impotent, which understandably frustrated the poor guy, so he ended up being ornery and couldn't even walk because of his permanent hard-on. Since he couldn't visit all the fields in person, farmers made statues of Priapus which were eventually pared down to his most prominent feature.

It's rare to be in a museum where jaw-dropping beauty, sex, and laughter blend together so well. But this is Naples, after all.

**Museo Archeologico Nazionale:** Piazza Museo 19, Wednesday-Monday, 9-7, www.cir.campania.beniculturali.it/museoarcheologiconazionale.

❧

**Golden Day:** Spend a couple of hours in the **Museo** and take a break at the nearby **Evaluna Libreria Café** (Piazza Bellini 72). Dine at **Pizzeria Bellini** (Via Costantinopoli 79/80, 081 459 774, closed Sunday) where the house specialty, spaghetti cooked in parchment with seafood, is fantastic.

# 17 Cloister of Santa Chiara—Naples

TUCKED AWAY FROM NOISY, DARKER **SPACCANAPOLI** is this calm bright oasis where the followers of Santa Chiara once prayed.

The cloister's main attractions are rows of seventy-two majolica-tiled columns, painted in pretty blue, green, and gold floral designs. Tiled benches below show scenes of peasants dancing the *tarantella*, hunting, and enjoying jolly times in the fields, along with myths featuring Neptune and his mermaids. Citrus trees and shrubs fill the gardens, adding sweet smells.

On the convent walls surrounding the cloister are faded jewel-toned frescos where angels float on arches next to women representing virtues such as Wisdom and Temperance. Murals picture action-packed battle scenes and Bible stories, including one of Judith looking innocent and content as she cuts off the head of General Holofernes.

It all seems a bit much for the nuns who called themselves The Poor Clares and were famous for living lives of poverty and self-denial. As they had no contact with the outside world, these images must have been as entertaining to them as high-def TV.

The cloister didn't look at all like this originally. It was built in the fourteenth century when the second wife of Robert D'Anjou (the church founder) decided she wanted to live vicariously through the lives of nuns in seclusion, so she had this convent added on to the Santa Chiara church.

Four hundred years later the innovative artist Domenico Antonio Vaccaro came in and renovated the cloister, inspired by all the Neapolitan frivolity of his day. The nuns enjoyed it all to themselves until 1924, when they traded places with their Franciscan friar neighbors. The Franciscans invited upper-class intellectuals and artists to see the cloister and finally in the 1970s the space was opened to the public.

Although this is still a quiet spot, who knows what Santa Chiara (to us Clare) would think of it. She was a twelfth-century girl living in Assisi who got very inspired when Saint Francis came and gave a sermon at her church. Though many noblemen wanted to marry her, one Palm Sunday night Chiara snuck out of her wealthy parent's home and headed to Saint Francis to ask to join his gang.

Francis took her in, shaved her head, and gave her sackcloth to wear. Though Chiara's parents tried to force her to come back home, she fiercely resisted. Instead she founded the Poor Clares order of nuns, and became a fanatic about vows of poverty. The sisters wore no shoes, existed only on alms, slept on the ground, spoke little, and could own nothing.

Chiara became the Patron Saint of Embroidery and Sore Eyes because she was a sickly type and while in bed managed to get a lot of sewing done, making altar cloths and vestments for churches all over Assisi. One Christmas Eve, ailing in her bed, she heard songs from the church below. Then, miraculously, an image of the Bethlehem manger appeared on her bedroom wall. That's why in 1958, the Pope declared that she should also be known as The Patron Saint of TV.

There are many impressive churches nearby, including the **Cappella Sansevero** with its famous statue of the veiled Christ. And don't miss **Pio Monte della Misericordia**, where you'll find Caravaggio's *Sette Opere della Misericordia* (*Seven Acts of Mercy*), with angels carrying the Virgin Mary into a Spaccanapoli street.

**Cloisters of Santa Chiara**: Via Benedetto Croce, Monday-Saturday 9:30-5:30, Sunday 10-2:30, www.monasterodisantachiaraing. jimdo.com.

࿐

**Golden Day:** Visit **Cloisters** and **Spaccanapoli**. For a wonderful lunch, go to **La Cantina della Sapienza** (Via della Sapienza 40, 081 459 078, lunch only, closed Sunday), a humble place for Neapolitan classics. Of the many other delicious stops in the area are **Scaturchio** pasticceria for *sfogliatelle* (Piazza San Domenico Maggiore 19) and **Sorbillo** for pizza (Via dei Tribunali 32, 081 446 643, closed Sunday).

# 18 Cave of the Cumaean Sibyl–Cumae, Campania

THE EARTH PERCOLATES IN THIS PLACE northwest of Naples called the "Phlegrean Fields" or "Burning Fields." Steam rises from volcanic craters and lakes. The Tyrrhenian Sea is the backdrop for ruins of temples and a trapezoidal-shaped forty-foot tunnel that leads to a chamber where poets say there lived the mysterious and powerful Cumaean Sibyl. Archaeologists say the tunnel was built as a defense structure, but what fun is that?

If you're a *Sopranos* fan you'll recognize this Cumae cave from a Season 2 episode. Annalisa Zucca, that bombshell of a mafia boss, brought Tony to this otherworldly spot to discuss family business. As they walked through the shadowy cave, the sexual tension between the two of them sizzled.

According to myth, thousands of years ago another bombshell of a young maiden was wandering around here and caught the eye of Apollo, God of the Sun. To win her over, Apollo threw her the "Your wish is my command" line. The maiden pointed to a pile of sand and said, "I wish to live as many years as those grains of sand." So Apollo gave her one thousand years of life, but she still wouldn't put out. To get back at her he found a loophole—she hadn't asked for youth. That's the reason why through most of her long life the Cumaean Sibyl was a bent over, warty old gal. In her later years, she shriveled into a small ball and hung like a bat in a jar from a tree. Kids would stand below her, taunting and asking: "What do you want, Sibyl?" Only her croaking voice was left and her answer was always: "I want to die!"

Apollo, who kept a soft spot for her, gave her the gift of prophecy. She was a sneaky one, writing enigmatic prophecies on oak leaves and leaving them on her cave's ledge. Often they were scattered to the winds, driving those looking for her answers crazy.

The poet Virgil wrote about the Cumaean Sibyl in the *Aeneid*, in a dramatic sequence where she inhales the smoke from burning laurel leaves and then "with wild hair, breast heaving, and foaming mouth" bellows to Aeneas that there's more trouble ahead for him.

All poor Aeneas wanted was to see his dead father. The Sibyl put him through a rigmarole of having to find a golden bough and burning animals in sacrifice. She finally escorted him into Hades, through a convenient door nearby in the foul-smelling, bubbling Lake Averno. The two of them rode across the River Styx and eventually got to Elysium, The Land of Joy, where Aeneas and his father had a tear-filled reunion.

Going to Cumae, you'll be visiting one of Italy's oldest settlements, founded by the Greeks in the eighth century B.C., way before Naples existed. It's free of tourist crowds, and marvelous to climb up curving, softly shaded paths, surrounded by bird songs and wild vegetation. Winding up from the cave, first you discover ruins of the Temple of Apollo, then a stone circle where Goddess Diana was once worshipped. At the top of the hill is the Temple of Jupiter. Settle in to the tranquil beauty, where the views of Cape Misenum inspire mythic thoughts.

**Sito Archeologico di Cuma:** Open from 9 until one hour before sunset, www.cir.campania.beniculturali.it.

❧

**Golden Day:** Go to the **Sito Archeologico di Cuma**, by car is best. While you're in the area, for the full Phlegran Fields experience, stop at **Volcano Solfatara** (www.solfatara.it), the mythical entrance to the Ancient Romans' Hell, where you can walk along the rocky surface, stopping at steaming jets to inhale hot, sulphorous vapors that have long been praised for their health benefits. Adjacent is a caffe and picnic area. Hiring a guide is recommended. Back in Naples, eat at **Da Dora** (Via Ferdinando Palasciano 30, 081 680519), where the house seafood pasta is divine and the waitress who bursts into song is so soulful you may find yourself teary-eyed.

# 19 Goddesses and Madonnas–Palermo

ACCORDING TO THE ANCIENT ROMANS, the Goddess Ceres brought abundance to Sicily, scattering seeds all over the island so fields of wheat, tomatoes, eggplant, zucchini, you name it, sprung up and thrived under the blazing sun.

In Palermo, Sicily's capital, Ceres stands majestically in one of the city's most beautiful outdoor places, the **Piazza Pretoria** fountain. Venus and a racy collection of nymphs and mermaids surround her. When this fountain was first brought here from a Florentine villa in 1575, the shocked Palermitani nicknamed it "The Fountain of Shame" because of all the nakedness.

The story of Ceres (Patron of Sicily, Motherhood and Agriculture) is interlocked with her daughter Proserpina, who caused Ceres tremendous grief. Beautiful Proserpina was picking flowers in a field near Enna in central Sicily when suddenly Pluto (God of the Underworld) caught sight of her, found her irresistible, swooped up, kidnapped or raped her (choose your version), and brought her down to Hades to make her his queen.

Distraught, Ceres left the heavens to wander Sicily in search of Proserpina, lured by the echoes of her daughter's cries. When she found out what Pluto had done, Ceres begged her husband (and brother!) Jupiter to get their daughter back. Jupiter had to oblige Ceres, because what with all her wandering and neglecting the fields, everything had stopped growing. Pluto let Proserpina go, but being a tricky god, he offered her a pomegranate to eat before she left. As soon as Proserpina bit into the fruit, a deal was sealed with that King of Hades: Proserpina would have to return to be Pluto's wife for four months out of the year.

That's one explanation for the change of seasons. Winter is a time when Proserpina does her stint in hell and Ceres mourns for her daughter. Spring comes when mother and daughter are joyfully reunited. To this day Sicilians hold festivals that mark Proserpina's leaving (in December) and returning (in March).

Beyond Palermo's Pretoria Fountain of goddesses and nymphs, there are wonderful sights that pay homage to the BVM. Close by and up some stairs from it is the tiny, sparkling **Santa Maria dell'Ammiraglio** church, originally dedicated to a Greek admiral and styled in a Byzantine-Islamic mix with fantastic mosaics of blue, deep red, and green set against a gold background.

Benedictine nuns, headed up by Mother Superior Eloisa Martorana, took it over in the sixteenth century, so it was renamed **La Martorana**. The nuns baroque-icized the church, which wasn't exactly the best thing, as they tore out some of those mosaics and replaced them with frescos. There's one pretty Annunciation, and we can forgive those nuns for their mistakes in redecorating, because they did keep the original mosaic columns and archways. The best thing they did was invent one of Palermo's tastiest treats: *frutta di Martorana*, marzipan molded into fruit shapes. These were so realistic when they were hung on a tree they were mistaken for the real thing and can still be found today in shops all over Palermo. You must have a taste.

More BVM treasures can be found in **La Kalsa**, my favorite Palermo neighborhood, where crumbling baroque buildings,

Spanish-Moorish architecture, and artists' studios blend together in a quiet area of the city that retains an exotic sense of the Arab port it once was.

In the Palazzo Abatellis, now the **Galleria Regionale**, you may think the *Annunciation* you see is mistitled, because there's no angel there. It's a close up of a gorgeous blue-veiled, dark-eyed Madonna, resembling the Sicilian women you'll see on the streets outside. Renaissance artist Antonello da Messina caught the moment where Mary receives her calling, with one hand raised from her book, in reaction to the offstage angel.

Also in this neighborhood is the awe-inspiring **Santa Maria dello Spasimo,** a sixteenth-century Romanesque church, named "Spasimo" to commemorate Mary's suffering at the crucifixion. What's amazing about the church is that it's roofless because a Turkish invasion kept it from being completed. Two huge sumac trees grow in the middle of what was once (almost) the sanctuary, forming a leafy cupola, opening to the Palermo sky. There's a natural grace to this setting and as you stand there looking up, you're likely to hear rehearsals going on in the attached music school that was once a monks' cloister. For a truly magical experience, get there for one of their evening concerts.

**La Martorana (Santa Maria dell'Ammiraglio)**: Piazza Bellini 2, Monday-Saturday 9:30-1, 3:30-5, Sunday 9:15-1.

**Galleria Regionale della Sicilia (Palazzo Abetellis)**: Via Alloro 4, Tuesday-Friday 9-6, Saturday-Sunday 9-1, www.regione.sicilia.it.

**Santa Maria dello Spasimo**: Via Santa Maria dello Spasimo 13, Daily 9-6, but opening times tend to be fickle here, with mornings being most reliable. For concert schedules, check out www.thebrassgroup.it.

᠅

**Golden Day**: Explore Palermo's **Kalsa district** and eat at **Antica Focacceria San Francesco** (Via A. Paternostro 58, 091 320264). To get a more luxurious side of Palermo, the pretty **Gattopardo Bar** at the **Grand Hotel et des Palmes** (Via Roma 398) is fun for a cocktail.

# 20 Nymphs, Goddesses, and Santa Lucias— Ortygia, Sicily

To step into a Wonderful Way Back Machine, head over a bridge in Syracuse to the island of Ortygia, one of Sicily's most intriguing and beautiful places. According to Homer, the sea nymph Calypso lured Odysseus here, and now amidst its remains of ancient civilizations and baroque architecture are treasures that pay homage to females, from nymphs to saints.

In Ortygia's main square, Piazza Archimede, is the baroque **Fontana di Diana**, that tells the story of the Greek Myth of Arethusa, a nymph dedicated to Artemis (Diana to the Romans), the Virgin Goddess of the Hunt.

Like Artemis, Arethusa loved frolicking about in nature. One fateful day she decided to take a dip in a lovely river, which just happened to be the god Alpheus's river. Trouble ensued, as he fell hopelessly in love with Arethusa, and went after her in hot pursuit. Desperate to keep her virginity, Arethusa begged Artemis for help, so the goddess swept in, lead Arethusa underground from Greece to Sicily's Ortygia island, and turned Arethusa into a spring.

Today the **Fonte Arethusa** spring at the Ortygia waterfront is a pretty papyrus-filled spot with swans floating about it. As for the rest of the Greek legend, Arethusa never did completely shake off her stalker, Alpheus. He remained connected to her through his river where she swam in Greece. When sacrifices were made there for the Olympics, the Fonte Arethusa here in Sicily would turn red. Even today it's believed that if you drop a cup into the Greek Alpheus River it'll turn up at this Ortygia spring.

The island's **Duomo** is built around the remains of a Greek Temple that honored the Goddess Athena, patron of Wisdom, Craftsmanship and Heroic Endeavors, who became Minerva to the Romans. Sprung from the head of Zeus, Athena was a real career goddess who did such great things as guide Odysseus home, think up the Trojan horse, and give Greece the olive tree.

The Duomo's Baroque and Norman designs blend around the massive Doric columns of Athena's temple. Once a sculpture of her graced the rooftop, where she stood with her golden shield, serving as a beacon to sailors. Now you'll see it's been replaced with a statue of the Virgin Mary.

Inside the Duomo, there's a chapel dedicated to the most celebrated saint in town—**Saint Lucy**, Patron of Syracuse and Eyes.

Lucy was born in the third century to a noble Syracuse family and early on decided to live for God and remain a virgin. This didn't sit well with her parents who wanted to marry her off, but Lucy managed to turn things around. She took her sick mother to pray at the tomb of Saint Agatha in Catania, and when her mother was miraculously healed, she took Lucy's side and stopped hounding her about finding a man. So Lucy could go about her saintly work, which was bringing food to Christians who were hiding out in underground tunnels. In order to guide her way through those dark tunnels, she wore a wreath of candles on her head, which is where the Swedes got the idea to always represent her with that wreath.

Despite herself, beautiful Lucy had many Syracuse admirers. One of them couldn't stop telling her how much he loved her eyes, so she plucked them out and handed them over to him on a plate, hoping he'd leave her in peace. But the guy was so insulted about being rebuffed, he turned Lucy over to the authorities for being a Christian. The governor's idea for a punishment was to drag Lucy to a whorehouse, but even with a team of oxen pulling her, Lucy miraculously could not be budged. When burning her at the stake didn't work, she was finally beheaded at a place on the Syracuse mainland where a church, Santa Lucia al Sepolcro, now stands.

If you're in Syracuse for Lucy's Feast Day (December 13), there'll be torch-lit processions and you'll be eating *cuccia*, wheat soaked in milk and sugar. The wheat commemorates a sixteenth-century Syracuse event, where the locals prayed to Saint Lucy to end a famine, and miraculously a ship sailed into the Ortygia harbor loaded with grain.

Finally, you shouldn't miss stopping by the **Museo Regionale di Arte Mediovale** (Palazzo Bellomo) to see Caravaggio's dark and intense masterpiece, the *Burial of Saint Lucy*. It was painted just a few months before Caravaggio died, when he was exiled to Syracuse, having been accused of murder in Rome. It's a powerfully haunting work, showing Lucy with her throat slashed, surrounded by mourners and gravediggers.

**Duomo**: Piazza del Duomo, Daily 8-12, 4-7.
**Museo Regionale di Arte Mediovale e Moderna (Palazzo Bellomo)**: Via Capodieci 16, Ortygia, Monday-Saturday 9-6:30, Sunday 9-12:30.

❧

**Golden Day**: Explore the sights of **Ortygia**, including the vibrant daily fish market, and eat at the extraordinary **Ristorante L'Ancora** (Via G. Perno 7, 0931 462 369) for fantastic seafood and lemon cake dessert. For a splurge, stay at the **Grand Hotel Ortigia Siracusa** (www.grandhotelortigia.it), a Liberty-style building set grandly on the seaside. Or go for good budget digs at **Domus Mariae** (www.sistemia.it/domusmariae), which is run by nuns and has simple rooms with sea views.

# 21 Temple of Segesta–Sicily

FOR AN UNFORGETTABLE, ROMANTIC EXPERIENCE OF the ancient world, head to **Segesta**, an hour's drive west of Palermo. There you'll find one of the most perfectly preserved temples in the world, from the fifth century B.C., set in the midst of a remote grassy field.

According to the Roman writer Cicero, the temple once held a statue of the Goddess Diana. When a governor ordered it removed, all the townswomen gathered to anoint the statue with perfume, cover it with flowers, and burn incense to give her a sacred send off.

Mystery surrounds this place. It's unknown why the Elymians, settlers who came before the conquering Greeks, never put a roof on it. Its thirty-six Doric columns clearly show Greek influence, and there's a theory that the Elymians built it to get on the good side of those powerful Greeks. At the time they were having a rivalry with their southern Selinunte neighbors, who'd aligned themselves with Syracuse. The Elymians, wanting the Greeks to think they were worth supporting, started building the temple because they knew a delegation from Athens would be coming through to check them out. Once the Athenians came and went, convinced the Segesta Elymians were rich and had good taste in architecture, they stopped work on the temple.

When the wind whips through the temple's columns, it sounds as if an organ is being played. And in spring, when it's surrounded by wildflowers, it's glorious. From the Segesta hilltop, there's a sweeping view of the valley towards the Gulf of Castellammare. Unlike places such as Agrigento, where modern developments break the ancient mood, in Segesta there are no such distractions.

A short walk away is an amphitheater from the third century B.C., where revivals of Greek plays, ballets, and avant-garde performances are staged in the summer.

**Segesta Temple**: Open November-March from 9-4 and April-August from 9-7, www.segestawelcome.com. It can be reached by driving an hour west from Palermo, or you can take a half-hour train or bus ride from Trapani.

**Golden Day**: Visit the **Segesta Temple**, and driving toward Erice, check into **Baglio Fontana** (www.bagliofontana.it), a wonderful agriturismo with an excellent restaurant.

# II

Ville, Palazzi,
and an Apartment

If these pretty walls could talk, you'd hear whispers of sweet nothings, laughing, crying, knock-down drag-out fights. The drama! In these grand homes, often adorned with masterpieces, heroines or courtesans or foreigners who moved here, lived and left a lasting legacy.

You may find yourself in the 500-room Palazzo Ducale, where Isabella d'Este, the brilliant gutsy Renaissance woman, became a patron of the arts and ruled Mantua. Or in a humble apartment in Florence, where Elizabeth Barrett Browning spent the happiest years of her life.

My first thoughts as I wander through these places always veer to: *Imagine the parties! A princess waltzing, a poet entertaining her writer friends, a courtesan playing a lute.*

Then my mind wanders.... *What about an ordinary day? A Savoy Queen waking up with that gigantic chandelier hanging over her bed. What would it have been like to have been Eleonora de' Medici, flinging open the curtains to her Boboli Gardens' view?*

History comes alive in these places. Go, admire, and indulge in your own imaginings as you walk in these women's footsteps.

# 22 Palazzo Barberini– Rome

IN *ROMAN HOLIDAY*, THE PRINCESS PLAYED by Audrey Hepburn escapes from this palace to end up on a romantic adventure with reporter Gregory Peck. It's sublime to play Audrey's moves backward and escape inside the Barberini to peacefully take in Renaissance masterpieces.

The palace was the digs of Maffeo Barberini, who transformed it when he became Pope Urban VIII in 1623. He went all out to make it *splendido*, calling in the best artists of the day, including Bernini and Borromini. You'll climb Borromini's spiral staircase as you enter. Inside you'll get a dizzying hit looking up at the Grand Salone ceiling, frescoed by Pietro da Cortona. Go ahead and lie back on a couch to admire this *Triumph of Providence*, where golden bees (the Barberini family emblem) ascend to the heavens.

Most of the rooms you'll be walking through were originally the apartment of Princess Anna Colonna Barberini, who had married the pope's nephew. She was the palace hostess and the most power-ful woman in Rome during the Barberini's seventeenth-century heyday. The family's fortunes got dispersed over the years, and the palace was sold to the State in 1949, becoming the National Gallery of Art.

In the galleries, you'll see beautiful women immortalized by masters, including:

### ⚘ *Fornarina* (Raphael's Girlfriend)

The subject of Raphael's most famous portrait is his longtime lover, Margherita Luti, who he called Fornarina, which translates to "little oven." The dark-haired, bare-breasted, mischievous-looking beauty was a Trastevere baker's daughter. She wears a bracelet with Raphael's signature on it, as if they were going steady.

### ⚘ *Beatrice Cenci* (Who Murdered Her Daddy)

With those legendary huge eyes and innocent over-the-shoulder look, it's hard to imagine this sixteen-year-old bludgeoned her father to death. That is until you hear the story of the man's atrocious cruelty to his whole family, who joined Beatrice in the murder. The painting is believed to have been completed the night before Beatrice was decapitated, in front of huge crowds on the Ponte Sant'Angelo. It's attributed to Guido Reni, but many believe Elisabetta Sirani, a female artist, is the one who painted it.

### ⚘ *Judith Beheading Holofernes* (Bible's Gutsiest Widow)

Master painter Caravaggio captures a gory biblical moment here. It's Judith, chopping off the head of General Holofernes, complete with spurting blood. Her maid stands by with a "Take that, you bastard!" look.

According to the Old Testament, Judith was a widow who got fed up with her Israeli countrymen in their fight against the Assyrians, so she took matters into her own hands, got all dolled up, and went to visit the enemy's General Holofernes. Clever woman that she was, Judith promised him helpful information and sexual favors, which she never made good on. The general lusted after Judith, and threw a banquet where he became "sodden with wine," expecting some nooky afterward. Imagine his surprise when Judith snuck into his tent, found Holofernes sprawled out drunk as a skunk, and lopped his head off.

Caravaggio's brilliant brush strokes illuminate Judith's conflicted expression. She's repulsed, curious, a bit repentant, but committed. For his model, he used one of Rome's most popular courtesans of the day, Fillide Melandroni. A few years after the painting was completed, Caravaggio got into a street brawl with Melandroni's "protector," Ranuccio Tomassoni. It's believed Caravaggio was trying to castrate Tomassoni, but instead gave his thigh a fatal artery-severing slash. Caravaggio was exiled from Rome for the murder, never to return.

**Palazzo Barberini:** Via delle Quattro Fontane 13, 8:30-7. Closed Monday, www.galleriaborghese.it.

**Golden Day:** Morning at the **Barberini** and lunch at **Colline Emiliane** (Via degli Avignonesi, 22, 06 481 7538, reservations essential, closed Sunday night and Monday) for specialties of the Emilia-Romagna region—the lasagna and *tagliatelle alla Bolognese* are out of this world.

**TIP:** *Don't miss the museum's backyard: a classic garden.*

## RECOMMENDED READING

*The Families Who Made Rome: A History and Guide* by Anthony Majanlahti
*Beatrice's Spell: The Enduring Legacy of Beatrice Cenci* by Belinda Jack

# 23
## Villa Farnesina–Rome

LE DELIZIE OR "THE DELIGHTS" was the original name of this villa, known back in Renaissance days as the best party house in Rome. It was built by Agostino Chigi, banker to the Popes, aka the Richest Man in the World. On the same site in 44 B.C. was a villa where Cleopatra had carried on with Julius Caesar.

Chigi was a generous patron of the arts, so in 1506 he called in Rome's top architect (Baldassare Peruzzi) and best painters to create luscious gardens and a villa packed with frescos of mythological love scenes to inspire his guests. Spectacles with singers and dancers were staged here, followed by opulent banquets. For the grand finale, Chigi had his servants toss his used china and silverware into the Tiber. Little did his guests know he kept a net down there to catch it all.

The stars of Chigi's parties were Rome's adored courtesans. These beautiful ladies, called "honest prostitutes," in addition to providing their expected services, could recite classical poetry at the drop of a hat and serenade their admirers with lutes or violins. They were treated well by Rome's many wealthy bachelors, who ranged from merchant traders to priests. Like movie stars, when courtesans rode through the streets in their fancy carriages, people would run out to gawk at their elegant get-ups, jewels, and hairstyles.

Imperia, one of Rome's most famous courtesans, was a favorite of Chigi's; he planned on living with her in this villa when he first decided to build it. The painter Raphael, who also spent quality time with Imperia, had her model for one of the first frescos you'll see here in the *Loggia of Galatea*. The image of the half-naked sea nymph (surprisingly muscular and fleshy) is a scene from a Greek myth that began with the Cyclops Polyphemus falling madly in love with Galatea. Unfortunately for Polyphemus, Galatea fell in love with a mortal shepherd,  Acis. When Polyphemus saw the two of them cavorting, he flipped out and threw a boulder at the couple, killing Acis. The blood of Galatea's dead lover turned into a river that she rides away on in this painting, triumphantly escaping Polyphemus.

Raphael's model Imperia was not so triumphant. The courtesan had many men besides Chigi, and fell in love with one of them. When he tired of her, Imperia feared she was losing her beauty, and at the age of twenty-six swallowed poison and died. The exact date of her suicide was August 15 (coincidentally, the celebration of Mary's Assumption into heaven), and in Rome there was a huge storm, with folks in the city saying Jupiter had thundered down to take away their beloved beauty.

Imperia's image appears again upstairs in this villa, where the artist Sodoma frescoed Chigi's bedroom with scenes from the life of Alexander the Great. There *The Wedding of Alexander and Roxanne* reeks with sexual anticipation, as Roxanne's clothes are tugged at by *putti* and Alexander stands awaiting his bride.

Chigi and Imperia had broken up before her suicide, and he'd gone to Venice and gotten himself another courtesan, Francesca. The couple moved in here and, after having four children, the Pope insisted they marry. Their wedding was one of the biggest bashes ever held in the villa, with Pope Leo and twelve cardinals in attendance.

For all the great parties at Le Delizie, guests would enter through the *Loggia of Psyche*, the villa's most beautiful setting, that originally opened to the gardens and wasn't enclosed like it is today. Raphael designed it, but had no time to paint it, as he was busy with other jobs and his romance with Margherita Luti, a baker's daughter who lived in the neighborhood. His students completed it, bringing in the surrounding nature with ornamentation of lush greenery, flowers, and fruits that surround frescos which tell the love story of Amore and Psyche. Here's a myth that fit right in with the Renaissance philosophy of joining the Divine (Amore) with the Mortal Mind/Soul (Psyche). The Goddess Venus is of course involved, and after many trials, the main characters are united in a marriage celebration painted on the ceiling.

After Chigi's death, the Farnese family bought Le Delizie, renamed it Farnesina, and planned on connecting it to their palazzo near the Campo dei Fiori. The proposed bridge was never completed, but part of it forms that beautiful, dripping-with-vines archway you'll see over the Via Giulia.

**Villa Farnesina**: Via della Lungara 230, Open Monday-Saturday 9-2, www.villafarnesina.it.

❧

**Golden Day**: Visit the **Farnesina**, eat at **Da Gildo** (Via della Scala 31, 06 581 0733, www.dagildotrastevere.it) for a seasonally changing menu full of delicious Roman classics, such as *vignarola*, a vegetable stew.

**TIP**: *This is one of the few museums in Rome that is open on a Monday.*

# 24 The Costume Gallery at the Pitti Palace— Florence

DUCHESS ELEONORA DI TOLEDO DE' MEDICI got fed up living in the gloomy Palazzo Vecchio. So in 1549, with her own money, she bought a palace on the other side of the Arno that the Pitti family had up for sale. What with her eight kids and failing health (hubby Duke Cosimo I had given her syphilis), Eleonora wanted someplace away from the city racket where she could have a garden. The choice was connected to her past: she'd been born in sunny Spain and grew up around lush gardens in Naples, the daughter of the city's Viceroy.

She was so raring to relocate she even moved in while renovations were going on, with architect Vasari doubling the palace in size. Right off the bat, she hired a landscaper for the backyard, which today we know as the Boboli Gardens.

Now the Pitti Palace Eleonora bought is home to six museums and those beautiful gardens. It's all too much for one visit, so I say go to the Costume Gallery for a change of scene from painting and sculpture. It's an absolutely glam place, the only museum in Italy dedicated to fashion design and is relatively new to the Pitti, opened in 1983.

You'll find it in the Palazzina della Meridiana, that was added to the palace and completed in 1858. Luscious chandeliers, gold-framed mirrors, and brocade walls decorate room after room (eighteen in all) that takes you through 300 years of Italian fashion.

Displays rotate every two years, as the collection is vast. One of my most memorable visits there began with eighteenth-century

Marie Antoinette styles—impossibly wide skirts of richly textured fabrics. There were fantastic silk Neapolitan wedding dresses, satin bustled ensembles worn by contessas in the nineteenth century, beaded Italian flapper wear from the 1920s.

But what I most adored were the 'post-World War II fashions, where Italian designers broke loose and the styles were outrageously chic—from scrumptious 1950s cocktail dresses to sparkling gowns by Florentine designer Cesare Fabbri, and choice vintage pieces from such greats as Valentino, Gianfranco Ferre, and Maurizio Galante. It's fun to imagine Italian women out and about flaunting these threads. Many come from the closet of an eccentric Bologna department store heiress, Cecilia Matteucci Lavarini, who's world famous for collecting couture and has sent some of her overflow to the museum.

The last room of the exhibit honors Eleonora. The dress she was buried in is displayed there. It's in tatters, spread out in a glass case, but you still can get an idea of the style of this fabulous woman, who kept a staff of ten weavers working full time to create her elegant get-ups.

Eleonora married Cosimo I de' Medici in 1539, when she was seventeen and he was just a year older. The Medici rep was at a low point, so it was a coup for them to have this beautiful woman descended from Castilian royalty added to their mix. Eleonora became a beloved first lady, winning the Florentines over with her generous patronage of artists and the peasantry. The marriage worked out: she put up with Cosimo's notorious mood swings, he put up with her penchant for gambling. He even named her regent when he'd take trips away from Florence, which was a most unusual position for a woman of those days.

Most importantly, Eleonora popped out heirs, bearing eleven children in their first fourteen years of marriage, five of them male. This was tough on her five-foot-tall body. By the time she was forty, she was emaciated, there were hairline fractures on her pelvis from the child-birthing, and her bones were deteriorating from syphilis she'd contracted from Cosimo. She took a trip with her son Garzia to see her older son Giovanni in Pisa, even though he'd warned them there was a malaria outbreak. One by one, first Garzia, then Giovanni, then Eleonora succumbed to the disease and died. From the looks of the dress, her funeral must have been grand.

Right down the steps from the gallery is the wondrous expanse of the Boboli Gardens. In the warmer months, you can stroll paths and terraces bordered by lemon trees and blooming flowerbeds, just as Eleonora did.

**Pitti Palace:** Houses the Palatine Gallery, Gallery of Modern Art, Silver Museum, Porcelain Museum, Boboli Gardens, and the Costume Gallery. Costume Gallery open daily 8:15-4:30 or 6:30, depending on the season. Closed first and last Mondays of the month, www.sbas.fi.it/english/musei/palazzopitti.

**Golden Day:** Enjoy wandering around the **Costume Gallery** and **Boboli Gardens**, linger in the **Oltrarno** and dine at **Il Santo Bevitore** (Via di Santo Spirito 64/66, 055 21 1264, reservations advised), an elegant/cozy place with a great wine list and refined Tuscan classics.

## RECOMMENDED READING

*The House of Medici, Its Rise and Fall* by Christopher Hibbert

# 25 *Casa Guidi–Florence*

WHEN WE THINK OF "HOW DO I LOVE THEE, let me count the ways," Elizabeth Barrett Browning's most famous line, it seems only natural that this romantic poet would wind up in Italy. It was *amore* that brought her to Florence, where she lived for fourteen years with her husband Robert Browning. Stop by their former Oltrarno apartment to get a hit of what life was like for these bohemians back in the nineteenth century.

When Barrett met Browning in London, she was thirty-eight and at an all-time low. Her poetry books were a smash, but she was a semi-invalid with lung problems that began with a spinal injury she got as a teenager and left her dependent on opium for the rest of her life. And she was in mourning for her beloved brother. He'd gone with her to a lovely lakeside spot to help restore her health, and ended up drowning in that lake.

In swooped poet-on-the-rise Robert Browning, who wrote her a fan letter that began, "I love your verses with all my heart..." It was a little too over the top for Elizabeth, but the two started writing to each other and after a few months Robert showed up at her father's house, where Elizabeth was living as a recluse. Robert was six years younger than Elizabeth, a strapping, healthy guy, and it was hard for her to even imagine he could love her. Elizabeth's wealthy, tyrannical father was dead set against any of his twelve children coupling, but after their first meeting, a secret romance between Elizabeth and Robert began.

A year later, in 1846, they eloped, and Robert whisked Elizabeth off to Italy for their honeymoon, along with her nurse and cocker spaniel. Elizabeth described it as "living a dream." After toodling around, they found this gem of a six-room apartment in Florence. They bargained with the landlord, giving him back the grand furniture the place came with, and getting the rent down to twenty-five guineas a year, which included free entrance to the nearby Boboli Gardens.

The apartment is on the *piano nobile* (what we think of as the second floor) of this fifteenth-century palazzo, once owned by Count Guidi. You pass through a big dining room to get to the main attraction: the drawing room where Elizabeth wrote and hung out with artists and writers like the Hawthornes and Harriet Beecher Stowe.

Thanks to an oil painting Robert had done, the room looks almost exactly as it was when the Barrett-Brownings lived here. It has a cozy Victorian style, with intense olive green walls, soft lighting, velvet upholstered furniture, and a little table with a mother of pearl tea set. In the middle of it all is a tiny writing desk where you can imagine Elizabeth composing *Aurora Leigh*—a love story of a woman writer making her way in the world. The gilt-framed mirror over the fireplace is the one piece that's original to Casa Guidi. Elizabeth wrote to her sister about how thrilled she was Robert bought it, even though to her the five-pound price was an extravagance.

Elizabeth got her strength back in Florence. At forty-three she gave birth to a son, whom she nicknamed Pen. She got passionately involved with the Italian fight for independence, and wrote the poem "Casa Guidi Windows" in support of the Florentines she saw from her terrace, who protested fiercely against Austrian occupation.

Though most biographies claim "they lived happily after," Elizabeth and Robert were real people, so it wasn't a fifteen-year honeymoon. Elizabeth was the poet star of the duo, paying all the bills for the house and many wonderful vacations, with her writing profits and money she'd inherited from an uncle. She got her way when it came to dressing Pen, outfitting him in effeminate velvet get-ups and having his hair grow in long curls like his mommy's. Robert didn't stand behind Elizabeth's passions—feminism, the fight for Italian unification, and most of all her explorations into spirituality, which involved consulting mediums. Add to that her four miscarriages and opium addiction to give some shadings to the "happily ever after" story.

A photograph of Elizabeth just months before her death shows her dressed in billowing black silk, with that signature cascade of curls surrounding a face that looks pained and cadaverous. The story goes she died in Robert's arms in 1861 in Casa Guidi, at the age of fifty-five. Some suspect Robert may have upped the dose of morphine to put an end to her suffering.

Robert left Florence after Elizabeth died and never returned. In England, he finally reached his success as a poet.

In Elizabeth's memory (no mention of Robert), the Florentines placed a plaque over the doorway of the Casa Guidi apartment building, honoring her for poetry they said "made a golden ring between Italy and England."

**Casa Guidi**: Piazza San Felice 8 (Oltrarno), Monday-Wednesday-Friday 3-6, April to November, 055 354 457, www.browningsociety.org.

**NOTE**: The attached rooms of the Barrett-Browning place that aren't being used for a museum have been turned into a **vacation apartment**, so you can sleep where the Brownings slept. It's three bedrooms, three bathrooms, and kitchen (www.landmarktrust.org.uk).

**English Cemetery:** Elizabeth Barrett Browning's grave, Piazzale Donatello.

**Golden Day:** Visit **Casa Guidi**, enjoy the **Oltrarno**, then have dinner at **Osteria del Cinghiale Bianco** (Borgo San Jacopo 43r, 055 215706, www.cinghialebianco.com), set in a thirteenth-century tower, serving robust versions of traditional Florentine dishes.

---

### RECOMMENDED READING

*Elizabeth Barrett Browning* by Margaret Forster

# 26 The Peggy Guggenheim Collection—Venice

PEGGY GUGGENHEIM WAS ONE OF THE twentieth century's great bon vivants. How fitting that her home base for thirty years was this airy palazzo on the Grand Canal. Today it's filled with a fabulous collection of modern art she acquired, including paintings and sculptures by such masters as Picasso, Kandinsky, de Chirico, and Mondrian.

Peggy's spirit lives on in these surroundings that resonate with the spicy times she and her artist friends had here from 1949 to 1979. You can imagine her stepping off the terrace into her private gondola for her daily ride, which she took religiously at sunset, wearing a flamboyant get-up and those signature butterfly-shaped sunglasses.

Born in New York in 1898, Peggy was the free-spirited rebel of the wealthy Guggenheim family. Her father died in the sinking of the *Titanic* when she was fourteen. When she came of age and inherited her fortune, she took off for Europe, and married writer Laurence Vail, who was nicknamed King of the Bohemians. They honeymooned in Capri, lived in Paris, and bopped around the continent, stopping in Venice where her lifelong passion for the place took hold.

By the time she was thirty-nine, Peggy was divorced, her two kids were in boarding school, and as she puts it, "I needed something to do." A friend suggested she open an art gallery.

Even though she knew nothing about modern art, she dove in, with Marcel Duchamp by her side to educate her. She made a vow to buy one painting a day and decided, taking Samuel Beckett's advice, that she would only buy the work of living artists. Duchamp and Beckett were not only friends who guided her along. They were just two of Peggy's myriad line-up of lovers she became famous for throughout her life. When asked in her later years, "How many husbands have you had, Mrs. Guggenheim?" she cracked back: "D'you mean mine or other people's?"

Her first gallery show in New York made a big splash—introducing the world to painters such as Robert Motherwell, Mark Rothko, and Jackson Pollack. It was Peggy's generous patronage of the American avant-garde that helped to bring international recognition to the movement.

"I have never been to a city that has given me the same sense of freedom as Venice," Peggy says in her autobiog-  raphy. In 1949, when she was fifty-one, she settled there, buying the Palazzo Venier dei Leoni in the Dorsoduro *sestiere*. The eighteenth-century, one-floor building was perfect for her to sunbathe on the roof and display her sculptures in the garden. Little by little, more and more of her home became gallery space, and while she lived there she opened it to the public a few afternoons a week. She willed the palazzo to her uncle's Solomon R. Guggenheim Foundation, so today it's been expanded and stands as one of the world's most important small museums of contemporary art.

The Peggy vibe throughout the museum is palpable. A fantastic silver headboard designed by Alexander Calder graces what was her bedroom. A pair of paintings by the surrealist Max Ernst feature monstrous half-naked female images, draped in orange capes, interpreted as being inspired by Peggy. She was married to Max from 1942 to 1946. It was a tumultuous relationship, largely because Max was still in love with Leonora Carrington, a surrealist painter whom he'd left behind in France when Peggy helped him to escape the Nazis and come to America.

One of the first sculptures Peggy bought for the villa appears center stage on her terrace: *The Angel of the Citadel* by Marino Marini. This Etruscan-inspired bronze features an ecstatic rider on horse-back—so ecstatic he has an enormous hard-on. Peggy loved peeking out from her sitting room to watch visitors' shocked reactions to the statue. And out of respect, because the terrace faced the Venetian prefect's home, she had the figure cast with a removable penis, so when nuns rode by on their way to get the patriarch's blessing, she'd remove it.

Peggy died at eighty-one and her ashes are buried in the muse-um's garden, alongside those of fourteen beloved Lhasa terriers she kept throughout her Venetian life. Nearby is an olive tree (a gift from Yoko Ono), and sculptures by such artists as Arp and Moore.

Along with the great collection, this place has wonderful docents. In contrast to most Italian museums, where employees typically slump on folding chairs and bark "No photo!" from time to time, here you'll find young, enthusiastic types. They're art stu-dents from all over the world on Guggenheim internships, thrilled to be in Venice, and delightful to talk to about what Peggy col-lected. Just as Peggy brought a fresh spirit of adventure to Venice, these docents keep her spark alive.

**Peggy Guggenheim Museum**: Daily 10-6, closed Tuesday, www.guggenheim-venice.it.

✣

**Golden Day:** Visit the **museum**, lingering a while in the **caffè** for a drink (hot cocoa on a wintry day is fab). Enjoy the Dorsoduro neighborhood, with a stop by **Cantinone già Schiavi** wine bar (Fondamenta Nani 992) and eat at **Ai Gondolieri** (Calle San Domenico, 041 528 6396, closed Tuesday, www.aigondolieri.it), a romantic old school place for such specialties as *Fegato alla Veneziana*, liver and onions. It's one of the few restaurants in Venice that doesn't serve fish.

**TIP:** *Speaking of contemporary art, every two years—the odd ones—there is the Venice Biennale, an international exhibition featuring artists from all over the world (www.labiennale.org).*

## RECOMMENDED READING

*Out of This Century: The Autobiography of Peggy Guggenheim* by Peggy Guggenheim

*Art Lover: A Biography of Peggy Guggenheim* by Anton Gill

# 27 Palazzo Fortuny– Venice

VENETIANS CALLED THIS PLACE "The House of the Magician." It's where Mariano Fortuny, who became world famous for his outrageously gorgeous fabrics, gowns, and lamps, set up his home and workshop in 1907. There was a woman behind his success: Henriette Negrin, who he met in Paris in 1897, when she was a French widow, a model and a seamstress. She became his muse, collaborator, and wife—after they lived together for twenty-two years. You'll see Fortuny's paintings of Henriette here—some nude, others with her dressed elegantly with her hair swept up, along with photographs of their trips to Greece and Egypt, where Fortuny got lots of inspiration.

In the museum where they once lived and worked together, you enter the world of this eccentric, twentieth-century Renaissance man. Fortuny was born in Granada in 1871, to both a father and grandfather (on his mother's side) who were highly acclaimed painters in Spain. His father died when he was three, so his mother took him to live in Paris, and also traveled about, until they finally settled in Venice, because Fortuny was horribly allergic to horses, and this was the only place around without carriages.

After his early artistic endeavors in painting and photography, and success in designing sets and lighting for theater, Fortuny, at thirty-six years old, began his work on printed fabrics here with Henriette. He'd already had an attic studio in the thirteenth-century palazzo, and then bought the building that had been cut up into apartments and gutted it, turning it into a free-flowing creative space.

The walls of the first floor's large rectangular room are covered with Fortuny's patterned fabrics, creating a warm, exotic, colorful ambience. His paintings and lamps surround displays of his gowns and capes that were worn by such illustrious women as Eleanora Duse, Sarah Bernhardt, and Isadora Duncan.

Fortuny broke into the woman's fashion world in 1907 with his Delphos gown, inspired by tunics from ancient Greek statuary. It was simple and finely pleated, in soft, shimmering colors. Women happily tore off their corsets to put on the sensational dress that elegantly draped their bodies. He packaged it rolled up in a hatbox, so it was easy and light for travel.

The second floor of the museum gives you an idea of what life was like when 100 workers were there producing Fortuny fabrics, under Henriette's supervision. In contrast to what's below, it's stripped bare with only huge worktables. Off to the side is Fortuny's library and personal workshop, where you'll get a hit of the practical side of this free-spirited artist. It's packed with volumes of books about artists who came before him, lots of journals where he catalogued designs and colors, his paints and tools. Fortuny's preferred entrance to this palazzo was climbing through the skylight, straight into his workshop.

Depending on what is being exhibited, you may get to see the expansive top floor of the palazzo. The views from here, through wavy glass windows, are some of the best in Venice: red roofs, church domes and steeples, the ever-changing dramatic sky...it's marvelous to imagine how he was inspired here.

Fortuny's fabric designs, of intricate swirls, animals, and geometric prints, on cotton, silk, or velvet, clearly show his influences from Spain and travels to Greece and farther east. But ultimately, they're completely Venetian, reflecting the cultural melting pot of the city, with rich colors muted by the city's fog, or glistening in gold or silver sunlight. He was called "the magician" because nobody could figure out exactly how he produced these fabrics, and his techniques are still kept secret.

You'll be so tempted to reach out and touch them in the museum, but you can't. For a tactile experience, head to the **Venetia Studium** stores in Venice, where you can even buy a scarf, pillow, purse, or lamp inspired by Fortuny, to take home and keep a little bit of the Venetian magician in your life.

**Palazzo Fortuny Museum:** Campo San Beneto (San Marco), Daily except Tuesday 10-6, www.fortuny.visitmuve.it.

**Venetia Studium Stores:** In San Marco, Calle delle Ostreghe and Ponte del Lovo, and in Dorsoduro at Calle del Bastion, www.venetiastudium.com.

❧

**Golden Day:** Visit the **Palazzo Fortuny** and have lunch or an aperitivo at **Acqua Pazza** (Campo Sant'Angelo, San Marco, 041 277 0688, closed Monday, www.veniceacquapazza.com), serving excellent seafood, cooked in the southern Amalfi Coast-style, with Campania wines to match.

**TIP:** *To enjoy more Venetian textiles, visit the Bevilacqua shops for gorgeous velvets and brocades (Fondamenta Cononica, San Marco and Campo Santa Maria del Giglio, www.bevilacquatessuti.com).*

# 28 Villa Valmarana Ai Nani–Vicenza, Veneto

SPRINKLED OVER THE VENETIAN PLAIN ARE beautiful villas from the sixteenth to the eighteenth centuries. They're the jewels of superstar Renaissance architect Andrea Palladio and his followers, which recall the symmetry and grace of Greek and Roman temples.

You can visit some of them pleasantly from Venice or Padua by taking a boat ride down the Brenta Canal, which stops at the waterway entrances to the villas and a restaurant for lunch. That's a Golden Day right there.

But to get the full Palladio hit, go to the town of **Vicenza**. This is where Palladio was born and it's packed with his treasures, including the not-to-be-missed **Teatro Olimpico**.

A walk or short bus ride away from Vicenza's historic center takes you to Palladio's famous **Villa Rotonda**, and further along a favorite of mine: the **Villa Valmarana ai Nani**. *"Nani"* means dwarves, and the name originated with this legend:

Once upon a time, a couple who lived in this villa gave birth to a daughter, who was a beautiful dwarf. Loving their child dearly, they wanted to protect her from feeling different, so they hired dwarf servants and kept her secluded in the villa and walled garden. For many years she was clueless and content, but when she was fifteen she got curious about what was going on in the outside world. When her dwarf servants were sleeping, she climbed the stone wall, and up rode a handsome fellow on horseback. It was love at first sight for the dwarf-girl, but when she reached out to ride away with him into the sunset, for the first time she realized, "Oh no! I'm a dwarf!" Horrified, she hurled herself off the wall to her death. The servant dwarves heard her cries, woke up, and ran to find her. When they saw their dead mistress, they froze in grief.

That's why you'll see statues of seventeen *nani* atop the villa walls. They're all inspired by Venetian Commedia dell'Arte characters—such as the Doctor, the King, the Knight, and the Turk. When Giustino Valmarana, a theater fan, moved here in 1720 he incorporated the *nani* story as part of his redesign.

The legend probably originated in the seventeenth century, when dwarves were popular characters in royal courts. They were perfect playmates for children, entertaining, and considered good-luck tokens. Many were the result of inbreeding, and they were treated like pets, often given away by their mothers, as they weren't considered part of the "real" family and wouldn't be inheriting anything. Cruel, but true.

Once you're past the *nani* and inside the walls, things get elegant: lovely gardens surround a *foresteria* (former farm-laborer's place) and butter-yellow *palazzina*. Inside the little palazzo is where superstar painter Giambattista Tiepolo created some of the most stunning works of his career.

Tiepolo was a Venetian master of rococo, who frescoed this place with theatrical gusto, finishing the *palazzina* interior in only four months. Using a dreamy pastel palate, he created breathtaking scenes from classical myths and legends.

When you enter, you're hit with his *Sacrifice of Iphigenia*, which packs the power of an opera climax. Center stage sits the Greek warrior Agamemnon, pleading to the heavens for mercy, as he holds a knife to his daughter Iphigenia's chest. The story goes that Agamemnon ticked off the Goddess Diana by bragging that he was a better hunter than she was. To punish him she silenced the winds, screwing up his fleet. A prophet appeared to Agamemnon and said he'd have to sacrifice his daughter to lift Diana's curse. In Tiepolo's unusual happy-ending version of the story, Diana (on the ceiling) has a change of heart and flies in to substitute a sacrificial deer for Iphigenia. On the surrounding side panels, Tiepolo painted new winds blowing through.

Action-packed love scenes fill the adjoining rooms. There are images from "Orlando Furioso," a Renaissance epic poem, where the gorgeous maiden Angelica makes Orlando absolutely *furioso*, because she can't help but attract the attentions of other men.

In the Foresteria, which was a guesthouse, there's one final Tiepolo masterpiece in the Olympus Room, where Venus is paired with her boyfriend Mars and Diana with Apollo.

The rest of the Foresteria was frescoed by his son, Giandomenico, who moved on to realism, and painted images from eighteenth-century life. There are scenes of peasants in the countryside, wealthy folks partying, a carnival—with both a monkey and an African servant serving chocolate.

Framed photographs of the Valmaranas, who still live here, are scattered about. One of their family's twentieth-century heroines was Amalia, who was a mover and shaker in the Italian women's movement after World War II. She helped to found the Catholic Centro Italiano Femminile, an organization that got women involved in the reconstruction of Italy, defending women's rights and helping them get health care.

There's a special charm to this small (for a villa) place that's been in the same family for over three hundred years. The comical statues, colorful garden, sweeping frescos, even the family photos, mix together magically in this exquisitely designed space.

**Villa Valmarana:** Open throughout the year, but different days and times depending on the season. Check www.villavalmarana. com for up-to-date hours and prices.

**How to get there:** Trains from Venice connect regularly to Vicenza and take about forty-five minutes (www.trenitalia.it). Or rent a car, so you can explore the outskirts (www.autoeurope.com).

**Golden Day:** Visit the **villa** and enjoy Palladio's masterpieces in Vicenza. For dinner, take a fifteen-minute drive to **Caldogno** and eat at **Trattoria Molin Vecio** (Via Giaroni 116, 044 585 168, closed Tuesdays). It's built around a mill from 1520, surrounded by a lovely landscape and huge herb garden. Sleep at **Hotel Campo Marzio** (www.hotelcampomarzio.com), a boutique hotel close to the historic center.

---

### TOURS

Boat tours of Italian villas are available from Venice or Padua at www.battellidelbrenta.it or www.ilburchiello.it.

# 29 Palazzo Ducale— Mantua, Lombardy

OF ALL THE 500 ROOMS IN the humongous **Palazzo Ducale**, the two teeniest, hidden away on the ground floor, are the most enchanting. They are the *grotta* and *studiolo* of Isabella d'Este, aka First Lady of the Renaissance. Here's where she'd come to leave the world behind and read the classics, play her lute, or have her friends over to marvel over the paintings, antiques, and gems she'd collected.

It was all the rage for Renaissance palaces to have a *studiolo*. The idea behind it was to move away from the sterile, monastic retreats of the Dark Ages and into a space inspired by the ancient Greeks and Romans, where the appreciation of beauty was the path to transcendence.

The treasures that once filled Isabella's rooms have been sent off to museums, but there's still a tantalizing magic here. Her *studiolo's* deep blue walls, stars, and gilded woodwork create the ambience of an evening sky in paradise. In the *grotta*, polished cabinets of wood inlays form pictures of idyllic cities and palaces. Alabaster carvings of mythological figures grace the moldings. Right out the door is her secret garden, a square patch of trimmed shrubs and pots of laurel. I'd love to move in.

Isabella moved into the Palazzo Ducale in 1490 when she was sixteen and married Marchese Francesco Gonzaga. His powerhouse family dominated Mantua for 300 years, and the town is full of Renaissance buildings built during their reign. Francesco was a

Captain General, off on fighting trips for long stretches, but came home enough so Isabella ended up having seven children. She was a faithful wife, while Francesco dallied about, even having a fling with the infamous Lucrezia Borgia.

Isabella let her husband's affairs slide and put her energies into

ruling Mantua while he was away. She was already highly educated, from growing up the daughter of the Duke of Ferrara, and then studied agriculture, architecture, and industry to get up to speed in other areas. Besides her brains, she had a natural talent for diplomacy, and could deftly swim in the shark tank of Renaissance politics. She did such a bang-up job that Mantua was raised in status to a Duchy.

While she was at it, she also made the palace a gathering place for poets, artists, and musicians, turning Mantua into a thriving cultural center. Leonardo da Vinci stopped by and made a sketch of her that now hangs in the Louvre. Titian painted her twice.

Her voracious appetite for beauty was where this almost perfect woman slid into naughty behavior. She insisted on wearing sables and elaborate costumes, even though the Mantua treasury couldn't afford it.

She left behind hundreds of letters and some are hilarious to read, showing her needy-greedy side. These are the ones she'd address to relatives of sick people whom she knew had precious collections. She'd begin with much sympathy, but soon enough stick it to them, all but begging to be informed immediately if their relative died, so she could get her hands on their stuff.

As an art patron she could be downright annoying. In one instance, she hounded the established master Perugino, demanding the painting she commissioned fit her standards exactly. The goddesses could not be naked. The theme had to be Chastity

(Minerva and Diana) triumphing over earthly love (Venus and Cupid). It was Isabelle's blatant way of standing up against that ne'er-do-well husband of hers, pushing a "Purity is Power" line.

All through the early years of her marriage, Isabelle filled her downstairs *grotta* with her growing collection. When Francesco retired from the army, he came back to Mantua debilitated and addled from syphilis, but still managed to grump about how Isabella had become the boss, which she didn't let bother her in the least.

Isabella was forty-six when Francesco died, which was old in those days. She'd always had weight problems, so climbing the palace stairs to her rooms was getting to her. Just like empty nesters who trade in their family home for a condo, Isabella moved out of her upstairs palazzo digs and redecorated this ground floor space which would be her beloved haven until she died eighteen years later.

Engraved in the wall is her motto, from the Roman poet Seneca: *Nec Speranza, Nec Metu: Neither Hope, Nor Fear.* It was this forge-ahead attitude that fueled strong, independent Isabella, who in an age when many women couldn't even leave the house, undeniably triumphed.

**Palazzo Ducale**: Tuesday-Sunday 8:30-7, www.mantovaducale. beniculturali.it.

❧

**Golden Day:** Visit Isabella's *studiolo* and *grotta* in the **Palazzo Ducale**, and don't miss the upstairs Camera degli Sposi and Hall of Mirrors. Eat at **Antica Osteria ai Ranari** (Via Trieste 11, 0376 328431, closed Monday), a casual family-run place for excellent local specialties. Sleep at **Casa Poli Hotel** (www.hotelcasapoli.it), a sleek boutique hotel about a ten-minute walk from the Palazzo Ducale.

# 30 The Royal Apartments in Palazzo Reale— Turin, Piedmont

CONSIDER MY FRIEND SOOZE, WHO ALWAYS recounts this story to me in amazement: "When I told my parents I wanted to have a home wedding with just the immediate family, they painted the dining room."

Sooze was talking about a dining room in a split-level in Kankakee, Illinois.

Now multiply that image by about a zillion-million and you'll get what happened when brides moved into the Palazzo Reale (Royal Palace) in Turin. From 1719 until 1930, whenever a king took a wife, massive redecorating ensued. So when you visit this thirty-room section of the *gigantico* palazzo, you'll be walking through a history of interior design—from baroque to rococo to neo-classical. For some brides, only a few elements were changed, others added entirely new rooms. It's all richly layered with the history of the women who lived there.

And it's all so very French. Why? Because this is where the Royal House of Savoy, a France-based dynasty reigned over the Piedmont region beginning in 1494. They also went on to conquer and rule other parts of Italy, and held the monarchy until they were exiled from the country in 1946, all way too complicated to get into right now.

Back to Palazzo Reale. As soon as you approach it—a magnificent vision of pale blue-gray stone with gold touches—you'll understand why Italians nicknamed Turin "Little Paris."

There were two Parisian-born women who were powerhouses behind building it as part of their "let's beautify Turin" projects: Madama Reale I and her daughter-in-law Madama Reale II. During the seventeenth century, they lived in the Palazzo Madama (next door to the Reale) and ruled Piedmont in succession, because their Savoy King husbands died young. Both were beloved by the Torinese, governing like intelligent *mammas*, bringing art and culture to the city. The Palazzo Reale's most famous feature, The Scissor Staircase, an ornate criss-cross design by Juvarra, was one of the artistic triumphs of the days of Madama Reale II.

The apartments you'll be touring are basically from after their reign. Here you're surrounded by birthday-cake chandeliers, giant gold-framed mirrors, and all those stiff, fancy furnishings that you couldn't imagine a soul slouching on. Fantasies of gala affairs spring up. You can picture Spanish-born Maria Antonietta Ferdinanda's 1750 wedding party in the baroque ballroom where a tapestry depicting a scene from *Don Quixote* hangs in homage to her. Duchessa Maria Teresa, who came here as a fifteen-year-old bride from Milan in 1788, had a Chinese salon put in, at a time when Europeans were intrigued with the Orient. When Principessa Maria Adelaide of Hapsburg arrived in 1842, exquisite wood-inlay floors were created and walls covered with pretty brocades.

Cut to 1930 to 1933 when the rooms were redesigned for Marie José of Belgium and her husband Umberto II. The charm of it is that it brings up thoughts of a contemporary fairy tale. Marie and Umberto were living in these grand old-fashioned surroundings when my mother was three—maybe Gershwin's "I've Got Rhythm" was blasting on the radio. Their *sala da pranzo* (lunch room) is a gorgeous design of pale green walls and gold ornamentation. In the center is a table set as if any minute the King and Queen would walk in and sit down for a plate of foie gras.

But the truth is, Marie and Umberto never ate together. The marriage was politically arranged from the time Marie was a girl, and when they officially tied the knot, she, like everybody else, knew Umberto was gay. Umberto went off to "honeymoon" with his friends in Courmayeur, and then the couple moved in to the Palazzo Reale and lived completely separate lives.

Marie launched into entertaining philosophers, artists, writers, and musicians in her Blue Room. Not caring about royal protocol, she'd jump in her car and drive off to enjoy concerts and festivals in Turin. She separated herself from the whole Savoy family by speaking out against Mussolini—when he ordered her to Italianize her name to Maria Giuseppina, she refused.

In the meantime, Umberto embraced the stiff traditions of his family, and loved redecorating the palace in grand style. He never visited Marie without announcing himself first, and always with someone accompanying him. Rumors flew that their four children had been conceived through artificial insemination, or maybe one of the guys Marie was hanging with.

World War II brought on great turmoil, and in 1946, when the monarchy was abolished, Marie was exiled with the rest of the House of Savoy. She went to Switzerland, Umberto to Portugal, and they remained apart for the rest of their lives.

Marie, who died in 2001, will always be remembered as the last Queen of Italy. Fondly remembered that is, for standing up against Fascism when all those around her were taking Mussolini's side. You may want to lag behind in the tour when you get to the Blue Room and picture Marie—a pretty blonde woman, sitting on her poufy couch with the fire blazing, surrounded by her artsy friends, having a grand time bucking the system in this beautiful place.

**Palazzo Reale:** The Palazzo Reale (Piazzetta Reale 1, Tuesday-Sunday 8:30-6, www.ilpalazzorealeditorino.it) can only be visited on guided tours, which run every fifty minutes. The tour of the Apartment of Princes (which many Italians call The Bridal Apartments) lasts around forty minutes, and there's also a great tour for the Royal Kitchen, which was recently opened. All tours are in Italian, but you can rent an English audio-guide.

**Golden Day:** Visit the **Palazzo Reale's L'Appartamento dei Principi** and the **Royal Kitchen.** The **Caffè Reale,** opposite the entrance to the palazzo, is the prettiest caffè ever and a wonderful to stop if you're waiting for your tour. For a splurge and terrific meal, eat in royal surroundings at **Del Cambio** (Piazza Carignano 2, 011 546690, closed Monday).

# 31 Oplontis–Torre Annunziata, Campania

TO GET PEACE AND QUIET AWAY from the city of Pompeii, rich and fun-loving folk would come to nearby **Oplontis** for banquets and bathing or just to chill out amidst the villa's gardens. Here's where you'll find room after room of amazing frescos that outshine most of what you'll see in Pompeii, and you'll get a good feel of what life was like in the suburbs before the whole shebang got covered in lava in that famous 79 A.D. eruption.

Unlike Pompeii, Oplontis (one stop away on the Circumvesuviana train line) is free of tourist crowds, so you can poke around in silence and let your imagination run free, picturing the intriguing woman who supposedly lived here, the Empress Poppea Sabina, Nero's second wife.

The Roman writer Tacitus described Poppea as bisexual and very ambitious. She married Emperor Otho to get close to Nero, soon became Nero's mistress, and then egged Nero on to murder his mother and divorce and execute his first wife. Poppea was a high-maintenance empress who insisted upon being carried about by mules shod with golden shoes, and needed to bathe daily in donkey milk, or, as some accounts say, the milk of 500 asses.

When Poppea married Nero, she gave birth to a daughter who died four months later. While Poppea was pregnant with their second child, Nero flew into a rage, accusing her of spending too much time flirting with gladiators. And then he kicked her to death. In another version of her story, made famous in the movie, *The Producers*, Nero jumped on Poppea. You may remember Leo Bloom screaming in fear to Max Bialystock: "I know you're going to jump on me—like Nero jumped on Poppea...Poppea. She was his wife. And she was unfaithful to him. So he got mad and he jumped on her. Up and down, until he squashed her like a bug."

But before all the horror stories, Poppea and her guests must have had luxurious times here at Oplontis. When you get here, you stand above the villa for a great view of the huge gardens, loaded with oleander. Inside is an atrium, salons and dining rooms with walls vibrantly frescoed to give a 3-D effect of marbled architecture, accented by colorful peacocks and theatrical masks. In the private spa, a painting tells the story of the Hesperides (daughters of the night) who lived in the garden of golden apple trees that Hercules visited when he was on one of his twelve assignments to gather fruits for King Eurystheus.

The portico corridors are more subtly painted with enchanting birds against ivory backgrounds. These open to curved indoor garden sitting rooms, where my favorite frescos have sumptuous paintings of fountains and ferns against an amber background, bordered by rich red. And then there's the huge rectangular outdoor pool that must have been dreamy to swim in with meadows in the distance back in those days.

On a memorable visit, one of the *signorina* guards had brought her dog to work, and the friendly mutt followed me around until an Italian tourist couple arrived with two daughters who were more thrilled with the pooch than the frescos. I left the group behind— the girls playing with the dog, as their parents wandered through just like I had, *ooh*ing and *ahh*ing as they turned corners to be met with discovery upon discovery of beauty in this most enchanting, evocative place.

**Oplontis:** November–March 8:30–5, April–October 8:30–7:30, www.pompeiisites.org.

**Golden Day:** On your way in or out of Pompeii, take a stop at **Torre Annunziata** to visit Oplontis. In Pompeii, be sure to visit the **Villa of Mysteries**, where you'll find a salon with fabulous frescos that tell the story of the bride Ariadne's initiation into the cult of Dionysus. Near the Villa of Mysteries exit, go for a simple drink or spaghetti at **Bacco e Arianna** (Via Villa dei Misteri 6, 081 536 2282, www.baccoearianna.eu), that's beautifully set in a garden. For something fancier, go to **Ristorante President** (Piazza Schettini 12, 081 850 7245) for elegant renditions of Campania classics.

# 32 Villa Romana del Casale–Sicily

ANCIENT ROMAN GIRLS IN BIKINIS? That's just one of the bizarre sights in this villa. It's a mosaic that covers the floor of the "Room of the Ten Girls," featuring a line-up of curvy, muscular young girls in two-piece suits pumping barbells and playing handball. Their outfits, which scholars say are actually their underwear, make them look totally contemporary, even though the mosaic is from the fourth century. It's a striking, entertaining change from the classical images we usually see of women in togas or lounging about nude in erotic scenes from those days.

The mosaic is just one of many in this villa where you'll find the world's largest and most amazing display of mosaics from Roman times. It's smack in the heart of Sicily, in the rural, hilly province of Enna. Here's where the beautiful Proserpina, daughter of Goddess of the Harvest Ceres, was wan-  dering around picking wildflowers when God of the Underworld Pluto pulled her down to Hades to make her his queen.

The massive 12,000-square-foot villa was built around the fourth century as a luxurious hunting lodge, which was surrounded by a farm estate. Not much is known about the original owner, except that he was a rich Roman, probably a member of the

Empire's senate or imperial family. It's obvious from the set-up that he threw great parties.

There's a huge triumphal military arch at its entrance and a sprawling bath complex. Best of all are the floors of the public and residential rooms, which were created by North African mosaic artisans in a vibrant style that's distinct from what you'll see in Pompeii or Italy's medieval churches. Along with fantastic geometric patterns you'll find dramatic action-packed scenes that capture moments from myths to wild hunting expeditions to contests at the Circus Maximus.

Not much remains of the villa's wall decorations, but considering the floors, what a place this must have been. It was buried in a mudslide in the twelfth century, and not fully excavated until the 1950s. In order to keep the mosaics in the well-preserved state they were found and still have tourists traipse through, catwalks have been built. When you visit you'll be walking along narrow planks attached to the sides of the rooms to get an overview of the floors, which is actually a better angle to admire them than guests had back in Roman partying days.

Some of the most spectacular you'll see include the one in the "Corridor of the Great Hunt," which depicts rowdy scenes of animals (lions, leopards, and antelopes) being captured and carted off to Rome for shows at the Colosseum. In the corner of the room is a dark-skinned, regal-looking woman who personifies India or Arabia, surrounded by an elephant, tiger, and phoenix in flames. Other rooms have whimsical scenes of cupids fishing, women dancing, and the Greek poet Arion playing his *chitarra*.

What would a rich Roman's villa be without a touch of erotica? In what's assumed to have been the master's bedroom a mosaic shows the voluptuous bare backside of a woman looking like she's giving a man on a throne a lap dance.

**Villa Romana del Casale:** Open daily from 9 to one hour before sunset, with evening openings in July and August, www. villaromanadelcasale.it.

**Golden Day:** Visit the **Villa** early in the morning, before crowds of tour buses arrive. Spend the rest of the day at **Piazza Armerina**, a medieval hill town nearby (3.5 miles/5.5 km away), which has a beautiful baroque **Duomo** and other impressive churches. Eat at **Ristorante Al Fogher** (Contrada Bellia, 093 5684123, www. alfogher.net), which serves Sicilian classics in refined style.

# III

## Gardens

Stroll through an Italian garden for a peaceful experience of *la dolce vita* (the sweet life). Here's where landscape architects tamed Mother Nature, harmoniously blending greenery, sculptures, and fountains.

Most Italian gardens are not about the flowers, but focused on a flowing design, created specifically for the pleasures of the villa's residents. And the topiary! Like expert tailors, gardeners clip Cypress trees, boxwood, and ilex bushes into fashionable, clean shapes. Serene green, precisely arranged, is what defines the country's garden style.

Some of the most memorable to visit are gardens of the Renaissance or Baroque periods. These gardens were planned as carefully as the villas they surrounded, artfully blending design with the natural landscape. They're comprised of sunlit paths, pergolas dripping with wisteria, belvederes for awesome views, and romantic niches fragrant with lavender. Fountains and statues add emotion to the mix.

Every garden you'll visit will have a distinct personality, reflecting the owner—whether it's the bursting, playful spirit of Niki de Saint Phalle or the idealism of Giovanni de' Medici.

Go and enjoy their pleasant fantasies...

**TIP:** *Many gardens close down November–March, so be sure to check schedules. As many of the gardens are not marked, if you're an avid gardener and want a more in-depth experience, buy a guide before your visit or sign up for a tour.*

Also, don't miss these springtime experiences:

**Rome: Roseto di Roma Capitale** (www.comune.roma.it): Late April to mid-June, you can enjoy 1,100 varieties of roses in a stunning location next to the Circus Maximus.

**Florence: Giardino dell'Iris** (www.irisfirenze.it): In late April through May, 2,500 hundred types of iris, the symbol of Florence, bloom below the Piazzale Michelangelo.

**L'Infiorata (Flower Art Festival):** These occur in late May or early June, traditionally nine Sundays after Easter. To celebrate the feast of Corpus Domini, small towns all over Italy pave the *vias* to their churches with "paintings" made of flower petals. Among them are Genzano in Lazio (www.infiorata.it), Spello in Umbria (www. infioretaspello.it), and Noto in Sicily (www.infioratadinoto.it).

---

### RECOMMENDED READING

*Italian Villas and Their Gardens* by Edith Wharton

*Italian Gardens: A Guide* by Helena Attlee and Alex Ramsey

# 33 Villa d'Este–Tivoli, Lazio

BEFORE YOU EVEN GET TO THIS GARDEN, you hear rushing water. Then you stand above majestic terraces filled with countless sculpted fountains, ponds, and grottoes. Water shoots up in grand columns, arcs out of a hundred animal heads, tumbles like a curtain over caves, pumps through a stone organ that plays a classical tune. On and on and on, it's High Renaissance Aqua-Theater.

**Villa d'Este** was Cardinal Ippolito d'Este's spectacular reaction to getting a booby prize. In the mid-sixteenth century, he lost out on becoming Pope. The powers that were in Rome shooed him away to suburban Tivoli and gave him the job of governor. Instead of living a life of luxury in the papal apartments, he was exiled to government housing: a plain ol' former Benedictine convent.

Being the rich Renaissance guy that he was, Ippolito embraced the "Man Controls Nature" philosophy of his day. Reaching back to the glory of ancient Rome, he built a massive aqueduct, diverting the plentiful waters of the Aniene River to his backyard. He pillaged the nearby Villa of Hadrian, using the former Emperor's marble and statues to make his home magnificent. He threw elaborate banquets, stocking his ponds with fish for his guests to catch and then hand over to servants to cook up. Folks came and marveled over the waterworks, calling it d'Este's "Garden of Miracles." *Living Well Is the Best Revenge* became his mantra.

Ippolito could have sulked and blamed his late *mamma*, Lucrezia Borgia, for his dreary Tivoli assignment. Lucrezia's father, Pope Alexander VI, had headed up a family of notorious Borgia villains who'd run the Vatican's reputation into the dirt. Lucrezia was the beauty of the clan, rumored to have worn a hollow ring filled with poison that she'd drip into cups of those the family found undesirable. Her first two husbands were gotten rid of by the Borgia men when they didn't cooperate with the family's evil plans.

The Duke of Ferrara (Alfonso d'Este) became Lucrezia's third husband, and father to Ippolito. Their marriage had glimmers of respectability. Sure, Lucrezia had her affairs—with the popular poet Bembo and, most naughtily, with the husband of that paragon of virtue, Isabella d'Este. But the Duke played around too and pretty much let Lucrezia's dalliances slide. To the outside world, the couple put on a classy royalty show. Lucrezia bore seven children and became zealously religious in her later years, until she died in childbirth at thirty-nine. Still, her *femme fatale* legacy would never disappear, which mucked up Ippolito's chance at becoming Pope.

Which is why at Tivoli he pumped up the fact that he was a d'Este. His whole paternal line had glorified themselves by wackily tracing their roots back to Hercules, so Ippolito filled his home and garden with allusions to the hero.

He had a villa room frescoed with a triumphant scene of Hercules in the Garden of Hesperides. According to legend, the strong man was challenged to go to this garden and pick an immortality-inducing golden apple that grew on a tree guarded by three "nymphs of the night," called Hesperides. All over Villa d'Este there are frescos including lemons, and lush pots of them in the garden, symbolizing those golden apples.

You'd hardly know this place was owned by a cardinal, or that it was even a former convent, as it has a smorgasbord of pagan images. Goddesses make their appearances in Ippolito's bedroom—there's a wall fresco of the gadabout Venus, and to balance things out, a chaste Diana on the ceiling. Ippolito put another version of Diana, as nature goddess of Ephesus, spouting water from what appears to be multiple breasts (actually they symbolized sacrificial bull's testicles), smack in front of the water organ. But conservative types that came in 1611 moved that Diana to the more discreet corner you'll find it in today.

Minerva, Goddess of Wisdom and Rome, crowns the Rometta fountain, a mini-model of the Eternal City. It's at the top of the terraces, facing Rome. You can imagine Ippolito standing right there, amidst his happy guests—from cardinals to courtesans—as they romped about his playground. No doubt he'd take in the whole scene, look past Minerva towards the city that rejected him, and smile.

**Villa d'Este**: Tuesday-Sunday 8:30-1 hour before sunset, www. villadestetivoli.info.

**Golden Day**: Visit the **Villa d'Este** and the nearby **Hadrian's Villa**. It's best to go to the latter with a tour group, because like the Roman Forum, it's a huge, sprawling place and practically none of the ruins are marked. Have lunch at **Antico Ristorante Sibilla** (Via della Sibilla 50, 077 4335281, closed Monday), an elegant restaurant from 1730, set overlooking the river beside the Roman Temple of Vesta and Sanctuary of the Sibyl.

### RECOMMENDED READING

*The Cardinal's Hat: Money, Ambition, and Everyday Life in the Court of a Borgia Prince* by Mary Hollingsworth

# 34 The Park of the Monsters—Bomarzo, Lazio

IN 1564 WHEN HIS WIFE DIED, Prince Vicino Orsini dedicated this place to her. He called it his Sacred Grove. In 1954, Giovanni Bettini found it abandoned, cleaned it up, and renamed it **The Park of the Monsters**—better for marketing.

It's actually a combo of the two names, which is what makes it so uniquely alluring. It's set on a wooded hillside where you meander along gravel paths under sun-dappled light and then along the way, popping up in haphazard places, you come upon immense bizarre statues of mythological creatures.

There are about two dozen of these creations in all, most carved directly from the hill's rocky outcroppings, which explains the unplanned arrangement. There's a winged mermaid, a sleeping nymph, a sphinx, a colossal Ceres, a tortoise, a whole house that's set up purposely tilted to astonish you. The most famous of all is a giant screaming monster's head—so giant you can walk into its mouth, where you'll find a tongue turned into a picnic table. The inscription carved into this sculpture sums up the park's surreal atmosphere: *All Reason Departs.*

There's a lot of mystery surrounding what the heck Orsini was thinking when he created this place. Some look at the statues' tortured faces and say it was his expression of grieving for his wife, Giulia Farnese. But Orsini began this project before she died.

Their marriage was a good one. He was a military officer, gone a lot while Giulia took over the small town Bomarzo reins. He, of course, had his share of other women, during the marriage and after she died. As far as he knew, Giulia was a perfect, faithful wife. Twenty years after the Sacred Grove was completed Orsini built a temple in her honor that's the most logical structure in this whole place.

The Sacred Grove seems to be more of an expression of Prince Orsini's intriguing, artsy character. While everybody else in those High Renaissance days was building grand, structured gardens to flaunt their wealth, the Prince turned his back on all that, wanting to create something that was not at all pretentious. It's not even attached to his castle, but farther down the hill. Also, he didn't have the money to compete with the Farneses and the d'Estes, so instead of grandeur, he went for shock and awe. Wherever a stone jutted out of the hill, he'd have his workers sculpt it according to his whim. He was a creative type who wrote poems and surrounded himself with the literati. This was his place for contemplation and meditation. It was his dream world where he mixed images from classical Greek, Roman, and Asian times.

Like every other prince who had a garden, Orsini had illustrious guests come to visit. But he was always glad when they left, preferring the pleasures of simple country life and his shepherd girls. While other Renaissance gardens were kept up by families over succeeding generations, his was forgotten. Only the locals knew of it, and believed it was a haunted place.

In 1938, Salvador Dali, in the midst of a creative crisis, heard about the Sacred Grove, left Spain, and cut his way through a tangle of weeds to see this "sleeping garden." He became so inspired he made a film that included it and painted *The Temptation of Saint Anthony* that featured an image of an elephant—clearly inspired by one of the park sculptures.

Giovanni Bettini bought the park in 1954 and restored it back to life. A visit here is a relaxing, enchanting experience, where you enter into the mythological dream world of the Prince.

**The Park of the Monsters:** Daily 8–1 hour before sunset, www. sacrobosco.it.

❧

**Golden Day:** Wander around the **Sacred Grove**. There's a casual snack bar there, where you can get a caffè and panino. Eat and stay a short drive north at *agriturismo* **Castello di Santa Maria** (www. castellosantamaria.it), a beautiful former convent surrounded by olive groves that serves up exquisite meals.

## RECOMMENDED READING

*The Garden at Bomarzo: A Renaissance Riddle*, by Jessie Sheeler

# 35 Gardens Outside Florence—Tuscany

LEAVE THE VESPA ROARS OF FLORENCE behind and head to the surrounding hills to discover lovely small gardens with fabulous views. Here's where Florentines have come to relax since the days of the Medici.

These are two that you can get to easily from Florence, by taking a short bus ride and walking about ten minutes. If you're feeling energetic, you could even hike up to them from the city, just like folks in olden days.

## ❀ Villa Medici—Fiesole

Three terraces of simple grace make up Italy's first Renaissance garden.

In 1461, Giovanni de Medici, the son of Cosimo, bought this land because he loved the view of the city below. His dad thought it was a cockamamie idea: Why spend a bundle for a steep, rocky plot that you can't even grow anything on? The Medici were originally farming people, and Cosimo's beloved spot was his country villa, where he'd tend vineyards and olive groves, hang with the peasants, and have friends over to read Plato.

Giovanni, a Medici banker, was of the new generation. From reading Pliny's ancient Roman writings, he got the notion that a garden was a place to combine home, nature, and an awesome view. Forget about growing food. Forget about the

walled medieval garden. His terraces would blend with the landscape and villa, like an outdoor room. This would be a beautiful
place to kick back, enjoy entertainments, and contemplate the
mysteries of life.

Giovanni's overeating and drinking got the better
of him and he died of a heart attack in his forties
before he had much time to enjoy this place. His
nephew, Lorenzo the Magnificent, took it over and
it became a meeting place for the Neo-Platonic
Academy. Here was where Lorenzo would lead
philosophical discussions centered around the
idea that perfection and happiness could be
attained right here on earth (not in the after-
life) through intellectual contemplation and
the appreciation of beauty. Lorenzo's artist
friends—Michelangelo, Leonardo da Vinci, and Botticelli—
along with philosophers, poets, and musicians were invited.
You can imagine Lorenzo in these gardens leading the group:
"Play the lute! Read me a verse from the *Aeneid*! What's life's
highest vocation? Tell me your ideas!"

The gardens have been relandscaped over the years, but the
original structure and remnants of it retained. Tall cypress trees
line the entrance and pots of lemon trees are neatly arranged
on the front lawn. Giovanni brought in lemons from Naples in
homage to the mythological Garden of Hesperides. According
to Greek legend, the earth mother Gaia gave this magical garden to Hera on her wedding day. In it was a tree bearing golden
immortality-giving apples, guarded by Hesperides—nymphs of
the night.

On a lower terrace, you walk under a pergola that's inter-
twined with roses. Four old magnolia trees spread shade.
Further along, you get the most stunning views of Florence.

And in that garden are circles of trimmed boxwood hedges that replaced Lorenzo de Medici's herb garden.

These terraces were relandscaped in the early 1900s. That's when one of Tuscany's most beloved women, Iris Origo, was growing up here. Iris was born in Britain, and when her father died, she moved with her mother to this villa in Fiesole.

The legacy of Iris Origo lives on in southern Tuscany's Val d'Orcia. That's where she and her husband had a farm during World War II, where they courageously and generously sheltered refugees. They transformed the property to a jewel-of-an estate called **La Foce,** that's now run by her daughters. It's comprised of a fifteenth-century villa and farmhouses that have been renovated into guesthouses you can rent.

The **Gardens at La Foce** are sublime. If you're in the area (near Montepulciano), stop by for a tour. In what had been a rugged place, Iris used memories of her past to create the garden's design. It's a mix of classic English style with influences of the Fiesole Villa Medici Renaissance garden she played in when she was a kid.

## ❁ Villa Gamberaia—Settignano

This place is so pretty it makes me feel prettier when I step into it. Landscape architects come here to study it. Painting classes set up their easels on the grounds. It's a vision of exquisite harmony: Cypress trees are immaculately clipped into soft, rounded shapes and archways. Crisp boxwood shrubs and rose bushes surround rectangular reflecting pools. A baroque stone niche imbedded with shells and fossils holds a statue of Neptune. A greenest of green alley of grass stretches out to a low stone wall. That's your photo opp perch, with a glorious view of Florence in the background.

All this on only three acres! A graceful mix of Italian baroque to Formal English styles.

The garden was first put together in the eighteenth century, when grottoes were built. Then in 1895 came Romanian Princess Jeanne Ghyka, part of the wave of foreigners who descended on Florence in those days. She made the garden her pet project, tearing out the raised flowerbeds and replacing them with the oblong reflecting pools. She was a mysterious sort, only occasionally having guests in for tea, and neighbors knew little about her except that she lived with an American companion, Miss Blood. In 1925 a widow from Detroit who'd been married to a German baron took over and she, Baroness Von Ketteler, is the one who's responsible for the amazing topiary that gives this garden such a distinct character.

It was almost completely destroyed in World War II, and then bought by the industrialist Marcello Marchi, who restored it. Still run by his family, the villa's been converted to guest accommodations. To stay here is a dream. Or just get here in April, when the blooming pink azaleas are a quasi-psychedelic vision.

**Villa Medici** Via Beato Angelico 2, Fiesole, 055 59164/59417, www.villamedicifiesole.it: The gardens can be visited by appointment only. From Florence: Bus #7 from the Stazione Centrale di Santa Maria Novella, Piazza San Marco, or the Duomo, to Fiesole's Piazza Mino, then an uphill walk.

**La Foce, Val d'Orcia** Strada della Vittoria 61, 53042 Chianciano Terme (Siena), 39 0578 69101, www.lafoce.com: The garden is open to the public every Wednesday afternoon, and on weekends from April to November. Check the website for guided tour times and information.

**Villa Gamberaia** Via del Rosselino 72, Settignano. Daily 9-6 by appointment, 055 697 205, www.villagamberaia.com: From Florence: Bus #10 from Santa Maria Novella or San Marco to Settignano, then a ten-minute walk to the garden.

**Golden Day:** See the **Villa Medici Gardens** and explore the other treasures of **Fiesole**—the Roman Theater and Duomo. Lunch at the loggia of **Belmond Villa San Michele** (Via Doccia 4, 055 567 8200, www.belmond.com), a former convent with a facade designed by Michelangelo that has become a romantic luxury hotel. Views from the restaurant are transcendent; the food refined and delicious.

### TOURS

**One Step Closer** (www.onestepcloser.net) is a Florence-based tour operator that provides arrangements for guided garden tours.

# 36 The Tarot Garden— Capalbio, Tuscany

BURSTING OUT OF THE FOREST IN this remote western corner of Tuscany is what artist Niki de Saint Phalle called her "Garden of Joy." It's a contemporary art park (opened in 1998), filled with twenty-two exuberant sculptures that represent her take on the major cards of a tarot deck.

The colors! The sculptures are made of a mix of day-glo mosaics, mirrored glass, and ceramics. They're curvy, oversized mythical creations, some standing three stories high. They entice you to reach out and feel their textures, or walk inside and find yourself surrounded by sparkling colors and mirrors. Fountains created by Niki's husband, the Swiss kinetic sculptor Jean Tinguely, add to the exceptional magic. Olive and oak trees, myrtle and rosemary bushes, blend with the art. The garden has a playful ambience, infused with Niki's childlike spirit. She even put a bright spin on the Devil—a smiling winged woman poised on a pedestal with a flame between her legs.

Towering over the whole scene is *The Empress*, a shining, blue, mosaic sphinx with enormous multicolored breasts. Niki lived inside it while the garden was being built—hard to believe because it's so glittery in there. One breast was the kitchen, and she slept in the other. The nipples are windows. She said it was her "protective mother" for the project she worked obsessively on, relying solely on her instincts to lead the way.

Niki was a drop-dead gorgeous woman—lithe, with high cheek-bones and delicate features. She was born in France in 1930, then moved to New York and modeled as a teenager, appearing on the covers of *Vogue*, *Harper's*, and *Life*.

When she was eighteen she eloped, and a few years later, moved with her husband and daughter to Paris. While studying acting there, she had a ner-vous breakdown. She'd been abused as a child by her father, and finally facing the trauma, started painting to work through it. She was self-taught and got encouragement to stick to her naïve style, showing her paintings in a Paris gallery in the mid-1950s. It was there  she met and fell in love with the sculptor Tinguely. They both divorced their spouses and became life-long partners.

Niki's "Shooting Paintings" catapulted her to worldwide recog-nition in the early 1960s. They were created in galleries, bringing out the performance artist in her. She'd strut out in a white jump-suit and black boots, whip out a twenty-two caliber pistol, and shoot at a blank board, where she'd imbedded bags filled with paint. Colors would explode and form spontaneous paintings. After three years of wowing fans from California to Amsterdam, she gave it up, saying, "I've become addicted to shooting."

Having worked the machismo stuff out of her system, Niki moved on to explore feminine archetypes. Inspired by a pregnant girlfriend, she created *Nanas*—huge pop-art styled fertility goddess sculptures. Expanding that theme, she rocked the art world with a room-sized Nana in Sweden. Visitors would enter through the sculpture's vagina and find inside a milk bar and screening room showing Greta Garbo films.

Ever since the 1950s when Niki saw Gaudi's Park Guell in Spain, she'd felt it was her destiny to create her own sculpture garden. In the 1970s she was given this land in Tuscany to begin the twenty-year project. She died four years after it was completed, in 2002. She was seventy-one and had suffered from emphysema, brought on by polyester fumes she'd inhaled while making those *Nana* sculptures. Her creations are exhibited all over the world, but the Tarot Garden is her greatest legacy.

To visit it on a sunny day, when bright light bounces off the sculptures, is spectacular. I have a great memory of strolling around amidst a gang of local elementary school boys, who ran to the big-bosomed statues, pawing and kissing them with glee.

My favorite story of a traveler discovering this place comes from my friend JoAnn Locktov, who showed up here in the midst of a thunder-and-lightning storm. Since there are loads of metal pieces in the garden's Tinguely fountains, the tour group she came with decided to stay in the bus, terrified they'd be struck by lightning. But JoAnn, a mosaics fanatic, was determined to get in no matter what. The guard who answered the door after twenty rings tried to stop her. JoAnn rushed past him and took in the marvels, running her hands over textured archways, awestruck by the rich designs. Caught up in JoAnn's enthusiasm, the guard turned on the fountains for her. She said to herself, "If this is where I was meant to die, it'd be O.K.!"

**The Tarot Garden:** Il Giardino dei Tarocchi, open April-mid-October, 2:30-7:30 and November-March, first Saturdays of the month, 9-1, www.ilgiardinodeitarocchi.it.

**Golden Day:** Visit the **Garden** and spend time exploring nearby **Capalbio**, a tiny medieval hilltop village. Eat there at **Tullio**, (Via Nuova, 27, 0564 896196, closed Wednesdays), to enjoy delicious

Tuscan classics. For luxury digs at the nearby seaside, stay at the **Pellicano Hotel** (www.pellicanohotel.com), a Relais & Chateaux property.

## RECOMMENDED READING

*Niki de Saint Phalle and the Tarot Garden*, by Niki de Saint Phalle, Pierre Restany, Mario Bolta, and Enrico Crispolti

*Niki de Saint Phalle*, by Christianne Weidemann

# 37 Villa Cimbrone– Ravello, Campania

WINDING UP THE CLIFFS OF THE AMALFI COAST, mesmerizing views of lemon groves and vineyards tumbling to the shimmering sea take your breath away. Then you arrive above it all, in Ravello. A quiet path from the piazza of this romantic village opens to the fairytale **Villa Cimbrone** gardens.

You're drawn like a magnet down a shaded path to a statue of Ceres, Goddess of the Harvest, and then onto the Belvedere of Infinity. On the sheer cliff of this terrace it feels like you're floating in paradise.

Behind you, the terraced gardens are a bewitching mix of umbrella and cypress tree-lined paths, manicured lawns, arbors dripping with wisteria, nooks of purple petunias and daisies, a rose garden, and a tearoom. Sculptures of smiling cherubs and a curvy Eve in a cave add to the enchantment.

All this was created under the direction of Lord Grimthorpe (aka Ernest William Beckett), who came through Ravello on the Grand Tour, and fell in love with this spot that had been abandoned. In 1904 he transformed it into what it is today, blending Moorish and Renaissance designs with the remains of the Roman villa it once was. His guest list included Virginia Woolf, D. H. Lawrence, and T. S. Eliot, whom I imagine must have had a grand old time here.

But the guest who came after Grimthorpe's reign, who I'm most intrigued by, is Greta Garbo. A plaque commemorates her famous month-long visit. In translation it reads: "Here in the spring of 1938, the divine Greta Garbo, fleeing the clamor of Hollywood, spent with Leopold Stokowski hours of Secret Happiness."

If you'd like to believe that read no further.

The true story starts off like the ideal romance. Garbo, the thirty-two-year-old glamour queen of Hollywood got wooed by Stokowski, a flamboyant fifty-five-year-old conductor. She thought "Stoki" would be the great love of her life. He invited her to meet him in Ravello, where he rented out the Villa Cimbrone just for the two of them.

According to a Swiss maid, Garbo arrived with one battered suitcase. All she'd packed were blue espadrilles, a bathing suit, lots of sunglasses, jars of jam, and a pair of pajamas, which the maid had to wash, iron and place at Garbo's bedside every evening.

Garbo's routine was morning calisthenics on the terrace, followed by a pool swim and strict vegetarian meals, except for the slathering of jam on her teatime cakes. She was in bed every night by eight.

Stoki had leaked to the press that Garbo was meeting him at the villa and hordes of paparazzi showed up, perching in trees, hoping to get shots of what could be the wedding of the decade. Garbo hired policemen and guard dogs to keep them out.

As for the grand love story, in *Garbo, Her Story*, Greta says she was happy to be there at first and learn all about Italian art from Stoki. But when he talked about his plans for the future things took a nosedive. Stoki proposed they make a movie together—he'd do the music, star opposite her and they'd finance the movie with their own money. That last part of his proposal was the straw that broke the affair for Garbo, who was a notorious tightwad.

She says Stoki attempted to woo her back in Capri's Blue Grotto, but his sexual advance was unsuccessful; he got nervous and cried. Unbeknownst to the reporters, the love affair was finished. Stoki confessed to Garbo that he'd told the reporters they were going to get married. Graciously Garbo agreed to meet the press in the Villa library, if they'd agree to then go away. True to form, she played the interview close to the vest. When questioned about the relationship, she shocked the reporters with: "I have never had an impulse to go to the altar."

Years later, Stoki married the twenty-one-year-old Gloria Vanderbilt, heiress to a 20-million-dollar fortune.

Though Garbo didn't actually have "hours of secret happiness" here, this is undeniably a romantic place.

**Villa Cimbrone**: Via Santa Chiara 26, daily 9 until sunset, www. villacimbrone.com.

**Golden Day**: Visit the **Gardens**, eat fresh seafood at **Albergo Ristorante Garden** (Via Boccaccio 4, 089 857226), and sleep at **Villa Cimbrone** (www.villacimbrone.com). The Vuilleumiers, a Swiss family who lived there for many years, now run it as a hotel, with ten luxurious rooms, a swimming pool, and the gardens to yourself after visiting hours.

**TIP**: *While in Ravello, also visit the **Villa Rufolo** gardens (www.villarufolo.it). Plan ahead if you'll be there in summer, to get tickets for the Ravello Music Festival, held in this splendid setting.*

# 38 *Parchi di Nervi– Liguria*

CATCH THE SPIRIT OF GUTSY, GORGEOUS Anita Garibaldi as you walk along the seaside path named in her honor. Waves crash against rugged cliffs, as you look out to stunning views of Portofino and the Cinque Terre. Flanking the other side of the Anita Garibaldi Path are three villa lawns that comprise the **Parchi di Nervi**. They are shaded by palm trees and pines, filled with exotic plants and Mediterranean flowers.

The Genoa elite used to come here to escape the summer heat, but now it's the place to blend with the regular folk. Couples stroll arm in arm, kids run for the trees with bags of nuts to feed the squirrels.

The dramatic seascape and exotic nature of the gardens express the essence of Anita Garibaldi. She was Italy's wonder-woman who fought alongside her husband Giuseppe in the nineteenth-century revolution that culminated in giving them the titles "Father and Mother of Modern Italy."

I first encountered Anita on Rome's Janiculum Hill, where there's a statue of her brandishing a pistol as she rides a wild mustang, with a baby tucked under her other arm.

Anita's life story is the stuff of a blockbuster movie. She was born in Brazil and learned horsemanship from her father, who died when she was twelve. At fourteen, she was married off to a local older man, Signor Aguiar, aka "the drunken shoemaker."

While her husband was off at war, who should appear, but Giuseppe Garibaldi, sailing in from Italy with a passion to help Brazil fight for its independence. The moment Giuseppe set eyes on dark-haired Anita with her extraordinary almond-shaped eyes, he walked straight up to her and said, "Maiden, thou shalt be mine." Even though she was still married, Anita took off to fight by Giuseppe's side in Brazil and Uruguay, firing cannons, teaching him gaucho guerilla warfare, and giving birth to their first son in the midst of all that. They married two years later, after Anita's first husband died.

In 1848, with four children in tow (between the ages of eight and two!), Anita and Giuseppe left South America to go to Italy and join the fight for unification. A year later, Anita died in Giuseppe's arms after a battle near Ravenna. She was twenty-eight and pregnant with their fifth child.

Giuseppe kept Anita's memory alive. When he rode in victory to the crowning of Emmanuel II as the first king of a united Italy, he wore a Brazilian poncho. And around his neck, Anita's striped scarf.

The Anita Garibaldi Passeggiata was created by Marchese Gaetano Gropallo in 1862, just two years after Italy's unification. It used to be a rustic path used by fisherman, but the Marchese fancied it up with lampposts and paving, so now it's an extended terrace to not only Gropallo's gardens, but also his neighbors, the Grimaldis and the Serras. The Villa Grimaldi rose garden is the most famous of the three and especially beautiful in spring. All are now owned by the state, house museums, and the grounds are used for outdoor ballets and theater in July.

**Parco Villa Grimaldi**, Via Capolungo 9, 8-dusk.

❧

**Golden Day**: Take a train (fifteen minutes) from Genoa to **Nervi**, and enjoy a leisurely stroll along the path and gardens. If it's beach season, go to **Bagni Medusa Genova** (Passeggiata Anita Garibaldi 27/A, 010 3728113, www.bagnimedusagenova.it) for delicious seafood or cocktail, or if you're there in cooler weather, nearby is a great pizzeria, **Halloween** (Via Caboto Giovanni 16/r, 010 3726154, www.pizzeriahalloween.net), which also serves traditional Genovese focaccia, with a seaside view.

## RECOMMENDED READING

*Anita Garibaldi: A Biography* by Anthony Valerio.

# 39 Gardens of the Isole Borromee–Piedmont

THE TRADITION OF A GROOM GIVING his bride a wedding present was taken over the top by Carlo III Borromeo. In 1632, he decided to transform one of his family's Lake Maggiore islands from a barren rock into a baroque-a-palooza wonderland and dedicate it to his wife-to-be. Fisherman living there at the time were none too happy when they were pushed aside as Carlo burst in with architects, loads of dirt, and exotic plants to begin his project, but wife Isabella must have been pleased. Especially when Carlo named the island Isola Isabella in her honor. The name was later changed to the easier-on-the-tongue **Isola Bella.**

Carlo's project took generations to complete, but by 1700 there stood an opulent villa above a pyramid of ten terraced gardens.

Getting to Isola Bella by ferry from the town of **Stresa** is half the fun of this garden visit. On misty days the island rises from the water like a pearl on the lake. Nearby are the Borromeo-owned **Isola Bella** and **Isola Madre** and the fisherman's island, **Isola dei Pescatori**, which is great for lunch. It's best to do **Isola Bella** on one day, with lunch on the fisherman's island, and save **Isola Madre,** where you'll find botanical gardens and a villa with an antique doll collection and puppet theater, for another day.

Among Villa Isola Bella's many elegant, art-filled rooms is the Sala di Napoleone, named in memory of the general who found this place perfect for romantic encounters. He stayed in this room with his first wife, Josephine, back in 1797.

Napoleon and Josephine had married the year before in Paris. She was a thirty-three-year-old widow with two children, described as "the voluptuous Creole" from Martinique, whose husband had been beheaded in the French Revolution. Napoleon, twenty-seven, was just beginning to gain fame. Three days after their wedding he had to head to war in Italy, and Josephine stayed behind in Paris.

Napoleon wrote Josephine passionate love letters (often two a day), with lines like "You are the eternal object of my thoughts. My imagination exhausts itself wondering what you are doing." Meanwhile Josephine was having quite the gay Paris time, celebrating hubby's victories with handsome escorts. She barely responded to his letters, which drove Napoleon absolutely insane. He finally convinced her to come meet him in Italy, and since they'd been apart practically a year, a rollicking time was had in this villa and gardens. Check out the etching of the couple's visit with their entourage, where the caption recounts how the local help complained that the French party gang practically trashed the place, they were having so much fun.

The most unique feature of the villa is its downstairs grottoes, done up floor to ceiling in elaborate black-and-white pebble and seashell mosaics—a fantasy of an underwater cave.

The grand finale is the gardens, which hit you like an *Alice in Wonderland*-vision come to life, with stretches of dazzling green lawns bordered by vibrant rose bushes, gushing fountains, fish ponds, and a spectacular curved stone theatrical backdrop with sculptures of gods and goddesses, crowned by a unicorn, the Borromeo family symbol. White peacocks strut about freely, opening their tails to punch up the experience.

Next, ferry to **Isola dei Pescatori**, a folksy fishing village, where you can wander the cobblestoned streets, and enjoy lunch or a drink at one of the many caffes or bars.

In *A Farewell to Arms*, Ernest Hemingway wrote about rowing to Isola dei Pescatori, and stopping in at a caffè for a Vermouth. It's toward the end of the book when he's deserted the army and goes to Stresa to hook back up with the British nurse he's crazy about, who's pregnant with their child.

"I kissed her neck and shoulders. I felt faint with loving her so much," Hemingway writes in a scene that takes place at their **Grand Hotel des Iles Borromees** room in Stresa. It seems like even Papa Hemingway, not typically a romantic guy, allowed passion to overtake him in this extraordinary place.

**Gardens of the Isole Borromee:** Open mid-March through mid-October, 9-5:30, www.isoleborromee.it.

**Stresa Apartment Info:** www.stresaapartments.com

**Golden Day:** From Stresa, take a ferry to **Isola Bella** (www.navigazionelaghi.it), and enjoy at least two hours there, then have lunch on **Isola dei Pescatori** at **Ristorante Belvedere** (0323 32292, www.belvedere-isolapescatori.it), to enjoy delicious lake fish on their terrace. Back in Stresa, a sunset *aperitivo* on the rooftop **Sky Bar of Hotel La Palma** (www.hlapalma.it) is a must. For a splurge, like Hemingway, stay at **Grand Hotel des Iles Borromees** (www.borromees.it).

**TIP:** *If you are with a group of four or more, rather than take the ferry, it's less expensive and more convenient to bargain with a boatman near the ferry station for a private round-trip ride.*

## RECOMMENDED READING

*Napoleon and Josephine* by Frances Mossiker

*A Farewell to Arms* by Ernest Hemingway

# 40 Giardino della Minerva–Salerno, Campania

"NOBODY COMES TO SALERNO," SAYS AWARD-WINNING cookbook author and southern Italy expert Arthur Schwartz. I'm grateful he's somebody who goes where "nobody" goes, and that he turned me on to this under-touristed town's treasure-of-a-garden, on the southern edge of the Amalfi Coast.

The immediate attraction for me was that it's named for Minerva, Roman Goddess of Wisdom and War, who sprung from the head of Jupiter. She was also worshiped as Minerva Medica, patron of doctors. This *giardino* was created by Doctor Matteo Silvatico in the early thirteenth century, with plants to be used in curative potions by the medical school that was next door. These were medieval times when practicing medicine centered around balancing the four humors of the body, as first written about by Hippocrates in ye olden days of ancient Greece. Hippocrates' premise, a departure from prayers and sacrifice, was that the body's four fluids (blood, phlegm, yellow bile, and black bile), needed to be balanced with the four elements and the four seasons for optimum health. Herbs were regularly used for cures, such as chamomile to lower the biles, making gardens near hospitals very convenient for doctors.

The Giardino della Minerva became the first botanical garden in Europe, and now has a total of 260 plant species, including such rarities as the legendary mandrake and ginseng. It's a delightful mix of six pretty terraces that rise above Salerno's historic center—making it lovely for strolling or bringing children along to run along the paths, surrounded by fig and lemon trees, palms, fish ponds, fountains, and aromatic herbs. There's a lot of local pride surrounding this spot, which was restored in 2001, and gardeners appreciate the well-labeled plant displays.

On the top terrace, is **La Tiseneria**, a tea room, where you can settle in and enjoy pretty views of the port and sea, while you sip teas made from the garden's herbs or, better yet, *limoncello*.

**Giardino della Minerva**: Via Ferrante Sanseverino 1, Salerno, closed Mondays, www.giardinodellaminerva.it.

**Golden Day**: Enjoy the *centro storico* of Salerno, that's full of luxury shops and an eleventh-century cathedral dedicated to Saint Matthew. Get to the **Giardino della Minerva** around sunset, for beautiful views of the sea. For dinner, here are two of Arthur's favorite places: **Antica Pizzeria Vicolo della Neve** (Vicolo della Neve 24, 089 225705, closed Wednesday), which besides pizza has great stuffed peppers and pasta fagioli, or the old-school **Osteria Dedicato a Mio Padre** (Via Giudaica 8, 089 23155) for excellent seafood dishes.

# IV

*Beaches*

Italians have mastered the art of a day at the beach. You've seen the photos: perfect lines of matching umbrellas and chairs, immaculately raked sand. It's summer theater with the sea as the show.

You pay a fee at these *bagni* (beach clubs), and your umbrella and chair is typically set up with flourish by an attendant. He may even come around and adjust your umbrella during the day, keeping you in the shade, so you'll feel like a real *principessa*. Fancy clubs have libraries, gyms, pools, and some even transform to discos at night. These places are packed in July and August, when Italians traditionally take their vacations. Show up then and you'll get seated in the back row—closer spots have been reserved by families for generations.

There are also lots of free public beaches, but they're typically not maintained up to *bagni* standards. Which means some will be right next to the clubs, looking like poor trash-ridden step sisters. Don't despair—with so much coastline you can find beautiful free beaches in every region, and even gems of hidden coves you could have all to yourself.

What to wear? What you wish, of course. Just FYI: You may be startled at how Italian women having what Americans may consider "non-bikini-body types" comfortably wear two-piece suits. The focus is on the fabulous sensation of feeling the sun on your body, so here you can throw concerns about sags or cellulite away.

Topless? No big deal, though it does depend on location. On the island of Sardinia, probably. On the coast of Tuscany, less likely.

I do hope that if you're in Italy between April and October, you take the time for a day at a beach. Settle in, taste the *granite* (fruit-flavored ices), and have a fresh seafood lunch with a glass of prosecco to make it all perfect. These are the places where you surrender to what Italians call *Il Dolce Far Niente: The Sweetness of Doing Nothing...*

## INFO

To enjoy the best beaches of Italy, head to Sardinia. If you're looking for "The Summer Party Scene," the beaches around Rimini on the Adriatic Riviera are where it's at.

**Bandiera Blu** (www.bandierablu.org) is an environmental organization that lists the best beaches in Italy, updated annually.

**Italian Naturist Foundation** (www.fenait.org) lists Italy's beaches where you can go *au naturale*.

# 41 Sperlonga, Lazio

"A ROMAN SUMMER ISN'T A REAL ROMAN SUMMER without a stay in **Sperlonga**," says my friend Gioia, an Eternal City native. She's been going there every August for twenty years. "It's where we all had our first boyfriends," she sighs.

Set high up on a seaside cliff, Sperlonga's historic center has the ambiance of an old Greek city: a pedestrian-only labyrinth of whitewashed stone buildings connected by stairways and arched alleys. Though now it's basically a tourist town, Sperlonga retains the quaint atmosphere of its fishing village days—pre-1957, before a road was built to reach this place. It's always attracted liberal, creative types like the Italian writer Natalie Ginzburg who had a home here. And because it's positioned halfway between Rome and Naples, it's a popular spot with visitors from both cities.

Stretching out below the town are immaculately raked beaches of golden sand and the tantalizing, rolling, cobalt sea. Modern beach establishments cover the area north of Sperlonga harbor, but to the south is where you'll find the treasures of free beaches and classic clubs, where rentals of umbrellas and chairs are about twenty euros. Gioia's advice is to head to **Lido Grotta dei Delifini**. "It's one of the quieter beaches, with beautiful wide white umbrellas, and room to spread out and enjoy everything."

In the evenings, the Sperlonga *piazzetta* is a charming place to relax with a cocktail and enjoy a sunset view. And in traditional

Italian beach town fashion, outdoor movies are shown—a different one every night to entertain the whole family.

For a break from the sun, walking south along the shore takes you to the **Museo Archeologico di Sperlonga** and ruins of a Roman villa and cave. Here's where the Emperor Tiberius, who reigned from 14 A.D. to 37 A.D. would come to party, before he moved permanently to Capri. The cave had an island inside it that was his banquet room, and submerged in the surrounding waters were sculptures that told stories from Homer's *Odyssey*. In the museum you can see those enormous sculptures, of such dramatic scenes as the multi-headed Scylla she-monster eating up Odysseus's crew or the blinding of the Cyclops Polyphemus.

**Sperlonga info**: www.sperlonga.it/english/

**Golden Day**: Get to **Lido Grotta dei Delfini** (www.grottadeidelfini.it). Enjoy a seafood dinner with a view at **Tramonto Bistrot** (Corso San Leone 21, 0771 549597). Stay in the historic center at **Hotel Corallo** (www.corallohotel.net), a cozy three-star.

**How to get there**: It's best to drive, which takes about two hours from Rome. Or take a train from Roma Termini to the Fondi-Sperlonga stop, and then connect to Sperlonga by bus or taxi.

# 42 *Forte dei Marmi— Tuscany*

COME TO THE PLACE THAT'S CALLED the Queen of the Versilia coast to luxuriate in one of Italy's chic-est beach experiences. Yes, it's in Tuscany, but erase all those quaint thoughts of cobblestoned streets and medieval architecture.

**Forte dei Marmi** is laid out in a flat grid, perfect for biking. Mid-century villas peek out behind clipped hedges, cypress, and palm trees. The town center is packed with designer shops, like Gucci, Prada, Versace, and Dolce & Gabbana. This is more like the Hamptons of Italy, where the elite meet to beach, dine, shop, and disco.

It has one of the mainland's best stretches of wide, fine sandy beaches, with shallow water that's perfect for the kids. If you go in season, you'll be mixing with well-to-do families who've been coming here for decades, along with the more recent trend of international jet-setters, who've taken their cue from folks like Miuccia Prada and Giorgio Armani, who have summer getaway homes here.

It wasn't always this way. Forte dei Marmi translates to "Fort of Marble," which is what that big brick building you'll see in the town's main piazza used to be. Back in the eighteenth century it was a storehouse for marble that was quarried from the Apuan mountains that backdrop the town. Now the jetty built to lug that marble out to ships is a promenade, flanked by beaches, and filled with glamorous tourists.

There are almost a hundred beach clubs to choose from to enjoy the Forte dei Marmi experience with starting prices of about fifty euro for your cabana, beach chairs, and umbrellas. A favorite for families is **Bruno** (V. Arenile 79 Riviera della Versilia, 058 489 972), or there is **Gilda**, (www.gildafortedeimarmi.it), which also has an excellent restaurant. If you want to splurge for the ultimate jet-set scene, head to **Twiga**, owned by the mega-businessman Flavio Briatore, renowned for dating models like Heidi Klum and Naomi Campbell. Here you'll find billowing Moroccan tents, chairs upholstered in leopard skin, and if you show up in the evening, a disco where you'll be dancing until the wee hours. Or you may go for one of Italy's top topless beaches, **Santa Maria** (V. Arenile 9), that's surrounded by pine trees.

Forte dei Marmi is a great place to settle into for at least a few days. Nearby is the town of **Pietrasanta**, filled with artists whose sculptures, paintings, and handcrafted jewelry make for fun shopping opportunities and gallery shows. Or you could visit **Carrara**, home to the famous marble quarry where Michelangelo chose his stone for the *Pieta*.

☙

**Golden Day:** Get to **Forte dei Marmi** for the Wednesday market that has designer goods at discount prices, choose your beach, and eat at **Gilda Ristorante** (www.gildafortedeimarmi.it). For luxury digs, stay at the **Hotel Augustus** (www.augustus-hotel.org).

# 43 *Sirolo–Marche*

TWO GIANT POINTED ROCKS, CALLED LE DUE SORELLE (the two sisters), symbolize the Riviera del Conero. They resemble two nuns dressed in white habits rising from the azure sea, as if blessing the most stunning stretch of Italy's northern Adriatic Coast.

Bright white limestone is what makes this place so spectacular. Towering over the scenery is **Monte Conero**, that wows you as you drive along a winding panoramic highway above jagged cliffs. Deep green pine forests and yellow broom add bursts of color. All this wild beauty is the backdrop for pebbled beaches, coves, and a handful of sweet resort towns.

Best of these towns is **Sirolo**.

Below it you'll find four sublime beaches. My friend Alessandra is a fan of the largest, **Grotta Urbani**. It's shaped like a crescent moon, with an enticing cave at one end. Shallow water makes it perfect for families with children. The scent of pine trees backing up the beach mixes with the sea air. There are three beach clubs, a restaurant, and bar on the jetty. From Sirolo, you can catch a shuttle bus to get there, or walk downhill through the forest, which takes about ten minutes.

Sirolo's other beaches are only accessible by foot or boat from Grotta Urbani. Boat is better, as the paths are treacherous and steep. **Le Due Sorelle** is the gem of them all, with the view of the "two sisters" rocks. **San Michele** has a rustic appeal, with wildflowers covering its borders. If you're in the mood to sunbathe *au naturale*, head to **Sassi Neri**, the Beach of the Black Pebbles. Keep in mind all the beaches are pebbly, so bring your beach shoes.

Sirolo is a beautifully restored medieval village, that's a happening spot during its beach season. Along its narrow alleyways are lively restaurants and bars. Everybody hangs out on the wide piazza, a tree-shaded balcony at the edge of the village that overlooks the sea. In July and August, two theaters stage operas and concerts. The most unusual is the **Teatro Alle Cave**, a quarry that's been converted to an open-air 1800 seat theater. More traditional is the **Teatro Cortesi**, a 220-seat ornate building from 1873.

Sirolo is also the entrance to the **Conero Regional Park** (www. conero.it), where you can hike to an archaeological site and find the **Tomb of the Queen of Sirolo**. Folks were amazed when this was excavated in 1989. They discovered jewelry, vases, and two carriages from the sixth century B.C., which must have belonged to this woman of mystery.

⁂

**Golden Day:** Choose your beach and enjoy the village of **Sirolo**. Stay at **La Libellula del Conero** (www.lalibelluladelconcero. com), an enchanting B&B, and dine on the terrace of **Ristorante Vittoria** (Via Accesso Spiaggia 2, 320 647 6610) for breathtaking views and fresh caught seafood. Be sure to taste the local dry red wine, Rosso Conero.

# 44 _Positano–Amalfi Coast_

THANKS TO PASITEA, AN IRRESISTIBLE NYMPH who lured in Poseidon, the dreamy seaside village of **Positano** was discovered. It has six beaches to choose from. There's the large, busy **Spiaggia Grande**, where you can watch handsome fisherman glide in and out. A short walk away is the quieter **Fornillo** beach, where you can enjoy drinks on the porch of Hotel Pupetto.

But for the feel of discovering your own private hideaway and a delicious lunch, head to **Arienzo**. It's a small cove bordered with giant rocks, with views of fishing boats bobbing along the horizon, ferries headed for Capri and, in the distance, the Li Galli islands. Legend says these islands were once mermaids whom Ulysses turned to stone so they'd stop trying to seduce him off his course.

I'm not talking great sand. It's volcanic and coarse with lots of black pebbles. But like almost everything you touch around here, Positano's black pebbles have a story behind them. If you find one with a hole in it, it means the BVM passed through it, and it's blessed. You'll see many Positanesi wearing necklaces of these black pebbles.

The sand situation means you should bring along beach shoes and rent an umbrella and lounge chair. Then get totally comfy, lie back and get lulled by the lapping of the calm water.

Melody, an American who's lived in Positano for years, tipped me off that Ada's gnocchi at Arienzo is famous in these parts. As you approach the beach you'll see Ada, a fifty-something-year-old *signora* with a radiant smile, bustling about in her walk-in-closet-sized kitchen.

The beach snack bar is set up on stilts, looking like something Thurston Howell III would have built on *Gilligan's Island*, perched to take in the view. A blackboard lists the day's specials, which along with Ada's gnocchi may feature spaghetti with clams, Caprese salad, fish caught that morning and granitas—flavored ices made from Positano lemons and whatever else is in season.

Around noon, locals start arriving on foot or pulling up on boats to enjoy Ada's lunch. Her gnocchi are light and beautifully textured, served with a delicate tomato sauce. The house red is rich and lively. On a visit there one warm October day, for dessert Ada served me a plate of ripe figs picked from a nearby tree, and poured me a glass of homemade limoncello.

Even if you don't find a pebble with a hole blown through it, at Arienzo Beach you'll feel Positano's blessings.

**Arienzo Beach** (www.bagnidiarienzo.com): To get here you can catch a small boat from Spiaggia Grande or walk down a zigzag path of 300 steps from the Arienzo bus stop.

**Golden Day:** Visit **Arienzo Beach** and then head to **Ada's** and have gnocchi for lunch. Stay at **Maliosa di Arienzo** (www.lamaliosa.it), a B&B nearby, with your private sea-view terrace. Arrange for complimentary car service to **Mediterraneo** ristorante (www.mediterraneopositano.com) for a dinner of fantastic seafood and a Neapolitan guitarist who strums classics.

# 46 Parghelia–Calabria

"THE ENTERTAINMENT AT PARGHELIA IS WATCHING the tanned, pudgy, eleven-year-old local boys jumping off the rocks—it's hilarious!" my friend Tania told me about her favorite beach. She lives in Tropea, the prettiest town on Calabria's coast. In summer, Tropea's wide, white sand beaches (rated among the best in Italy) get packed with tourists.

That's when Tania takes a two-minute drive north to the little fishing village of **Parghelia**, and heads to the secluded **Spiaggia di Michelino**. Giant craggy rocks border it at one end. The pale turquoise water is so clear you can see all the way to the bottom of those rocks, and the light and sparkling sea playing against the intricate stone formations is hypnotic. It's a perfect place for snorkeling.

This beach is not in the least luxurious. There's no fee, no umbrella or chair rentals, no snack bar. As you walk the shaded, woodland path and steps to get down there, birdsongs mix with the sounds of waves crashing against rocks. Just like so many other stunning places in Calabria, no big deal is made out of this rustic spot of natural beauty. The rocks give it a deep, old world mysterious vibe. Locals of all ages who come to relax here give it the authentic Calabrian flavor.

The **Spiaggia di Michelino** is part of a whole Tyrrhenian sea stretch called "The Coast of the Gods." Odysseus ran into loads of trouble in these waters. Just south of here, the she-monster Scylla, a twelve-legged, multi-headed creature, snatched up his six best men and gobbled them up. Poseidon's son, **Aeolus**, gave him a bag of winds that steered him off course. That's how the Aeolian Islands, that lie off this coast, got their name.

From the **Spiaggia di Michelino** you can see the closest of the five Aeolians, Stromboli. With its smoking volcanic peak that erupts with a brilliant orange-red display from time to time, Stromboli adds a dramatic touch to the beach view.

Every time I look at Stromboli I'm reminded of the movie of the same name starring young, glamorous Ingrid Bergman. While it was being filmed, Bergman and director Roberto Rossellini fell madly in love, their affair causing a scandal, as both of them were married to others at the time. Once again, a spicy romantic story seems inescapable wherever you go in Italy.

To be at **Spiaggia di Michelino** for a sunset—when shadows fall on the rocks, the orange ball slips into the deepening turquoise sea, and (if you're lucky) Stromboli shoots off its fireworks, is spectacular.

**Spiaggia di Michelino**: The beach is about a twenty-minute walk from Tropea. If you're arriving by train or driving, take a left from the Parghelia *stazione*, follow the road beneath an underpass, and keep going until you see steps that lead to the beach.

᛭

**Golden Day**: Head to **Spiaggia di Michelino**, stopping on the way at **La Piccola Rosticceria** at **Piazza Ruffa** to pick up Calabrian lunch goodies like *polpette di melanzane* (eggplant balls).

# 46 Santa Teresa di Gallura–Sardinia

IT WAS QUEEN MARIA THERESA'S IDEA to name this town on the north coast of Sardinia Santa Teresa, to honor the Spanish mystic. Plus, it happened to be her middle name. In 1808, her husband, King Vittorio Emanuele I, obliged. He happened to be ruling the island. This spot had been prime territory for smugglers, as its curved harbor made it naturally perfect for doing sneaky things. King Vittorio wanted to clean things up, so he had the town rebuilt in a neat grid plan and even offered free plots of land to respectable folks who wanted to move in.

These days **Santa Teresa di Gallura** is a pretty resort spot, more relaxed and less expensive than Costa Smeralda that lies to its east. The former famous-for-smuggling harbor is filled with ferryboats that go to the Maddalena Islands and Corsica.

And, on this island that has the best beaches in Italy, the **Rena Bianca**, that's steps down from Santa Teresa di Gallura, is prime. My friend Elizabeth spent two weeks here with her family, and loved Rena Bianca. During the long stay, she scoped out surrounding spots, and though it was fun to watch windsurfers or go snorkeling on other beaches nearby, as far as classic beachfront, Rena Bianca was certainly the best.

It's sheltered from the winds by the harbor and has fine white sand, opening to clear waters that change in color from pale blue to turquoise to deep cobalt at the horizon. If you get there when the tide is right, the shoreline is tinged with pink from coral fragments that wash up. There's a restaurant, bar, and umbrella and chair rentals.

This is a beloved spot for Italian vacationers, which Elizabeth found out when she arrived there in August. "I never felt so white," she told me, as she and her blonde family placed their towels amidst the alligator-tanned Italians. August may not be the best time to go, as Elizabeth told me it was towel-to-towel packed—so much so that in order to get a good space, her husband would get up early and take the steps down to the beach to claim the family turf. But still, she found it divine, with her two boys, aged eight and ten, staying in the water for the entire day while she and her husband read and drank prosecco. There also were a few topless *signorine* who made quite the impression on her boys. Elizabeth said, "a few topless." Her husband, remembering the vacation fondly, chimed in, "There were four."

If you're not up for the August crowds, come here another time during the May to September resort season. But August can be fun, as that's when there are celebrations honoring the town's founding, with musicians in the piazza and evening classical concerts in churches.

**Tourist Info**: www.santateresagalluraturismo.com

**Golden Day**: Relax at **Rena Bianca** and eat at **Pape Satàn** (Via La Marmora 20, 078 9755048), where the pizza is out of this world and they also serve up fantastic seafood pastas.

## RECOMMENDED READING

*Sea and Sardinia* by D.H. Lawrence

# 47

*Scopello–Sicily*

"SCOPELLO IS ONE OF SICILY'S HIDDEN GEMS," my writer friend Maria Lisella told me. She lives in Queens, New York, and visits Italy often with her Sicilian-American husband. They're always getting off the beaten path to seek out unusual places. **Scopello**, a two-*via* fishing village on the west coast, is one of her most beloved spots.

It has a horseshoe-shaped beach that's free and tiny, made up of a mix of white pebbles and fine sand. Warm, transparent turquoise waters, framed by *faraglioni* (limestone towers), cover an amazing seabed, where colorful sponges and anemones cling to the rocks.

If you're up for diving to see *astroides* illuminating caves or a World War II shipwreck, the **Cetaria Dive Center** (www.cetaria. it), rents out equipment and is even kid-friendly, offering classes for those over seven years old. But just swimming around here is spectacular, and in spring and fall you may be joined by *stenelle*, a breed of dolphins who migrate through the area.

Though the village of Scopello is tiny, it's rich in history. Two medieval watchtowers and the *tonnara*, a twelfth-century tuna processing building that was in use until the 1980s, accent the surroundings. The piazza has charming B&Bs and restaurants, where you should definitely order the *tonno* (tuna). Not many Americans get here, but it has become a popular spot for Italian and German tourists.

Adjoining Scopello is **Lo Zingaro National Park**, a fantastic seaside nature preserve. There are easy hiking trails set along the

4.5-mile/7.5-km rocky shoreline, where you get breathtaking panoramic views from the cliffs. Paths are surrounded by dwarf palms and wildflowers—from sea lavender to crocuses, irises, and orchids. It's also great for bird lovers, who'll enjoy watching eagles, peregrine falcons, partridges, and owls.

You may want to use Scopello as your base to explore the nearby hill town of Erice, the salt towers of Trapani, or the Temple of Segesta.

But best of all, as Maria puts it, "Scopello is the perfect place to end a vacation and let go of your tourist agendas. Just flop there, relax and swim."

೫ఁ

**Golden Day:** Settle in for relaxing swimming and sunning at **Scopello** beach. For lunch, stop by the best bakery in the village, **Panificio di Stabile e Anselmo** (Via Gallupi 5), and pick up a *pane cunzato*, the town's signature *panino*, freshly baked bread saturated with local olive oil and filled with eggplant, tomatoes, olives, and anchovies. A pretty bed and breakfast in town is **Pensione Tranchina** (www.pensionetranchina.com). It's owned by a Scopello native and his Chinese wife, Marisin, who speaks English. The couple are passionate about sharing all they know regarding the region with travelers and they serve up delicious dinners of catch-of-the-day seafood.

# V

## Beauty Treatments and Spas

Treat yourself to one of Italy's oldest traditions: taking the waters at a spa. That's SPA, as in *Salus Per Aqum = Health Through Water*. Spa, as in *AH...that feels soooo good.* If any "I'm in Italy, I should be at a museum" thoughts come up, shut them down. You're having a valuable cultural experience.

Every region of Italy has curative thermal springs gurgling below. The Ancient Romans, experts at enjoying sensual pleasures, built elaborate bath houses around these waters. They were social centers where spirits were lifted; aches and pains soaked away.

Today, these places are taken seriously by Italy's health care system. So say you're Italian and you have arthritis or some other ailment. Instead of popping pills, a doctor will write a prescription for you to spend time at a spa, where you'll go through a supervised program of soaking and massage.

Italians and visitors from all over Europe and Russia flock to these places. Many of them are grand old hotels. And there's a growing number (especially in Tuscany) of spas that are closer to the American model, offering yoga classes and acupuncture. American travelers haven't caught on to them yet, even though there are bargains to be had, especially in the early spring and fall off season. Hotel packages that include treatments cost a fraction of what you'd pay for the same thing in America. Well, not exactly the *same* thing: think Italian food and wine. Plus, there's a gentler philosophy here—rarely are there hard core gyms or punishing diet offerings on the menu. And don't be surprised if you see a few folks smoking.

For the best bargains, head to the country and seek out Italy's *wild* spas—free places where you just walk in and soak with the locals.

Wherever you end up taking the waters, you'll come out rejuvenated in body and spirit, just as the Romans did. So relax, slow down, enjoy...

# 48 *Hair Salons and Spas*

IF YOU'VE SEEN *ROMAN HOLIDAY,* the fantasy of impulsively stepping into a salon and becoming magically transformed à la Audrey Hepburn may stick with you.

I confess it happened to me. I wound up in a chair with a very enthusiastic Marco chopping and circling, telling me he was giving me "Hair for the pillow—Sexy!" When I got home my husband greeted me with: "Hey! Liza Minelli!" No offense to Liza, whom I adore, but it wasn't what I was going for.

So now I rely on my beauteous Italian girl-friends for advice, which I pass on to you.

If you're just in need of a shampoo and style, most of Italy's major cities and even small towns have Jean Louis David or Aveda salons. But for great cuts, beauty treatments Italian style, or massages to give you that boost while you're traveling, here are some places in major metropolitan areas.

## Rome

* **Hotel de Russie**, Via del Babuino 9, 06 32 8881, www.roccofortehotels.com

  An amazing oasis, perfectly set between the Spanish Steps and Piazza del Popolo. Indulge in their anti-jet lag massage, soak in the dreamy pool, enjoy a cocktail in the hotel garden, and you'll be fabulously energized to take on the Eternal City.

* **Contesta Rock Hair,** Via degli Zingari 9, 06 478 23717, www.contestarockhair.com
  In the under-touristed Monti neighborhood, this modern shop is not just for rock and rollers as the name might imply. It's a great place to get a chic, reasonably priced cut, color, or blow-out.

* **Spazio Beauty,** Via dei Chiavari 37, 06 686 9800
  A simple "Beauty Place" off the Campo dei Fiori, where you can get massages, body scrubs, facials, and waxing for reasonable prices.

## Florence

* **Simonetta Pini,** Viale Antonio Gramsci 27r, 055 247 7713, www.simonettapini.com
  How lovely it is to slip into this lively salon, joining in with Simonetta's loyal followers: beautiful Florentine women who have been coming here for decades. Simonetta gives exceptional cuts, the colorists are great, and you could also get your nails done.

* **SoulSpace,** Via S. Egidio 12, 055 200 1794, www.soulspace.it
  The ground floor of a nineteenth-century palazzo has been transformed to a cozy spa oasis, with a warm pool and hammam to hydrotherapy your travel aches away. A wide range of massage and facial treatments are offered by the charming, English speaking staff. Check the website for special offers.

❀ **Four Seasons Hotel Spa**, Borgo Pinti 99, 055 26261,
www.fourseasons.com/Florence
If you're up for a splurge, this is your spot. Behind the luxury
hotel is a two-story modern wonderland, surrounded by gorgeous gardens, where treatments feature products from the
beloved *Santa Maria Novella Farmacia*. There are even Full-Time
Mom treatments, custom designed for mothers and children to
relax together.

## Venice

❀ **Michele Doardo Hair Stylist,** Salizada del Pistor Santi
Apostoli (Cannaregio), 041 528 7217
Make an appointment with in-demand stylist "Miky"—who
can doll you up for a Venetian ball, wedding, or give you an
inspired style and cut.

❀ **Bauer Palladio Spa,** Giudecca 3, www.palladiohotelspa.com
In dreamy Venice, this place ranks up there as one of the
dreamiest. The Renaissance master architect Palladio designed
the building in the sixteenth century as a sanctuary for unmar-
ried women. They learned lacemaking here, a craft that kept
them from heading out to the canals to join in on the world's
oldest profession. Their sanctuary has been restored to a luxurious hotel with enchanting gardens and a spa that has a Turkish
bath and treatment rooms for facials, massages, or body treatments. All is top-of-the-line, with a gorgeous view of mainland
Venice from its relaxing room.

# 49 *Spas—Viterbo, Lazio*

IN HIS *INFERNO*, DANTE WROTE OF "SINFUL WOMEN" who once hung out in the thermal springs outside the town of Viterbo, a verdant, hilly area north of Rome. Besides working girls, these *terme* have been enjoyed by the Etruscans, Roman emperors, and became favorite spots for popes in the middle ages, when they were kicked out of Rome and the Papal Seat moved to Viterbo. The sulfur-rich waters are renowned for soothing the skin, relieving aching bones, and working miracles on the respiratory system. These days you'll find a mix of spa offerings here, from wild, free spots to luxury hotels. Of the many choices, a couple of suggestions...

## Free Spa

* **Piscine Carletti**
  You'll discover these bubbling pools in a flat field, just 1.5 miles from the center of Viterbo. It's a no-frills set-up, where you park in the adjoining lot, change in your car, then join in with the local pensioners and a smattering of tourists. What's wonderful is the pools' varying temperatures, which give you the opportunity to experience a genuine Roman bath ritual—going from cool to progressively hotter—without spending an euro. It's a great place to go in cooler weather, and unless you bring an umbrella, not recommended during summer's high heat, as there are no trees around for shade. Also best to go before lunch to avoid the crowds.

## Hotel/Day Spa

❋ **Terme dei Papi**

This vast hotel spa, named in honor of the popes who once soaked around here, has a bustling thermal pool scene. It's fun to join in with the boisterous Italians—many locals come here weekly—and rent a foam noodle to enjoy a curative float. There are also saunas, a grotto, and treatment rooms where you can get massages and facials for low prices. Terme dei Papi's mud treatments are tops—featuring one mud variety for muscle therapy and another type for cosmetic treatments.

If you have a car, and are up for more adventure, head toward Rome for a visit to Italy's most bizarre town: **Calcata**. From a distance it may look like just another tiny medieval hilltop village. But once you enter its walls, you'll discover it's full of artists, from all over Italy and the world. This place was practically abandoned sixty years ago, until these creative types moved in, dug in their heels, and saved it from the government wrecking ball. I got to know the town through writer David Farley, who lived there for a while and wrote *An Irreverent Curiosity*—a fascinating and hilarious story about his search to solve the mystery behind the theft of Calcata's famous relic: Jesus's foreskin.

**Info for Viterbo Spas:** www.termediviterbo.it

**Terme dei Papi:** Provides direct round-trip bus service from Rome's Piazza Mancini daily, for a morning visit—perfect to prepare you for an afternoon of sightseeing. Bring your own towel, rubber slippers, and cover-up. Closed Tuesdays. www.termedeipapi.it

❧

**Golden Day:** Soak in **Viterbo**, then head to **Calcata**. Eat at **La Grotta dei Germogli** (Rupe San Giovanni; 0761 176 9438, open Friday dinner and for lunch and dinner on weekends), a nouvelle Italian restaurant in a mosaic-lined cave. To spend the night, check out **I Sensi della Terra** (340 505 2322, www.calcata.info) for room and apartment rentals scattered throughout the village.

### RECOMMENDED READING

*An Irreverent Curiosity: In Search of the Church's Strangest Relic in Italy's Oddest Town* by David Farley

# 50 Spas—Tuscany

As if Tuscany isn't marvelous enough—cities bursting with masterpieces of art, charming hill towns, and a countryside that's world famous for vineyards and olive groves, the region also has the most thermal springs of any in Italy.

Here are some favorites:

## Free Spas

* **Saturnia Terme**, in the province of Maremma, is Tuscany's most famous free spa. Myth has it that the springs were created when Jupiter became enraged at Saturn and shot lightning bolts down to Earth. The god's fury created the **Cascate del Mulino**, (www.cascate-del-mulino.info), a fantastic hot bubbling waterfall that tumbles down into a complex of warm thermal pools, surrounded by lush vegetation. Sulphur is the major mineral component of these water (good for skin and joints), so a rotten-egg smell will lead you to this glorious spot. Be advised that it gets mobbed midday and in summer. It's wonderful to go at night, with a flashlight, when clouds of steam rise from the pools and you can soak under the stars.

* **San Filippo** (www.bagnisanfilippoterme.it), named after a Florentine hermit, is a less dramatic option in the province of Siena. A short hike from the road through the woods brings

you to **Fosso Bianco,** a large white rock formation created by the springs. Further along are terraces of pools that range in temperature from 75 to 125 degrees. It's a serene spot, where you can soak with local families, amidst tall shade trees and butterflies.

## Spa Towns

* **Montecatini Terme** (www.termemontecatini.it) is an enchanting Art Nouveau-styled town, easily reached by train from Florence in about an hour. It rose to fame as Italy's top spa destination between the eighteenth and twentieth centuries, and now has over two hundred spa hotels that pump in curative waters from local springs renowned for their curative effects on the liver and digestive system. My favorite place is **Terme Tettuccio**, a grand pavilion that sits in the beautifully land-scaped park at the center of town. You're given a cup when you enter, and can fill it up at gorgeous marble bars, mingling with the mix of hipsters in their gym clothes and pensioners steadying themselves on canes. A jazz orchestra plays on the central bandstand, there's a caffe, bookshop, and inner flower gardens that blend to create a blissful, Old-World scene.

* **Bagno Vignoni** is a perfectly preserved medieval village in the Val D'Orcia. Its central piazza is a stunning rectangular thermal pool, where such greats as Saint Catherine, Saint Francis, and Lorenzo the Magnificent soaked. My favorite place to take the waters near the center is **Hotel Posta Marcucci** (www.hotelpostamarcucci.it), a welcoming, family run three-star, with a large outdoor thermal pool, set perfectly for gorgeous views of the valley. You can come for the day and enjoy a delicious Tuscan lunch at the restaurant, beloved by generations of locals.

## Luxury Spa Hotels

For the most elegant Tuscan spa experience, spend a day or more immersed in rich history at one of these beauties. All three offer state-of-the-art treatments, blending Eastern medicine and traditional Mediterranean spa styles to balance body-mind-soul. And their dining rooms are run by top chefs, bringing in the finest wines of the region and traditional Tuscan specialties with modern twists.

❀ **Fonteverde Spa**, San Casciano dei Bagni, (www.fonteverdespa. com): How about sitting on a marble throne submerged in a warm thermal pool with hydro-jets massaging your back and the soles of your feet, while taking in a view of rolling hills of vineyards and olive groves? It's good to be Queen here, where Grand Duke Ferdinando I de' Medici and his family frolicked in the seventeenth century. The reactivating hydrotherapy treatments set me off to take in the sights of Florence completely renewed, an unstoppable art fiend from dawn till dusk.

❀ **Grotta Giusti**, Monsummano Terme, (www.grottagiustispa. com): Composer Verdi called the thermal cave here the Eighth Wonder of the World. It was discovered in 1849, during a renovation of this elegant villa, home of poet Giuseppe Giusti. One of the workers exploring it suddenly felt his joint aches disappear. Doctors came in to study the phenomena and a spa hotel was built soon after, attracting travelers on the Grand Tour. It's amazing to wander through the grotto levels, named Paradiso, Purgaturio, and finally Inferno, where you settle into a lounge chair and relax with the healing vapors. There's a large outdoor thermal pool, and the gracious hotel is surrounded by a lush, landscaped park.

⊛ **Bagni di Pisa,** San Giuliano Terme, (www.bagnidipisa.com): A twenty-minute train ride from Pisa delivered me to this quaint spa town that's centered around a stupendous villa that was the summer home of the Grand Duke of Tuscany in the eighteenth century. Now a grand spa, it was marvelous to soak in the central courtyard's Minerva Bath, surrounded by sculpted archways and urns. There are outdoor and indoor pools, a small grotto was recently discovered, and magnificently restored frescos all around, particularly in the Shelley Bar, where I lifted a glass of prosecco to toast the view of the Leaning Tower in the distance.

# 51 Grand Hotel Abano Terme–Veneto

I CAME HERE FOR THE WINE THERAPY. Wine therapy is not downing a bottle, having a good cry, and healing your inner child. Wine therapy is a super ingenious body treatment invented in this place east of Venice. While all the region's winemakers are using the vineyards to produce such favorites as prosecco and amarone, these spa scientists have different ideas about the grape.

Which is why I am laying here as Lianna paints me with slick goo from toe to neck. The goo is made from fermented grapes and contains a *prezioso* ingredient: *resveratrolo*. *Resveratrolo* that will exfoliate me, anti-inflammatory me, re-collagenize me, and pump up my serotonins so my mood will be lifted. It's the "aroma-emotional path" of the **Grand Hotel Abano Terme** and I am on it.

"Your miracles, Abano, give speech to the mute," sang Claudius when he soaked in the waters here thousands of years ago. Roman emperors, thrilled to find 130 thermal springs in the surrounding Euganean hills, built baths. They slathered themselves with mud and sang the praises of its miraculous healing properties. They indulged in their own version of wine therapy, guzzling it and honoring Bacchus. They named this spot Abano, from the word *aponos,* without pain.

Now what you find here is *termalismo moderno,* modern thermalism that puts a cutting edge style on what Romans adored in olden days. Thermal waters pump through hydro-jets in curative Jacuzzis. Mud is treated like wine, maturing so it develops algae that has unique anti-inflammatory properties. And as for the grapes, it's all about extracting that miraculous *resveratrolo.* A recent addition, the Venezia Spa, is a wonderland of mosaic rooms with a series of saunas, cold alley, aromatherapy showers, and chromotherapy lighting that's all set up to recharge body and soul.

The Grand Hotel Abano Terme is the only five-star amidst the many hotel/spas in Abano, and its focus is anti-aging treatments. I winced as I put myself in for it, being from Los Angeles, land of the obsessive quest for eternal youth, where places like this can get pushy and expensive. But there's a kinder, gentler spirit to it here. The three-hour wine therapy, that went from that *resveratrolo* to mud-packing to massage cost me about a third of what I'd pay for anything that would come close to it back in the States.

Why haven't we Americans heard of this place, when Germans and Russians are joining the Italians to fill it up? Because the town of Abano gets a grade of charm-minus. The forested hills that surround it are lovely, but it was built up for tourism in the 1970s. Its streets are lined with concrete-block multi-storied hotel/spas, like a low-key Vegas. Everything is prettily landscaped with palm trees and other tropical plants, but there's zilch Old-World ambience or fabulous art like you'll find in abundance everywhere else in the Veneto region. The appeal here is the bargain deluxe digs, extraordinary spa treatments, and lovely service every step of the way. It's a great base to explore the treasures of Padua (ten minutes by train), or the hotel can arrange for you to get to prettier places nearby and go horseback riding or golfing.

The Grand Hotel Abano Terme is grand in an Empire Louis XIV meets Sheraton-of-the-1970s way. There are grand chandeliers all over the place, meals are lavish buffets, loaded with fresh fish, lots of nicely prepared vegetables, and the finest Veneto wines.

There are also corny details to add amusement. Right off the lobby is a formal glassed-in smoking room—in a spa! Opposite it is a matching room furnished with felt tables for card games, where I got a nostalgic hit thinking of my mother's bridge club, when I peeked in to see a senior-citizen foursome enjoying themselves. At dinner, there was a fashion show, where sleek-haired goddesses with legs up to their ears strutted around modeling furs—a big business for designers of the area.

The stellar thing about this place is excellent treatments for excellent prices. When I arrived home a week after my wine therapy, and met my friend Monica for a welcome back glass of wine, the first words out of her mouth were: "You're glowing!"

**Grand Hotel Abano Terme**: www.gbhotelsabano.it

# 52 Spas—Ischia, Campania

AN HOUR'S FERRY RIDE FROM NAPLES takes you to this lush island, formed long ago by volcanos. Though there are no longer eruptions, there is lively action underneath the island's surface that creates springs of mineral rich water and smoking plumes of air, that shoot through fissures, turning caves into curative saunas. Much of this goodness is fed into treatment facilities—from luxury spa hotels to thermal parks, totaling over three hundred, making Ischia the largest thermal-water destination in Europe. Along with the spas are rolling hills of vineyards, lively port towns, and remnants of the ancient Greeks and Romans who soaked here.

Women have left their mark all over Ischia. As you approach by boat, you'll see an Aragonese castle where Vittoria Colonna, a beloved Renaissance poetess, lived and surrounded herself with an elegant court. She later moved to Rome where she became Michelangelo's soul mate and he wrote poems to her, addressing her as "thou spirit of grace." In the town of Forio is **La Mortella**, an exotic garden created by the late/great Lady Susana Walton. She was born in Argentina, came to Ischia with her music composer husband in the early 1950s, entertained such illustrious visitors as Vivian Leigh and Maria Callas, and then turned a barren plot of land into a showpiece that's visited by thousands every year.

Here are some favorite places to take the waters:

## Free Spa

* **Sorgeto, Panza** (www.sorgeto.it): It's an adventure to discover Sorgeto—either by boat from Sant'Angelo or taking the bus to Panza, then zig-zagging down about two hundred steps. You arrive in a marvelous cove where thermal springs gush into the sea, creating shallow hot bubbling pools. Go ahead and join in with the pleasure seekers—that may range from local housewives to Australian tourists. Standing by will be Nino, a hippie dude, with a bucket of thermal mud, which he'll slather on you for a small tip, and then he may even offer you a cooked potato he's boiled in one of the pools. There's a club set above the rocks with changing rooms, lounge chairs and umbrellas, and a restaurant that serves fantastic fried seafood and bruschetta made with the delicious tomatoes grown in the fertile soil of the island.

## Thermal Park

* **Poseidon Thermal Park**, Forio, (www.giardiniposeidonterme. com): I love bringing groups of women here for a spa day during our Golden Week in Southern Italy tour. Poseidon is Ischia's largest and most popular thermal park, with over twenty pools of varying temperatures, set into the hillside, with palm trees, gardens, a sauna carved into the rocks, and an idyllic beach on the Bay of Citara. Among the many great treatments, a favorite is reflexology, for deep relief from days of walking on cobblestoned streets.

## Luxury Spa Hotels

* **L'Albergo della Regina Isabella**, Lacco Ameno (www. reginaisabella.com): Queen Isabella of Spain came to the springs around here in the nineteenth century, pregnant and

needing R&R. Before her visit the waters were named after Santa Restituta, a Christian martyr whose body washed ashore nearby in the third century, but the Queen's stay was apparently such a major deal they became known as Regina Isabella in her honor. The sprawling Spanish-style resort was built by film producer Angelo Rizzoli in the 1950s over the ruins of ancient Greek and Roman baths. It immediately became a hot spot for celebrities like Ava Gardner, Gina Lollobrigida, and Anna Magnani. These days it still has a mid-century retro vibe and is one of Ischia's most exclusive places, hosting an international film and music festival every June, with outdoor movies and concerts. I stayed in a room with my very own thermal tub on the outside terrace, got treated to mud baths, relaxing massages, and the delightful atmosphere of laid-back resort by day and old-world formality at night. Restaurants include the Michelin-starred Indaco.

❀ **Mezzatorre Resort and Spa**, Forio (www.mezzatorre.it): This former fifteenth-century watchtower is now a tranquil, romantic oasis, offering spectacular views from its promontory setting, a heated sea water swimming pool and a private beach. I loved floating under the pine trees and then taking their indoor thermal circuit, an ingenious system of pools with massage jets that progressively target different areas of the body—from my shoulders to feet. They also offer outdoor massages, under a gazebo, where the sound of the waves and soft breezes enhance the relaxing experience. Dining here is divine, especially in the French-inspired Chandelier restaurant. It's perfect for honeymooners.

❀ **Terme Manzi Hotel and Spa**, Casamicciola Terme, (www.termemanzi.com): Tucked into the island's green hills is this dazzling place, designed as an homage to Ischia's history—with Roman-inspired statuary, Arabic mosaics, vibrant paintings of dancing Neapolitan peasants, and everywhere colorfully painted tiles that this area of southern Italy is famous for. The heated indoor pool is all glittery, and the outdoor one is set facing the island's largest peak, Mount Epomeo. Waters pumped in from the nearby Gurgitiello springs have been praised since Roman times for their anti-aging mix of minerals that the spa signora told me, "turn back the clock." Restaurants include the elegant **Gli Ulivi**, featuring a patio where pizzas are cooked in wood burning ovens and the 2-Michelin-starred **Il Mosaico**, where you can have a fabulously entertaining culinary experience with a seat at the chef's table in the kitchen, in view of master Chef Nico Di Costanzo. Among my dinner's many memorable courses was *crudo* (raw fish), served on glimmering blocks of Murano glass, and a dessert, presented to me with ear buds, so I could listen to Neapolitan music over a delightful plate of sweets.

# 53 Masseria Torre Maizza-Puglia

I'M LYING ON A MASSAGE TABLE, feeling like Cleopatra, getting rubbed with warm olive oil. Here in Puglia, it's the most logical thing to use. All around are old olive trees, lots of them from 700 years ago. Their thick, gnarled trunks twist up like sculptures from shimmering green fields, with the calm Adriatic Sea as a backdrop.

Athena, Goddess of Wisdom, is the gal responsible for olives. She and Poseidon were fighting over who should rule the Greek region of Attica when Papa of the Gods, Zeus, stepped in and said, "Whoever brings the best gift to humanity gets the job." Poseidon stuck his trident into the earth and out popped a galloping horse. Pretty impressive. Then Athena stuck in her trident and out popped an olive branch, which must have looked puny by comparison.

But then the goddess talked her way through it: "This will grow into a tree that will live hundreds of years. There will be fruit on it, wonderful to garnish martinis. And the oil from that fruit will be what humanity will go crazy over. They'll light lamps with it, cure boo-boos, and no good kitchen will be without it. And by the way, this olive branch...will be the symbol of peace." No contest. Athena won. The capital of Attica was named Athens and the Parthenon built in her honor.

Thank you Athena, for this olive oil massage. And for peace. Centuries ago this place where I'm getting my rubdown was regularly invaded by Turks. It was a farm estate and the spa its watchtower, where folks hovered anxiously, looking out to sea for pirate ships. Now it's a most tranquil spot, where not only olive oil, but herbs and vegetables grown on the property are incorporated into their treatments. My friend Sheila is in the next room getting slathered with a creamy paste of fava beans. Sounds weird, but it's an age-old tradition in these parts. Post-slathering, she takes a steam in the Turkish bath (one good thing that came from those mean Turks), and comes out all aglow when we meet up for a Jacuzzi soak.

We go back in to get non-traditional (for an Italian spa) Kembiki Do facials. It's an ancient Japanese deal where the sweet technicians "reorganize the facial architecture" according to the write-up. This means such an intense massage they even put on rubber gloves to stick their fingers in our mouths to rub out marionette lines. I'm amazed looking in the mirror afterwards. Maybe I should try this at home.

Like many similar *masserie* (farm estates) in this stretch south of Bari, the Torre Maizza has been luxuriously renovated. Simple whitewashed stone buildings, that were servants' quarters and stables in the sixteenth century, are now spacious suites with arched ceilings, all airy and furnished in elegant style.

All this white and perfect blue sky and sun makes Sheila and me feel extra energized. The air is perfumed with the scent of jasmine and myrtle bushes. Bougainvillea adds a splash of crimson to the buildings. There's an infinity pool a pleasant walk away that looks tempting, but we want to get to the private beach. We have the choice of taking a five-minute shuttle van or riding a horse there, but we decide on biking it, stopping on the way to gawk at those amazing old olive trees.

The sea is calm, shallow, and warm enough for a swim, even though it's October. There's a restaurant that blends right in to the beach, all white of course, and done up with chic bamboo furniture. They serve sushi, but we go for the salt-encrusted *orata*.

And why not a glass of white wine from the nearby Locorotondo vineyards to match? We clink our glasses. We feel pretty.

**Masseria Torre Maizza**: 72015 Savelletri di Fasano, 080 482 7838, www.masseriatorremaizza.com. The spa also offers yoga and Pilates sessions. The **Coccaro Beach Club**, open to guests of Torre Maizza, is a happening spot on the Puglia coast in the summer.

# 54 *Hammam—Palermo, Sicily*

HOW DID MY FRIEND PETULIA DEAL with the hustle-bustle of Palermo? She stepped off the street into this luxurious and relaxing hammam for a few hours.

It's a dreamy callback to Palermo's Arabic past. In the ninth century, Moors from North Africa conquered Sicily, bringing their sophisticated culture to the city, which included the hammam, or what we call a Turkish bath. The Moors were shocked to see what the Romans were doing: "Bathing in their own filth!" Their cleaning style was a more intimate set-up of heated rooms, where they'd splash themselves with water, then scrub their skin and get massaged with perfumed oils.

This hammam has received rave reviews for giving visitors the calming pleasures of that thousand-plus year-old tradition. It was designed by Andre Benaim, a Florentine who's internationally famous for his theater sets. He stuck to the classic cozy set-up, putting a sleek, magical spin on it. There are lots of candles surrounding two octagonal-shaped heated rooms of shiny white marble. One is domed with red brick and has openings that filter in a pale light. Between splashing yourself, you lounge around on warm marble slabs, going from the *tepidarium*, to the hotter, steamier *calidarium*. It's great for clearing up the respiratory system, sweating out toxins and stress, and getting your skin all set for a perfect tan. The pro staff sets you up with pretty water buckets, olive-oil soap, and a scrubbing mitt. All kinds of massages are available—from "comfort soul" to shiatsu.

In keeping with the Moslem way, the hammam is open on separate days for men and women. Over a thousand years ago, when the tradition started, women couldn't get near these places. That changed soon enough, and the bath became the prime spot for gals to socialize, as they could rarely leave the house. Mothers would go to check out prospective daughters-in-law, even kissing them so they could warn their son if the woman had bad breath. The hammam was especially popular in Turkey, where women would throw off their veils, smoke, laugh, and put on makeup. If a husband denied his wife the chance to go, she legally had grounds for divorce.

The scene is not at all as rowdy in this Palermo hammam. The experience ends in the relaxing room, where you curl up on colorful Moroccan pillows and get served herbal tea and sweets made with local honey.

**Hammam:** Via Torrearsa 17/d, 091 320783, www.hammam.pa.it. Women's days: Monday, Wednesday, and Friday.

# VI

## Indulge Your Tastebuds

Transplendent flavors await. Not only in restaurants where you're treated to the main events of your Italian days—those course-after-course feasts—but in simpler, one-taste-at-a-time moments. These are the treasured times when you indulge with a focus on just one of the delicious things Italians create so artfully—be it coffee, gelato, chocolate, or wine.

You might pursue your passion for tasting by heading to the country and visiting a winery, where you could be welcomed by one of the new wave of Italy's female wine producers.

Or any day during your visit to any Italian city, from morning until night, you can indulge your tastebuds as you tune into delicious daily rhythms: the morning buzz of activity at the caffè, the leisurely afternoon pace you'll slip into as you stroll down the street with a gelato in hand. Finally, there's the evening's relaxed pre-dinner interlude, when you settle in at a cozy wine bar. And Italian chocolate? That's a treat that gives a zing of pleasure anytime.

Savor these simple, one-taste-at-a-time moments, so easily found...

# 55 Caffès

"THE DEVIL'S DRINK" IS WHAT COFFEE was called when it first came to Venice on trade ships from North Africa in the sixteenth century. While wealthy Venetians were having a gay old time getting hopped up on it, pious peeps ran to Pope Clement VIII and urged him to ban it. The Pope figured he should at least have a taste first. He took one sip, declared it would be a sin *not* to drink this delicious gift from God, and blessed it. Now Italians drink 14 billion cups of coffee a year.

Caffès are happening places in Italy. In a Verona caffè in 1983, Howard Schultz looked around at everyone enjoying themselves so much that he went home to America and created Starbucks.

As far as Italy's caffè styles, you have many to pick from for your postcard writing, people watching, Devil's Drink break.

If you're in the mood to go fancy, you can splurge in one of Italy's historical caffès, some of which have been around for 300 years. Every Italian city has at least one of these classic places, where you're seated in a jewel-box of a salon and waited on by tuxedoed waiters. All have lists of illustrious travelers who have come before you—from queens to writers like Oscar Wilde to stars like Eleonora Duse. They are also great stops for evening cocktails, and offer delicious sweets and snacks. You'll pay a lot less if you stand at their counters, but come on, you're on vacation, so you might as well settle in. You're not going to end up some old lady eating cat food and muttering, "Oh, if I only hadn't spent ten euros for that cappuccino at the Florian..." Go for it.

If you're feeling more like having the Italian bohemian experience, there are caffès that have rich traditions of being gathering places for artists and intellectuals, which are typically also popular with locals.

And finally, if you want to go to a place that's legendary for serving the absolute best coffee in each city, I've listed them below. After you elbow in with the natives at the bar for your drink, you can buy a bag of beans to bring home.

## Rome

* **Fancy: Antico Caffè Greco,** Via Condotti 86 (near Spanish Steps)
  This caffè was founded by a Greek man in 1760, thus the name. Amidst the elegant surroundings, check out the photo of Buffalo Bill, whose 1906 visit caused a sensation.

* **Bohemian: Antico Caffè della Pace,** Via della Pace 3 (near Piazza Navona),
  From 1891, there's a theatrical atmosphere here—both in the interior dark wood bar and on the patio flanked by ivy-covered walls. In the evenings it becomes a hipster gathering spot.

* **Best Coffee: Caffè Sant'Eustachio,** Piazza Sant'Eustachio 82, or **Tazza D'Oro,** Via degli Orfani 84 (both near Pantheon).

## Florence

* **Fancy: Caffè Gilli,** Piazza della Repubblica 39r
  This began as a confectioner's shop in 1733, and moved here in the early 1900s. Now it's the place to have your espresso in

airy belle époque surroundings with wonderful pastries and buy their *delizioso* chocolates.

⚘ **Bohemian: Gran Caffè Giubbe Rosse,** Piazza Repubblica 13/14R
A *caffè storico letterario* (historic literary caffè) where the Italian futurist movement blossomed in the early twentieth century. It's traditionally been a meeting place for intellectuals from around the world, and hosts book signings, art exhibits, and performances.

⚘ **Best coffee: Ditta Artigianale,** Via dei Neri 32r, Via dello Sprone 5R (Oltrarno)
Superstar barista Francesco Sanapo founded this modern institution in 2013, which features carefully selected sourced beans, a variety of brewing options, and even American-style breakfasts—eggs and pancakes.

## Venice

⚘ **Fancy: Caffè Florian,** Piazza San Marco
Opened in 1720, this is Italy's oldest and most divine caffè. Casanova enjoyed coming here because it was the only place at the time that admitted women. It's marvelous to tuck into one of the velvet banquettes inside on a chilly morning, and in the evening take a table outside with a view of the piazza—when the orchestra starts up it feels like you're in a dream world.

⚘ **Caffe with Great Pastries: Rosa Salva,** Campo San Giovanni e Paolo (Castello)
Since 1879, this family-run operation has been the top catering company in Venice. Settle in for tea, hot chocolate, or *caffè* and refined Venetian pastries.

- **Best Coffee: Caffè del Doge,** Calle dei 5 (Rialto) and Ponte del Lovo (San Marco)

## Naples

- **Fancy: Gran Caffè Gambrinus,** Piazza Trieste e Trento 2
  Since 1850, here's where you can sit ensconced in a stunning art nouveau atmosphere, and enjoy an orchestra on Saturday nights.

- **Bohemian: Evaluna Libreria Café,** Piazza Bellini 72, closed Sunday
  A lively caffè, tea salon and bookshop, run by the wonderful Lia Polcari. It's headquarters for the Evaluna Association that, since the 1970s, has been publishing books by women authors.

- **Best Coffee: Mexico,** Piazza Dante 86, Piazza Garibaldi 72

## Turin

- **Fancy: Baratti & Milano,** Piazza Castello 29
  Since 1858, hot chocolate, thick as pudding, is what to order here, and they've got great house-made chocolates, like *gianduiotti* (hazelnut chocolate) and liqueur-filled goodies to bring home. My friend Emanuela, a Torino native, called it "the caffè for *principessas*" when she was a child.

- **Bohemian: Caffè al Bicerin,** Piazza della Consolata 5
  Since 1763, this teeny, welcoming place has served *bicerin*, Torino's famous drink of espresso, chocolate, and whipped cream. Though founded by a man, it has been operated by women since its start, and traditionally welcomed female customers to stop by after mass at the church across the piazza.

❋ **Best Coffee: Lavazza**, San Tomasso 10
This is where the famous company originated in 1895. Lots of
other locations in Turin.

## RECOMMENDED READING

*Café Life* series (Rome, Florence, and Venice) by Joe Wolff

# 56 *Gelato*

THE FLORENTINES CLAIM GELATO WAS INVENTED by the Medici's family architect, Bernardo Buontalenti, in 1565, when he churned it up during a banquet for Francesco I. Coincidentally, 1565 happens to be the same year Francesco married the seventeen-year-old Austrian Duchess Joanna, so I fantasize this was where the great tradition of hubby offering wife ice cream to bring a smile to her face began.

This is just my imagination, because the facts are that Joanna was miserable all through the marriage—homesick for Austria and fed up with Francesco's philandering. He's suspected of poisoning her; she died in childbirth at age thirty, and Francesco quickly married his mistress.

Still I think it's in the best interest of gelato folklore to imagine they had one happy gelato moment together before the crash and burn.

There are countless places for happy gelato moments in Italy, with just a couple of caveats. Be sure to check for a sign that says *Produzione Propria, Nostra Produzione, or Produzione Artiginale*, which mean "homemade" in Italian before you go in. And never buy from a shop that has overflowing tubs of gelato—that means they've been artificially pumped. Finally avoid yellow banana or bright green pistachio gelato, which means somebody tossed some imitation coloring in there.

Like all Italian food, gelato flavors vary with what's in season and whatever's growing in the region. I've found amazing *cipolle* (red onion) in Tropea, truffle-flavored gelato in Alba, and *carciofi* (artichoke) in Venice. Be adventurous.

Here are some suggestions for the best:

## Rome

❀ **Fatamorgana,** Via Laurina 10 (near Spanish Steps), Via Roma Libera 11 (Trastevere), Via Leoni IV (Vaticano), Piazza degli Zingari (Monti), www.gelateriafatamorgana.com
This mini-gelato empire was created by Maria Agnese Spagnulo, aka "The Ice Cream Fairy," a native of Puglia. Her childhood in the countryside, surrounded by fruit and nut trees, inspires her to make gelato with fresh, vibrant flavors and whole spices.

❀ **Gelateria del Teatro,** Via dei Coronari 65 (near Piazza Navona)
Tucked in a charming alley off Via Coronari, here owners Stefano and Silvia whip up delicious classic flavors (pistachio and dark chocolate), along with unique creations (lavender or sesame), and bite-sized pastries.

❀ **Il Gelato Claudio Torce,** Viale Aventino 59 (near Circus Maximus/Colosseum), Piazza del Risorgimento (Vaticano)
Master gelato maker Claudio is the genius that began Rome's artisan gelateria boom. His chain of shops feature over 100 flavors, including 12 varieties of chocolate, and savory options, including gorgonzola or mortadella.

## Florence

❀ **Vivoli** (near Santa Croce)
At the first gelateria in Florence (founded in 1929), lovely Silvana follows in the footsteps of her grandfather, making simply flavored masterpieces, including *crema* and *riso*.

- **Carapina,** Via Lambertesca (near Uffizi), Piazza Oberdan
  Superstar Simone Bonini is the force behind these modern
  gelaterias, using the highest quality ingredients to create intense
  and delicious flavors. The gelato panini is divine.

- **La Carraia,** Piazza Nazario Sauro (just over Ponte Carraia on
  Oltrarno side) and Via Benci 24/r (near Santa Croce)
  Another local favorite where the prices are low and quality is tops.

## Venice

- **Alaska,** Calle Larga dei Bari 1159 (Santa Croce)
  Owner Carlo is a fanatic who gets his gelato ingredients fresh
  from the Rialto market every day and is always churning up
  flavors of the season, along with great renditions of standards.

- **La Mela Verde,** Fondamenta de l'Osmarin (Castello)
  Passionate and handsome gelato makers—Davide and Johnny,
  create fabulous flavors, including their most famous: Green
  Apple (*Mela Verde*). The shop is near the Church of San Zaccaria,
  once home to a Benedictine convent, famous for its naughty
  nuns, and beautiful Bellini altarpiece inside.

- **Il Doge,** south end of Campo Santa Margherita (Dorsoduro)
  In a lively location, typically filled with students, here the
  Crema del Doge, flavored with bits of orange is great, along with
  the standards and specialties of the season.

## RECOMMENDED READING

*Gelato! Italian Ice Creams, Sorbetti and Granite* by Pamela Sheldon Johns

# 57 Chocolate

"LET THEM EAT CHOCOLATE," was the kind proclamation of Madame Reale. There she was, thirty years old, widowed during her first year of marriage, with a three-year-old boy to raise and the Piedmont region to rule from her palazzo in Turin. This was back in 1678 when the French House of Savoy governed the region.

Chocolate came to Italy through the Spanish explorer Cortez, who found it in South America. In Madame Reale's day it was a precious novelty served only to royalty and priests. When a Turin baker asked her permission to make chocolate for regular folk, I imagine she figured, "Why not?" She probably frequently needed the seritonin fix to deal with the hassles of being a female ruler and wanted to pass on the high to keep her popularity ratings up with her underlings.

The baker began making hot chocolate—a drink called *bicerin* that's still "what to order" in Turin caffès today. A love affair with chocolate began and Turin became Europe's top producer, even inventing a machine that made the world's first candy bars.

Italy's chocolate-making tradition has continued ever since, and you can thank Madame Reale as you visit these establishments:

❀ **Rome: Moriondo & Gariglio, Via del Piè di Marmo 21-22 (near Pantheon)**
This fairy tale-styled shop near the Pantheon was founded by a family from Turin over a hundred years ago. Sales *signorine* wear old-fashioned lace caps and box up bon-bons, marzipans, or fruit glaces into beautifully crafted boxes at an old world pace... so don't say I didn't warn you.

❀ **Florence: Vestri, Borgo degli Albizi 11r, www.vestri.it**
There's a lively energy at this tiny shop where *molto bello* owner Leonardo doles out treasures that include chocolates made with flavors like Earl Grey and chile, along with thick hot chocolate. The gelato here is *fantastico*, which you should order *affogato*, topped with to-die-for chocolate sauce. Candies are packaged in Tiffany-blue boxes and make great gifts.

❀ **Tuscany: The Chocolate Valley**
The most exciting developments in Italy's chocolate scene are happening in an area bordered by Prato and Pisa, where since the 1980s artisans have taken on chocolate production like meticulous Tuscan winemakers. It all started with **Roberto Catinari in Pistoia** (www.robertocatinari.it), and now includes **Andrea Slitti** (www.slitti.it) in Monsummano Terme, **Simone de Castro** in Montopoli, and **Paul De Bondt**, who teamed with Cecilia Iacobelli to create a success story in Pisa. The most well known among them is **Amedei** (www.amedei.it), whose factory outside Pontedera has become so successful it sells to specialty food shops worldwide.

The creators behind Amedei are Cecilia Tessieri, a brilliant chocolate maker, and her brother Alessio, who takes care of the business side. They were children of Tuscan candy makers with no chocolate experience, who decided to give it a go over twenty-five years ago, experimenting with great dedication. In 1991, they brought their findings to the pinnacle of the chocolate world, Valrhona in France, and tried to partner with them. Valrhona flatly turned them down.

Insulted but not discouraged, Alessio set out to find the best beans he could to make Amedei chocolate. In Chuao, Venezuela, where a perfect microclimate supports excellent cacao, Alessio took a risk. He offered the farmers three times as much as what Valrhona had been paying them. Now all of Chuao's cacao goes to Amedei. It's what's called Sweet Revenge.

⚜ **Venice: Vizio Virtù, Calle Forneri, Castello, www.viziovirtu.com**
Award-winning Mariangela Penzo is the master chocolatier of this shop that opened in 2005. Her scrumptious artistic creations include chocolate flavored with pumpkin, artfully designed candies, and hot chocolate, which makes this a fun place to snuggle into on a chilly Venice day. Tastings and chocolate workshops can be arranged.

⚜ **Perugia: Home of Baci, www.perugina.it**
This artsy town in Umbria is home to the famous **Perugina** chocolate company that's now owned by Nestlé. Perugina goodies abound around here, and hard-core types may want to head out to the suburban factory for chocolate-making classes, along with tours, a gift shop, and museum.

Baci, Perugina's most famous chocolates, were invented in 1922 by Luisa Spagnoli, and were an immediate hit when first introduced that Valentine's Day. Luisa, the wife of Perugina's founder, fell in love with the much younger Giovanni Buitoni, who also worked at Perugina. She'd write secret love notes on the chocolates she sent to Buitoni for inspection. When she died he

renamed her chocolates Baci (which means kisses) and had them
packaged with romantic musings, in memory of those notes.
Which is why when you unwrap one, you'll find such Luisa say-
ings as: *Non esiste salvaguardia contro il senso naturale dell'attrazione* (There
is no safety-net to protect against attraction). Luisa was also the
inspiration for those beautiful Luisa Spagnoli clothing stores
you'll find all over Italy.

### ✸ Modica: Sicily's Chocolate Center

This pretty baroque town in southeastern Sicily is famous for
its Aztec-style chocolates that are granular, like what you'd find
in Mexico. Its origins go back to seventeenth-century Spaniards
who brought over the tradition of grinding cocoa beans to a
paste that's mixed with cane sugar, cinnamon, or other spices.
Top shops are **Bonajuto** (Corso Umberto I 159, www.bonajuto.
it), that's been around since 1880, and **Casa Don Puglisi**
(Corso Umberto I, www.laboratoriodonpuglisi.it), a newer
place created by former pastry chef Lina Lemmolo. Don Puglisi
is in a building that was a *casa di accoglienza*, in other words, a
house for women with criminal records. Lemmolo staffs her
shop with these gals, and their lives have been turned around
by chocolate-making, giving them focus, a sense of dignity and
accomplishment.

### ✸ Turin: Where It All Began

Grace Kelly loved *gianduiotti*, the chocolate-hazelnut candies of
Turin, so much she used them as her wedding favors when she
married Prince Rainier. The creamy candy was invented during a nineteenth-century recession, when cocoa imports were
limited. Clever candy makers figured out how to blend the
little they did have with the plentiful nuts that grow all over the

region. The **Caffarel** company patented it in 1865, and the rest is delicious history.

**Peyrano** (Corso Vittorio Emanuele 76, www.peyrano. com), near Turin's train station, has been around for almost a hundred years and serves up fantastic *gianduiotti* and dark chocolate that's roasted in olive wood. The award-winner in the new generation of chocolate artisans is **Guido Gobino** (Via Lagrange 1, www.guidogobino.it), whose small shop with a sleek tasting room offers the master's inventions of mint or orange chocolates, and *cremini al sale*, a new hit on *gianduiotto*, perfectly blended with sea salt.

**Eurochocolate**, the world's largest international chocolate festival, is held in Perugia every October. For details and other chocolate events in Italy: www.eurochocolate.com

## RECOMMENDED READING

*The Great Book of Chocolate* by David Lebovitz

# 58 *Wine Bars*

ONE OF THE BEST WAYS TO BLEND into the Italian social scene is to go to a wine bar. They're down-to-earth places, where along with great wines, delicious nibbles are offered, differing from region to region. They make perfect pre-dinner stops or may even fill you up for the evening.

Wine bars are also the best places to buy good *vino* to take home. Most will ship you a case if you fall in love with one of their vintages.

Here are a few favorites:

## Rome

In ancient Rome there were *enoteche* at every corner, but as the city transformed, the tradition slipped away. In the 1970s a wine bar revival began in the Eternal City. These days, *enoteche* fill up with working people meeting friends after a long day. Along with your wine, you'll enjoy such delicious Roman treats as *suppli* (deep-fried rice croquettes stuffed with cheese) or pecorino cheese wrapped in chestnut leaves.

- **L'Angolo Divino**, Via dei Balestrari 12, closed Monday, www.angolodivino.it
  A romantic spot behind the Campo de' Fiori clamor, where you can get great snacks like *tuna carpaccio* or a delicious meal by candlelight along with choice, reasonably priced wines.

* **Il Goccetto**, Via dei Banchi Vecchi 14, open Noon-2, 6-Midnight, closed Sunday, www.ilgoccetto.com
  It's always packed with locals, many filtering out to the sidewalk, aka the smoking section. Order up at the front counter, then tuck yourself into the cozy backroom, and have owner Sergio pair a cheese plate to match your wine.

* **Cul de Sac,** Piazza di Pasquino 73 (near Piazza Navona)
  One of the first of the new wave of Roman wine bars, this place has a list of 1,500 vintages. Get there before 9 P.M. to score an outside table and order a variety of house made pates—a specialty they do well.

* **Vino Roma**, Via in Selci, 84 (between Colosseum and Termini), www.vinoroma.com
  Thanks to Roman food expert **Katie Parla**, for turning me on to this wonderful, welcoming spot, where charming sommelier Hande Leimer and her team host tastings and events to educate English speakers around the world about Italian wines.

## Florence

What with all those wonderful vineyards surrounding the city, Florence has a long-standing tradition of wine shops that would always serve their customers glasses of *vino* and snacks. These old-style wine bars are called *fiaschetteria*, from the word *fiasche*, meaning straw-covered chianti bottles. I'll date myself with the sweet memory of turning those bottles into candlesticks to add a romantic touch to a dorm room. Whether you get to a *fiaschetteria* or newer place, you'll be drinking some of the best wines in Italy and eating delectable Tuscan cheeses, salamis, and panini.

* **Casa del Vino**, Via dell'Ariento 16/r (San Lorenzo), open 9:30-3:30, closed Sunday

This humble place, tucked behind the San Lorenzo Market, hasn't changed since I first walked in twenty-five years ago. Then I stood alongside the workmen, had a tumbler of wine and anchovy panini, and got an ecstatic feeling that I'd discovered a hidden treasure. It's in every guidebook now and gets crowded with tourists. But the Migliorini family, who's owned it for seventy years, keeps things traditional.

❀ **Cantinetta dei Verrazzano**, Via dei Tavolini, 18-20, www.verrazzano.com
I love this location, between the Duomo and Piazza Signoria, where it's delicious to stop by for a great selection of wines by the esteemed Tuscan Verrazzano winery—a family that's also famous for its explorer who navigated North America's Atlantic Coast. You can get table service or perch on a bench to enjoy stuffed focaccia, a cheese-and-salumi tasting plate, or even dessert wines, as well as enjoy excellent biscotti and pastries.

❀ **Le Volpi e L'Uva**, Piazza de' Rossi 1r, open 11-9, closed Sundays
The sommelier and his partners who run this place are committed to be like *volpi* (foxes) and seek out new, high-quality, small wine producers. Get in on their discoveries that you'll enjoy with gourmet nibbles: delicious cheeses and cured Tuscan meats.

## Venice

In the place that does everything differently, here wine bars are called *bacari*, the snacks (including fab seafood) are called *cicchetti*, and a drink of wine is called an *ombra*, which means shade. That's because back in the old days, wine sellers in San Marco would move their carts to the shadow of the Campanile to keep their wine cool, and workers would take a wine and panini break there. In warmer months, you'll want a *spritz*—sparkling water, prosecco, and Aperol or Campari.

* **Cantinone Già Schiavi**, Ponte San Trovaso
On a quiet canal in the Dorsoduro *sestiere*, near a gondola workshop, this classic family-run spot is where old-time regulars go elbow-to-elbow with foreigners. I had my first *baccala mantecato* (whipped *baccala* on toast) here and they've hooked me ever since.

* **All' Arco**, Calle Arco, San Polo 436, open 8-2:30, closed Sunday
A popular spot with the workers of the Rialto market, here owners Francesco and Matteo make excellent *cicchetti*, including delicious vegetable selections, depending on the seasons, such as marinated artichokes or green beans.

* **La Cantina**, Campo San Felice, Cannareggio, closed Sunday
There is no menu at this wine bar/restaurant, but anyone looking for great fish must come here. The *crudo* is especially fantastic and they offer a wonderful selection of Veneto. The atmosphere is one big party, and service can be hit or miss.

## TOURS

**Context Tours** (www.contexttravel.com) offers wine walks in each of these cities. These are fun ways to discover the best places, learn about wine from an expert, and perfect to join in on if you're travelling solo. It's especially great to take a wine walk in Venice, to be guided to hidden places and not worry about getting lost.

## RECOMMENDED READING

*Vino Italiano: The Regional Wines of Italy* by Joseph Bastianich and David Lynch

# 59 Women-Owned Wineries

LUCILLE BALL LIFTING UP HER SKIRT, jumping into a barrel, and stomping grapes with the peasants might be the first image that comes to mind when you think of Italian women and winemaking. As entertaining as that is, cut to the twenty-first century's more sophisticated and inspiring phenomenon: Italian women have jumped into the art of winemaking and joined the ranks of the country's top producers, winning awards and high scores in wine journals.

It all started in the 1980s, when gutsy Italian women began to move away from their traditional roles. Instead of simply helping out on their family's farms and with marketing, they enrolled in winemaking schools, often where they'd be the lone female in their classroom. In 1988, an organization called *Le Donne del Vino* (Women of Wine) was formed, and now it has over seven hundred members from all over Italy.

*Che coincidenza* that ever since that time Italian wines have become some of the most beloved in the world. Not only have women brought fresh insights into production, they've also pumped up the marketing, traveling internationally as multilingual ambassadors for Italy's major export. Big wineries like Antinori, Lungarotti, Planeta, Argiolas, and Zenato all have women running them or in top-level positions.

If you're planning on visiting wineries, keep in mind that most aren't set up Napa Valley-style with elaborate tasting rooms and souvenir shops. Once again, a woman, Donatella Cinelli Colombini (profiled below), was on the forefront of Italian wine tourism, founding an organization in 1993, called Movimento Turismo del Vino. It now includes over eight hundred wineries which host events throughout the year. The most famous is Cantine Aperte on the last Sunday in May, when these wineries open their doors to the public. For now, even if a winery's tasting hours are posted, it's best to call ahead to confirm or make an appointment.

Here are a few of the many places where women reign:

## Tuscany: Val d'Orcia-Brunello

South of Siena, the landscape opens to rolling hills graced with stately cypress trees, stone farmhouses, olive groves, and vineyards. Here's where Brunello di Montalcino, one of Italy's most prestigious wines, is born.

### ❉ Casato Prime Donne, Donatella Cinelli Colombini

This place is exceptional for two reasons: It's the only winery in Italy (maybe anywhere) that has an all-female staff, and it produces award-winning Brunello that made history as the first to be designed by an all-female panel of experts.

Trailblazer Donatella Cinelli Colombini moved on from her family's renowned wine business in 1998 to create two Tuscan wineries. Both have brought her great success, including the Best Wine Producer in Italy award from the Italian Sommeliers Association.

It is a joy to meet her at Casato Prime Donne, a converted sixteenth-century hunting lodge. She's an elegant, generous woman, and despite all her accolades, surprisingly soft-spoken and humble as she leads tours and tastings. Adding beauty to her vineyards are contemporary art installations and engraved quotations from winners of the Casato Prime Donne award, given annually to a female who has promoted women's roles in society. Among previous awardees are the Cabrinian nuns and the ballerina Carla Fracci. Fracci's engraved quotation says: "Look around, you are in the moral center of the world."

Guided tours in English are available Monday-Friday, and by appointment on Saturday and Sunday (www.cinellicolombini. it).

### ● Fattoria Resta, Anna Lisa Tempestini

"Earthy and soulful," is what I'd call Anna Lisa's Martin del Nero Rosso Orcia wine. I would describe her the same way. Her passion for sharing her passion of the Val d'Orcia is deep. In only half a day with her, I felt plugged into the spirit and flavors of this place.

Though she grew up in cities, Anna Lisa is a country girl at heart. She was born in Chicago and moved to Florence with her family when she was four. Her love for wine began when she was nineteen, working in the PR department of Florence's Chianti Consortium and slipping next door to taste top DOCG wines. Yearning to work in the vineyards, she quit her job and headed to the Val d'Orcia.

I meet her decades later, with a husband and three kids, living in a converted monastery that overlooks her very own vineyard. We taste her wonderful wines, freshly pressed olive oil, and she proudly shows me how she's converted one of the monastery rooms into a yoga studio. As Anna Lisa is part American, she especially enjoys visitors from the States, and she's sought after for her custom-designed winery tours and cooking classes. "Each tour is a different adventure for me, as well as my guests," she said.

My tour included lunch at the **Vineria Le Potazzine**, in the heart of the nearby medieval town of Montalcino. Wine bottles surround us as we dig into homemade *pici al sugo di cinghiale* (thick spaghetti pasta with a sauce of tomato and wild boar). We taste a rich, delicate Le Potazzine Brunello, made by Anna Lisa's girl-friend Gigliola and her husband. *Potazzine* are the little, colorful birds that flit about these parts, and also a word used as a term of endearment for children. As we're sitting there, Gigliola's two young *potazzine* burst in from the school bus. They're wear-ing matching grape-colored turtlenecks. Full of energy, the girls spin around, kiss their parents, then settle down for lunch. That's just how idyllic life can be around here.

By appointment. Winery tours and cooking classes also available (www.fattoriaresta.it).

## Piedmont: Le Langhe-Barolo

West of Alba, the northern Italian town that's famous for its white truffles, is a graceful wide valley of lush vineyards—Le Langhe—where Barolo, the "King of Wines" is produced. It was a woman, Marchesa Giulia Colbert, who made Barolo famous in the nine-teenth century. She wanted something better than the wine that was being produced from the grapes growing around her Piedmont castle. So she called in a French wine expert to make wine similar to a Bordeaux. She was so happy with the result, she sent cartloads of it to the King of Savoy in Turin. It became a hit there and all over the courts of Europe.

❁ **Marchesi di Barolo, Anna Abbona**
Anna is the wife of Ernesto Abbona, whose family has owned this prestigious winery since the early twentieth century. She's a glam-orous VIP of the wine world and when I met her she graciously

took a break from a meeting with producers to sit with me in the dining room, which she also oversees. By the way, you must make a reservation to have lunch here to enjoy Piemontese specialties such as *brasato*—veal braised in Barolo. "My husband is home resting from the weekend," she said. "We women are stronger!"

The winery is a grand butter-yellow complex that sits across from the Barolo castle where Marchesa Giulia Colbert once reigned. It originated as the headquarters for the Opera Pia Barolo, a charitable foundation Giulia created to help the town's needy, which the Abbona family keeps going. On a tour, you get to see the original barrels used in Giulia's day, and there's an incredible wine library, with a bottle of Barolo from 1859 as well as shelves that hold vintages from 1938 on up—totaling 35,000 bottles.

Call for appointment and restaurant reservation: 017 356 4491 (www.marchesibarolo.com).

⊛ **Pira & Figli Estate, Chiara Boschis**
"The Barolo Boys and One Girl" was written on a t-shirt for a promotional tour for Barolo in the 1980s. That one girl was Chiara Boschis, who was put in charge of this place in 1990.

Chiara says that since her parents never treated her any differently than her brothers (who taught her winemaking), working in the male Barolo world has never been a problem.

Chiara's an exceptionally attractive woman who makes a silky and refined Barolo. It's won many awards and turned a spotlight onto this small winery that puts out a limited production. The winery offers accommodations in a renovated farmhouse on the outskirts of Barolo—a perfect agriturismo base to explore the abundance of delicious wines in the region. (www.pira-chiaraboschis.com)

**Movimento Turismo del Vino**: www.movimentoturismovino.it

## RECOMMENDED READING

*Barolo* by Matthew Gavin Frank; also excerpted in *The Best Travel Writing 2008* and *The Best Travel Writing 2009* edited by James O'Reilly, Larry Habegger, and Sean O'Reilly

*Adventures in Wine* edited by Thom Elkjer

# VII

*Shopping*

One of the reasons Italian vacations are so relaxing is because we allow ourselves to slow down and look at beautiful things. Not only masterpieces in museums, but in shop windows where artisans' craftsmanship is on display. These handicraft traditions have been passed down for generations. Shopping becomes more than piling up souvenirs. You're brushing up against history.

Shopping is also your chance to interact with the natives. You may feel pounced upon when you enter a small store and the owner greets you, enthusiastic to help. You're probably looking at something they've made, or a display they spent hours creating. It's as though you're a guest in their home. So always ask before you touch.

The magic word for Italian shoppers is *saldi = sale*. The second weeks of January and July are generally when *saldi* begin in stores all over Italy. They last a month or so, but you'll get the best stuff if you show up early. And there are **designer outlets** all over Italy, where you can score pretty good bargains. Remember we are talking Italy's top designers, which are marked 50-60% off at these outlets, meaning the Prada wallet that sells for 500 euros will cost you 250 euros. New outlets are popping up all the time, so check out the web site (www.factoryoutletsitaly.com) to keep up.

Bargaining is expected when you're shopping at outdoor markets. It's also O.K. to try in a small shop, especially if you're buying in quantity. I use the tried-and-true bargaining style: carry only small bills, go through the show-interest-then-walk-away-get-called-back routine. A line that rarely fails is: "I wanted to buy this for my mamma..."

However you play the shopping game, savor the experience, whether you walk away with just a memory, a treasure, or both.

**TIP:** *The Mall (www.themall.it), one of Italy's most popular luxury designer outlets, is easy to reach from Florence, via a fifty-minute bus ride on the #17, that runs regularly from Via Santa Caterina di Siena, near the central train station.*

## RECOMMENDED READING

*Made in Italy* by Laura Morelli, and her *Authentic Shopping* series, found on www.lauramorelli.com

*Lo Scopri Occasioni* by Theodora Van Meurs (available in Italian bookstores, lists discount places in Italy, written in English and Italian)

*The Fearless Shopper* by Kathy Borrus

# 60 *Shoes*

WE HAVE SALVATORE FERRAGAMO TO THANK for being the grand-papa of modern Italian shoe fashion. These days his widow Wanda is queen of the company he began in 1938. She's so beloved by Italians they've even named a rose in her honor.

The Ferragamo story is legendary. Salvatore was a man of humble beginnings, the eleventh of fourteen children, born in 1898 in the mountain town of Bonito, outside Naples. He apprenticed with a cobbler there, making his first pair of shoes when he was nine for his sister to wear at her confirmation. He took off for America when he was seventeen, and set up a little shop in Santa Barbara, California, that caught the eye of silent film stars like Mary Pickford. Within a few years he was a Hollywood sensation. Besides designing for movies like *The Ten Commandments*, actresses clamored for his creations to wear off the set. What's always separated Ferragamo's shoes from the pack is that he never wavered from his conviction to combine glamour with comfort. He was so obsessed he even took anatomy classes at the University of Southern California, so he could learn all about the foot.

As for Wanda, she met Salvatore in 1939 when he'd moved his successful business from California to Florence. Always remembering his roots, he was sending money back to help out his Bonito hometown. A doctor from Bonito wrote to Salvatore, telling him he should visit and see all the good his donations had done. When

he arrived, Wanda, the doctor's nineteen-year-old daughter
answered the door. Since her mother had died, Wanda was the lady
of the house, and she shyly thanked Salvatore for all his wonderful
work. Salvatore turned to his sister who he was traveling with and
said, "I am going to marry this woman."

Three months later, Wanda wed Salvatore,
who was twenty-two years older. They had six
children, lived in Florence, and the retail business thrived, along with Salvatore being named
"Shoemaker to the Stars," designing for such
beauties as Marilyn Monroe, Ava Gardner, and
Audrey Hepburn.

In 1960 Salvatore died of cancer. Wanda was
thirty-eight, had no business experience, and could have sold the
company. But instead, she took it on, with her eldest child, nineteen-year-old Fiamma, becoming the new creative force. Fiamma,
who'd quit high school to learn shoemaking from her father, went
on to design the award-winning Vara pump—that fabulous square
toed, chunky 3-inch heel number with the grosgrain bow. As the
rest of the family joined the business, Fiamma continued to design.
Sadly, she died of breast cancer in 1998.

Now the **Ferragamo Museum**, in the lower level of his Florence
store, pays homage to Salvatore with fantastic displays, molds he
made for the stars, videos, and photos of celebrities showing off
their shoes—from Carmen Miranda to Katharine Hepburn to
Andy Warhol. It's in a medieval palace that Ferragamo bought in
1938. It even has an original well in a back room, called the Pozzo
di Beatrice, named after the girl Dante went gaga over when he first
laid eyes on her on the Florence bridge that's steps away from the
palace.

Shopping upstairs from the museum is a treat, especially in the
boutique, where you'll find limited edition copies of such beauties

as the heels Ferragamo designed for Marilyn Monroe for *Some Like It Hot*. You've got to at least try a pair on and have sales people measure your feet like when you were in grade school, and fit you to your exact width.

**Ferragamo Museum and Store:** Piazza Santa Trinita 5r, open 10-7:30, www.museoferragamo.it.

The list of fantastic ready-to-wear shoe shops in Italy is endless, while finding places that custom-make shoes as Ferragamo did in the old days is becoming rarer and rarer. But here are a few where you'll find artisans still going at it with Ferragamo's passion:

## Rome

* **Petrocchi,** Vicolo Sugarelli 2, www.calzoleriapetrocchi.it
  Bruno Ridolfi has taken over the shop his uncle started in Rome's 1950s *la dolce vita* heyday. He handcrafts classic designs for men and women made with leather that's "like buttah."

## Florence

* **Calzature Francesco da Firenze,** Via Santo Spirito 62
  Stop by this family-run Oltrarno shop for reasonably priced handmade leather shoes or sandals that they can customize for you in twenty-four hours.

## Venice

* **Giovanna Zanella Atelier,** Calle Caminati, 5641 Castello
  www.giovannazanella.it
  Giovanna was a student of the famous, eccentric Venetian shoemaker, Rolando Segalin. Her creations show his influence—including wacky styles of curved pointed shoes and ones

that look like gondolas. She's always blending originality and comfort, using fine leather and fabrics, along with bold colors. She can custom-design shoes for you, or enjoy browsing and buying from what's on the shelves of her adorable boutique.

## Positano

❀ **La Botteguccia,** Via Regina Giovanna 19,
www.labottegucciapositano.it
A perfect souvenir of this heavenly village on the Amalfi coast are sandals handmade by Giovanni, that he'll custom-design to suit your fancy (from glitzy to folksy), just as he has for such stars as Jackie-O.

**Golden Day:** Visit the **Ferragamo Museum** and store, stop for wine and a truffle butter panino at **Procacci** (Via de Tornabuoni 64, www.antinori.it), a gem of a place from 1885 that also sells wines, olive oils, etc, from the esteemed Antinori winery.

# 61 *Leather*

WHAT IS IT ABOUT US WHO SWOON when we run our hands over a smooth leather handbag and then stick our noses inside for a sniff? Probably it's best not to analyze. It's probably better to just go to leather heaven on earth: Florence.

As you walk through the streets in the Santa Croce district you're hit with intoxicating smells and sights—everything from luxurious coats to purses and belts in appealing styles and colors. Here's where leather making in Florence all began, in the days of the Renaissance Artists' guilds, when this was the primo Arno riverside spot for tanning cow hides.

## Florence

* **Scuola del Cuoio,** Piazza Santa Croce 16, www.scuoladelcuoio.com

  This store and workshop was once a monastery built by the Medici, tucked behind the Santa Croce church. And by the way, when you stop by to see the wonders of Santa Croce, notice (as you exit) the statue of Florence Nightingale, who was born here and named after the city.

  Shopping at the Scuola del Cuoio has a step-back-in-time feeling, where you can watch artisans at their hallway wooden work stations crafting leather boxes or, with torch in hand, magically bordering them with gold filigree. Everything for sale is cut and sewn right here, using leather tanned from Tuscan experts. There are desk sets, wallets, lovely designed purses, and jackets. They have expert tailor services on hand who'll mail your jacket back home after it's fitted perfectly, or you can work with them to have one custom-designed just the way you like it.

✿ **Madova,** Via Guicciardini, 1r (Oltrarno), www.madova.com
The Donnini family has been creating leather gloves in Florence since 1919. Their tiny shop, just over the Ponte Vecchio, is crammed with beauteous cashmere and silk-lined leather gloves, that you'd pay twice the price for back home. Customer service is ultra-attentive. You place your hand on a green velvet pillow and the shopkeepers measure and fit you. For a moment, you feel like a queen.

## Rome

✿ **Ibiz,** Via dei Chiavari 39, www.ibizroma.it
Elisa Nepi, a young Roman artisan, is the designer of every chic thing in this fun shop. She also (bless her) keeps her prices for handcrafted wallets, purses, and belts reasonable. Her parents started the business in 1972, making satchels for local workmen that became popular with backpackers. In 2002, Elisa was all set to fly the coop and become a physical therapist. But when she flunked her university exam, she decided to put her hands into the business and has brought the shop into the fashion limelight.

✿ **Sirni,** 33 Via della Stelletta, www.sirnipelletteria.it
The Sirni family has been in the Rome leather business for over a hundred years. In this sophisticated, tiny shop, Mamma Rosanna (along with her son and daughter), handcraft exquisite

luxury bags, some done up in crocodile or ostrich leather. Roman women adore Sirni for their customized services; you can have them make a purse for you with every compartment you'd ever desire. It'll take a month, since it's a small workshop, but to have something beautifully styled by these folks is worth the wait.

* **Palazzo Fendi,** Largo Goldoni, www.fendi.com
You've got to stop in to this shrine to leather and fur. It all began with Adele Casagrande who created a little fur shop back in 1918. She married Edoardo Fendi in 1925 and then encouraged her five daughters to join the business. The Fendi daughters brought a whole new energy to the company, that's turned it into a worldwide success.

## Venice

* **Arnoldo e Battois**, Calle dei Fuseri 4271, San Marco, www.arnoldoebattois.com
Silvano Arnoldo and Massimiliano Battois met in architecture school, and bring their passion for contemporary design to creating unique, high-quality handbags, beloved by Venetian women.

* **Fanny,** Calle dei Saoneri (San Polo), San Leonardo (Cannaregio), www.fannygloves.it
Here you'll find everything from polka dot to fur-lined funky gloves, in every color imaginable. Snatch a pair up to take the Venice chill away.

✤

**Golden Day:** In Florence, visit **Santa Croce** and shop at the **Scuola del Cuoio**. Eat at **Trattoria Cibreo** (Via dei Macci 122r, 055 2341100, closed Monday. No reservations, cash only). This adorable trattoria is the budget branch of the revered Cibreo, headed up by Fabio Picchi, a superstar Florentine chef who changes his menu daily according to what's freshest at the nearby Sant'Ambrogio market.

# 62 *Ceramics*

LEAVE IT TO THE ITALIANS TO TURN a bathroom tile into a work of art. Vibrant colors and timeless designs turn their ceramics into irresistible treasures.

The craft took off during the Renaissance, mainly in small towns close to hills full of perfect-for-pottery clay. These are the towns to shop in—where you'll see artisans following centuries-old traditions and can pick up ceramics for much lower prices than in big city stores.

The major ceramics towns (over thirty) are scattered up and down the boot and have been officially designated "Cities of Italian Ceramics."

I have to warn you about some of them (such as Deruta and Vietri sul Mare). These places are packed with shop after beautiful shop. In other words, do not take along a not-interested-in-ceramics partner or child. Or plan ahead to have them enjoy themselves at a restaurant as you blissfully poke about. They also generally have ceramics museums, which are great to stop by before your shopping excursions to get an idea of the traditions being followed in each town.

Just like pasta shapes, ceramic styles differ from region to region. Along with every style there's a fascinating back story. One of the all-time most startling comes from Sicily.

If you've ever wandered around the island, you'll have seen planters on balcony ledges that were shaped and painted to look like Moors' heads—mustachioed, dark-eyed, turbaned guys. The legend of the Teste di Moro goes that around the year 1000, in Palermo's Kalsa neighborhood, there lived a beautiful virgin. Like all young Sicilian girls, she was forbidden to leave the house and could only watch the world from her balcony as she tended her garden.

One day, a handsome Moor passed by, looked up, and declared his love at first sight for the young maiden. She instantly fell for him, gave up her precious virtue, and passionate lovemaking ensued.

But then the girl discovered the horrid truth: the Moor was married with children and on his way back to his family. To get her revenge, on their last night together, she slit his throat and cut his whole head off. She put the head on her balcony, scattering basil seeds into it. The plant grew so lush that every girl in town wanted to have a planter just like it. Since cutting off real Moors' heads was awfully inconvenient, ceramic ones were made, and a new design for Sicilian pottery was launched.

Whether you're shopping for a planter or plate, keep an eye out for authenticity. Like Italian D.O.C. wines, ceramics that conform to government standards for following Italian traditions are stamped: *Ceramica Artistica & Tradizionale*. If it's not stamped, check for an unglazed ring at the bottom, which means it's been traditionally fired, and look at the decoration. If the brushstrokes are uneven, it's handpainted. Whatever you do, don't make the mistake my friend Tita did, when she bought a bowl in Positano and didn't discover a "Made in Japan" stamp on it until it was shipped home.

It's impossible to narrow down places for you to shop for ceramics, because Italy is so rich with them they'd fill another book. But do keep in mind such off-our-beaten track ceramic towns, such as **Castelli** in Abruzzo, **Faenza** in Emilia-Romagna, **Bassano**

**del Grappa** in the Veneto, and **Caltagirone** in Sicily. In the meantime, I've provided some suggestions...

## UMBRIA

### Deruta

Italy's most famous ceramic town is chockablock with hundreds of shops. Among the designs you'll find are the *bella donna* (beautiful woman), created in the sixteenth century, featuring profiles of beautiful women. You'll also see *albarelli* (old-fashioned pharmacy jars) decorated in Raffaellesco style, with golden dragons and mythological beasts. These got their name from the artist Raphael, who copied the images from frescos in ancient Roman villas that were excavated during his Renaissance days. Among the loads of high-quality shops, are:

* **Bettini Germano**, Via Tiberina 322,
  www.terrecottederuta.com
  Popular with locals and tourists as *the* place to go for everyday ceramics at great prices.

* **Ubaldo Grazia**, Via Tiberina 181, www.ubaldograzia.it
  One of the oldest family-run businesses in the world, Grazia started out in the sixteenth century making pottery for churches and now their clients include department stores like Neiman Marcus. The shop is huge and my friend Patty tipped me off that to the left as you enter there are seconds available for discount prices.

### Gubbio

In this serene, magical hill town, you'll find a style called *bucchero*, influenced by Etruscan pottery, with a black background and copper-colored decoration. Gubbio is also known for *lustreware,* pottery painted with vivid colors that has an iridescent sheen. Check out:

- **La Fornace del Bucchero,** 10 Federico da Montefeltro, www.bucchero.it

- **Magnanelli,** Via XX Settembre, 31, www.ceramichemagnanelli.com

## Orvieto

Along with *bucchero,* Orvieto's styles feature unusual colors like *verde ramina,* which resembles the green oxide of copper church bells. Right next to the magnificent Duomo are these two shops:

- **Ceramicarte,** Via del Duomo 42, www.ceramicarteorvieto.carbonmade.com

- **Jolanda Artigianato,** Via del Duomo 66

# AMALFI COAST

This region's lemon trees, flowers, fish, and cobalt sea appear in the *maioliche* found in such towns as:

## Vietri Sul Mare

This major ceramic center is known for its beautiful decorative tiles, which are exported worldwide.

- **Ceramica Artistica Solimene,** Via Madonna degli Angeli 7, www.ceramicasolimene.it
  The Gaudi-style exterior of this huge warehouse sets this shop apart from the cutesier places in town. The selection is

overwhelming, including adorable tableware featuring animals—
from chickens to pigs.

## Ravello

* **Ceramiche d'Arte Pascal,** Via Roma 22
In this gorgeous shop, near the piazza, the work of top artisans
includes giant platters that are absolute masterpieces.

For a list of places certified by the Association of Italian Ceramic
Cities: www.ceramics-online.it.

**Golden Day:** Go to **Gubbio**, not only to shop for ceramics, but
to enjoy this gem of a peaceful medieval town. Eat at **Ristorante
Federico da Montefeltro** (Via della Repubblica 35, 075 927
3949) and stay at **Hotel Relais Ducale** (www.mencarelligroup.
com), a restored Duke's palace.

### RECOMMENDED READING

*Deruta, a Tradition of Italian Ceramics* by Elizabeth Helman Minchilli

# 63 *Jewelry*

As you can tell from the statues of ancient Roman empresses, crafting jewelry has been going on in Italy for a very long time. The tradition not only includes gold and silver, but micro-mosaics, glass beads, and even eye-catching *plastique* costume pieces. Artisans still carve shells or coral to create intricate cameos.

These days, Italian women are enchanted by Dodo jewelry. It all started in 1995, when the Pomellato company created its first Dodo bird miniature gold charm, with a portion of the price going to the World Wildlife Fund in Italy to protect endangered species. Every year since, there's been a new animal, and each symbolizes a sentiment. For example, the Dolphin's is "Take Me With You," and the Frog's is "Kiss me, I am your prince." You can feel just like a native, stopping by one of their shops (found in big cities and major department stores) and creating your own necklace or bracelet with your choice of animals.

Here are some suggestions for beautiful bauble shopping:

### Rome

❂ **Studio Gioielleria R. Quattrocolo,** Via della Scrofa 48, near Campo Marzio, www.quattrocolo.com
This antique jewelry shop has pretty displays of gold, coral, cameos, and gems. Most unique are the micro-mosaic pieces, created to replicate souvenirs from the days of the Grand Tour, with scenes of ancient ruins, mythological figures and landscapes.

❋ **Diego Percossi Papi,** Via Sant'Eustachio 16 (near the Pantheon), www.percossipapi.com
Sophia Loren and Naomi Campbell are fans of Percossi's shimmering, colorful creations. He uses a unique cloisonné enamel technique, incorporating precious and semi-precious gems and pearls into his beautiful designs.

❋ **Massimo Maria Melis,** Via dell'Orso 57, www.massimomariamelis.com
You can watch Massimo's staff of goldsmiths crafting exquisite pieces in the back of this tiny shop. He uses twenty-one carat gold incorporated with gems, antique coins, engraved stones, or bronze fragments for designs that are crafted using techniques inspired by the Etruscans.

❋ **Sancesario Bijoux**, Via dei Banchi Vecchi 19, Via dei Coronari 223, www.sancesariobijoux.it
It's a delight to buy a souvenir from this dazzling store, where crystals, pearls, coral, turquoise, and Murano glass are incorporated into elegant designs inspired by Roman tradition. Welcoming and budget friendly.

## Florence

❋ **Fratelli Piccini,** Ponte Vecchio 23r, www.fratellipiccini.com
All the jewelry shops on the Ponte Vecchio used to be vegetable and fish stalls. Then the Medicis decided to build the Vasari corridor over the bridge to connect their two palaces. "That stench!" they said to the merchants, kicked them out, and replaced them with goldsmiths. These days, according to Florentines, the only place to shop among the bridge's many choices is Fratelli Piccini, owned by the same family since 1903 and now under the leadership of Elisa Tozzi Piccini. Elisa has created a "Moments" collection for wedding rings, that includes

a dinner or aperitivo on their Ponte Vecchio terrace for presentation of the special gift.

✸ **COI Spa,** Via Por Santa Maria 8n, www.coi-firenze.it
For those looking for quality 18-carat gold by contemporary designers including Marco Bicego, Nanis, and Fope, this shop has an extensive collection at competitive prices.

✸ **Angela Caputi**, Via S. Spirito 58r, Oltrarno and Borgo SS. Apostoli 44/46, www.angelacaputi.com
This bold designer has been creating fantastic *plastique* costume jewelry since 1975. It's high fashion, exotic pop art—fun and colorful. I love shopping here, elbowing in with Signora Caputi's fans, as we slide out drawers full of goodies and try on different designs.

✸ **Museo Bottega del Maestro Alessandro Dari**, Via S. Niccolo 115/r (Oltrarno), www.alessandrodari.com
As I walked by the fifteenth-century building that's home to Dari's shop, I was drawn inside by the sounds of a classical guitar. The player was the master goldsmith Alessandro Dari himself, sitting there in a muscle shirt, surrounded by cases of his jewelry that are inspired by Florentine architecture. His rings and pendants, shaped like domes or castles and studded with gems, are extraordinary.

## Venice

✸ **Gloria Astolfo,** 1581 Calle Frezzeria (San Marco),
www.astolfovenezia.com
There are so many jewelry shops in Venice, they can all start to blur together. But the late great Marcella Hazan steered me to seek out this one that's totally original, with exotic beaded designs that have a playful feel to them.

✺ **Venetian Dreams**, Calle della Mandola (San Marco),
www.marisaconvento.it
Owner Marisa Convento is a marvelous woman and an *Impiraressa*
(traditional bead worker), who showcases this Venetian jewelry
tradition with fabulous imagination and skill. Her shop dazzles
with intricate beaded jewelry, and upon request, she'll guide
you on a "Bead Walk" in the Castello *sestiere*, to tell you all about
the fascinating history of women bead workers of Venice. She
speaks perfect English and generously shares her passion for her
native city with tourists—whether you want to know the latest art
opening, where to eat, or are completely lost—Marisa is there
for you.

## Naples

✺ **Giovanni Ascione e Figlio**, Galleria Umberto, 081 421111, by
appointment only, www.ascione.it
Torre del Greco, outside of Naples, is the world's biggest producer of handcrafted cameos. The Ascione family's workshop
there (since 1855) is the oldest in town. You can see an amazing display of their cameos in this Naples showroom and shop.
They also make elegant, art-deco-styled jewelry using mother of
pearl, turquoise, and tortoiseshell.

## Sorrento

✺ **Miele Gioielli**, Via Fuoro 57
A highlight of Sorrento's pedestrian only centro storico is this
shop, where sweetheart/owner Rosalba sits delicately crafting
gorgeous creations—blending corals, cameos, and semi-precious stones. You can have her custom design something for you
or even arrange to have a jewelry-making lesson so she can show
you how to make your own pretty souvenir.

**Golden Day:** In Rome, shop at **Diego Percossi**, visit the **Pantheon**, and eat at my favorite restaurant in Rome, **Armando al Pantheon** (Salita Dei Crescenzi 31, 06 688 03034, Reservations essential, closed Saturday night and Sunday).

# 64 *Fragrances*

ITALY SMELLS GREAT. NOT ONLY THE FOOD, gardens, forests, and sea. There's the perfume they make.

The whole perfume-making deal started with monks in the Middle Ages who gathered flowers and herbs from the countryside and turned them into health and beauty potions. Their secret recipes are still used, so as you shop you can get in on the alchemy.

## Rome

* **Ai Monasteri,** Corso del Rinascimento 72

   A simple two-room spot where dark polished wood cabinets are stocked with varieties of monk-made beauty products, along with chocolates, honey, liqueurs, and marmalades made in abbeys all over Italy. It's been around since 1864 and still run by the Nardi family who started it all when they teamed up with the Benedictine Order.

   Favorites are Antica Acqua di Colonia perfume, a bergamot-and-musk blend created for the 1900 World Exhibition, and soap scented with violets of Parma. Everything is beautifully packaged and reasonably priced.

* **Laura Tonatto, Profumi-Galleria**, Piazza di Pietra, www.tonatto.com

   Laura Tonatto, aka the "Italian nose," is an award-winning perfume maker who began creating her own fragrance line in

1986, at the age of twenty-three. She takes inspiration from such diverse sources as literature, painting, film, and music, imagining smells they evoke—such as her spicy "Cleopatra" or floral "Birth of Venus." This sleek shop is also an olfactory gallery, with changing exhibitions to illustrate Tonatto's philosophy and process. You can buy a variety of scents, bath products, room sprays, or have the glamorous staff custom design a perfume for you.

## Florence

* **Officina Profumo Farmaceutica di Santa Maria Novella,**
Via della Scala 16 (near Santa Maria Novella), www.smnovella.it
Don't miss this place. Here gorgeously frescoed ceilings, sculpted columns and arches, stained glass windows, and a staff dressed in chic black takes a shopping experience to a mystical level.

The shop was a fourteenth-century Gothic church of Dominican friars, which was turned into a *farmacia* to sell their potions in 1612. Today scent scientists reproduce the monk's recipes and their creations are shipped all over the world.

Santa Maria Novella potpourri, a blend of ten different herbs and flowers from the surrounding hills, comes in monogrammed satin pouches and makes a perfect gift. The top perfume choice is Acqua di Colonia, a citrus and bergamot blend created for Catherine de' Medici when she went off to Paris to marry Henry II. There's also Acqua di Santa Maria Novella (aka anti-hysteria water), which was created when tight-corset-wearing gals needed relief from the vapors. Today it's touted as a cure for digestive problems.

* **Aqua Flor,** Via Borgo Santa Croce 6,
www.florenceparfum.com
The Renaissance Antinori Palace has been restored to a shop and laboratory under the direction of master perfume maker

Sileno Cheloni. You can make an appointment to create a bespoke perfume, or buy from the shop's grand collection of fragrances and scented candles.

## Venice

### The Merchant of Venice, Campo San Fantin,
www.themerchantofvenice.net
The esteemed Venetian Mavive perfume company created this line to pay homage to the Renaissance days when Venice was famous for its perfume laboratories. The shop is in a beautiful centuries-old pharmacy, selling perfume bottled in Murano glass.

## Capri

❀ **Carthusia,** Via Federico Serena, 28, Via Camerelle 10
This pretty shop embodies the bewitching purity of Capri, with light polished wood floors and white archways, along with black and white photos of celebrities who've shopped here, including Ingrid Bergman and Jackie O.

The legend goes that back in 1380 a Carthusian monk got caught off guard by the arrival of Queen Giovanna d'Anjou of Naples, and ran off to gather flowers all over the island for her. Three days after she left, the monk smelled the vase's water, found it delightful, and went to an alchemist to figure out how to reproduce it. In 1948 a monastery prior discovered the monk's recipe, and got the Pope's blessing to begin the commercial production of Carthusian perfumes.

Everything here is made from Capri's flowers, such as *Fiori di Capri*, a combo of wild carnation, lily of the valley and oak. Some scents have been designed by the aforementioned Laura Tonatto, such as *Ligea La Sirena,* a light perfume inspired by the legend of a mermaid who tried to lure Ulysses to Capri's shore.

❧

**Golden Day:** In **Capri**, stroll the **Gardens of Augustus**, continue on the path to **Carthusia**, eat at **Ristorante Villa Brunella** (Via Tragara 24A, 081 837 0122, www.villabrunella.it) and stay at their beautiful hotel with a fantastic view.

# 65 Lingerie

WINDOW DISPLAYS OF ITALIAN LINGERIE will stop you in your tracks. And then you just might purr. There's a range of fantastic styles to content your inner kitty cat—from cutesy to romantic. Or if you're looking for something especially alluring, Italy has what it takes to give you the power of Venus's golden girdle, which she'd whip on to attract mortals she had the hots for.

You'll see **Intimissimi** shops all over. The fun, quality, affordable brand is now carried by Victoria's Secret, but you'll get a bigger variety of selections in Italy, and a chance to elbow in with the natives who adore this company. In the same price bracket, is **Yamamay**, another chain store which gets its name from a Japanese silkworm, and offers flashier designs.

But the real treasures you'll find are luxury Italian lingerie, where silk, satin, lace, and embroidery are combined to make masterpieces. The most famous brand is **La Perla**, which began in 1954 when Ada Masotti, a Bologna housewife, started a part-time business in her home, making corsets for wealthy women. Her son, who was a cardiologist, took over the business and now it's a multi-million-dollar enterprise, turning out exquisite creations, with boutiques in big Italian cities and worldwide.

Another top designer is **Flora Lastraioli**, a Florentine company that was founded in 1932 by a family whose great-grandmother was the embroideress for the Grand Duke of Tuscany in the nineteenth century.

All these luxury labels are usually carried in Italian department stores (Coin and Rinascente). Many you can now find in stores in the States. But the most enjoyable shopping experience will be at lingerie boutiques. They're sweet shops that carry these well-known luxury brands, wonderful up-and-coming designers, great swimwear if you are in need, and the sales help are typically kind and attentive.

## Rome

❋ **Brighenti,** Via Frattina 7, near Piazza di Spagna
This two-floor old-world wonderland is the prettiest lingerie shop I've ever seen. Crystal chandeliers hang over rooms of dark polished wood, layers of gorgeous lace bras and panties fill shelves and cabinets. Upstairs are racks of gelato-colored silk negligees, displayed with matching jewel-ornamented mules. The dressing rooms, frescoed in pale turquoise and gold, entice you to try something on.

❋ **L'Ingerie D'Elia,** Via Sistina 119, near Piazza di Spagna, www.lingeriedelia.com
Two sisters from Argentina opened this shop in 1983, where you can splurge on high-quality, exquisitely designed lingerie, made with silk and lace in their Florence workshop.

## Florence

The stores listed in the Lace and Embroidery section (**Loretta Caponi** and **Giachi Grazia Ricami**) carry fabulous negligees and robes. You'll also find lacy funwear at **Stellini**, Via Nazionale 104 (near Mercato Centrale) and **Segreta Malizia** (Via del Giglio 74).

## Venice

🌻 **Cristina Linassi**, Calle delle Ostreghe 2434 (San Marco), www.cristinalinassi.com
Designer Cristina Linassi's negligees range in style from *La Dolce Vita* silks to graceful soft muslin gowns, accented with hand embroidery.

## Naples

You'll find two old-fashioned shops on the chic Via Chiaia that stock colorful selections: **Carmagnola** (Via Chiaia 261), that's been around since 1904, and **Elena Abet** (Via Chiaia 124), from 1840.

**Golden Day:** In Rome, shop at **Brighenti** or **L'Ingerie D'Elia**, head to the nearby **Via Condotti** if you're up for more shopping fun, then eat at **Ristorante Museo Canova Tadolini** (Via del Babuino, 150/a, www.canvatadolini.com), a space that was once the atelier of the sculptor Canova, now stuffed with his dramatic statues. As it's open without a break from noon to 11 P.M., it's perfect for caffe, *aperitivo*, or full meal.

# 66 *Embroidery and Lace*

WHY HAS THIS TRADITION LASTED FOR SO LONG? Isn't it way more practical to do this by machine? Thankfully, patient Italian women, dedicated to making life pretty, have kept the tradition alive.

Embroidery and lacemaking began over a thousand years ago as nuns' work, with busy-as-bees holy women decorating priests' vestments and altar cloths. Embroidery came first, in 1000, when Arabs taught it to Sicilian women and then the craft spread to the mainland. Lacemaking eclipsed embroidery in the frou-frouier Renaissance, when the rich nobility wanted it on everything from their tables to their shoes. Lace became as valuable as cash—farm estates were traded for it; wealthy girls' dowry trunks were stuffed with it.

Demand became so great all over Europe in the seventeenth century that middle-class women began to take on the work—it was a good, honest way to make a living back then. Many got sent to lace-making schools (run by nuns) at age five. They'd start out cutting thread and move on to master a specialty pattern, stitching the same design for the rest of their careers. The work was intense, studios were dimly lit. Many went blind.

Most of the *signore* who craft embroidery and lace today are in their eighties. They learned from their grandmothers, many who were employed in workshops set up during World War I, so women could make a living while the men were off fighting. If you have the chance to watch one of them crafting a small piece that takes hours to create, you'll never balk at the prices for handmade doilies or embroidered tablecloths again.

Here are places where you can get the real thing:

## Burano–Venice

The island of Burano has been world famous for lacemaking since the 1500s. The Venetian legend goes that it started when a man who was heading off to sea gave his beloved an intricate piece of seaweed. Pining for him, she took out her needle and copied the design. The more practical story is that these island women were experts at mending their husband's fishing nets, so when lace making came along they took to it naturally.

Now Burano, a twenty-five-minute vaporetto ride from the Fondamente Nuove in Venice, is covered in lace shops. Though many sell machine-made pieces from China or Eastern Europe, the handmade tradition lives on in places such as:

* **Museo del Merletto,** Piazza Baldassare Galuppi 187, closed Monday, www.museomerletto.visitmuve.it
  Copious displays of antique lace and videos telling the story of lacemaking in Burano make this a great place to begin your Burano shopping expedition. Best of all is an area where senior citizen *signoras* sit and make lace, happy to be showing off their skills—they are usually there from about 10 to 3:30, except for lunchtime. The superstar of them all is Emma Vidal, who celebrated her 100th birthday in February of 2016. Emma began lacemaking in 1926, and she miraculously does not need glasses to do her perfect stitching.

* **Martina Vidal**, Via San Mauro 308, www.martinavidal.com
  This impressive shop is close to the ferry landing, where you'll find everything from bed linens to tablecloths to handkerchiefs

and blouses. It specializes in custom orders and the staff will also proudly show you their antique collection. Their back garden is a pleasant place to enjoy a caffè and Venetian cookies. Check the website for guided tours and courses in lacemaking.

### Florence–Tuscany

● **Grazia Giachi,** Via Borgo Ognissanti 6r, www.graziagiachi.it
Grazia Giachi began embroidering at the age of eight in the 1940s, and today, stepping into her luxurious store, you're surrounded by beautiful displays of silk lingerie with accents of lace, children's wear, and reasonably priced embroidered tea towels and table linens. She also has a store in the center of Greve in Chianti and a workshop where it all began—in the Chianti countryside, which can be visited by appointment.

● **Loretta Caponi,** Piazza Antinori 4r, www.lorettacaponi.com
Wow! Seven glorious rooms in the former Palazzo Aldobrandini show off awesome hand- and machine-made embroidered pieces—from table linens, outfits for newborns that make grandmamas swoon, and elegant lingerie. The business began with the late great Loretta in 1967, when she opened up a small Florence shop, and now is run by her daughter, serving loyal clientele, including celebrities such as Nicole Kidman and Madonna.

### Offida–Le Marche

● **Il Gioiello, Piazza Valorani**
Come to this jewel-of-a-village near Ascoli Piceno to see lacemakers sitting outside their doorways working away, carrying on a tradition that's been going on here for over five hundred years. Signora Rosina of Il Gioiello is a star of the village, welcoming you to her studio/shop, where she displays prized lacework and sells lace earrings and small pieces on the spot.

## Rapallo–Liguria

❁ **Emilio Gandolfi**, Piazza Cavour 1, www.gandolfilaces.com
In the elegant Italian Riviera town of Rapallo, you'll find
Gandolfi's family-run shop from 1920, with women in the
backroom stitching away, turning out refined embroidery and
lace that's shipped all over the world. The tradition had its
heyday in the nineteenth century, when 8,000 Rapallo women
were employed as lacemakers.

## Isola Maggiore–Umbria

Taking the ferry to this small island in Lake Trasimeno is a step-
back-in time adventure. Isola Maggiore is a mini-Burano, where
senior citizen *signoras* sit on rickety chairs on the vias branching out
from the main piazza making lace. Elena Guglielmi was the first
to open a workshop here in the early 1900s, creating a style called
*irlandesi*, which was inspired by her Irish servant.

❁ **Lace Museum**, Via Guglielmi 1, 075 8254233
Start here to get to know the island's lace tradition and shop for
beautiful handmade creations.

**TIP**: *For special events focusing on lacemaking around Italy, go to: www.
merlettoitaliano.it*

**Golden Day**: Visit **Isola Maggiore**, by taking the *traghetto* from
Tuoro Navaccia or Passignano sul Trasimeno (info on www.umbri-
amobilita.it). Eat and stay at **Hotel Da Sauro** (075 826 168, www.
dasauro.it), which serves lake-caught fish such as eel and trout. The
hotel is a basic ten-room family-run place, near a private beach.

## 67 Paper

IT'S A MYSTERY TO ME HOW T'SAI LUN, a Chinese eunuch, was sitting by a river one day in 150 A.D., saw some plants and a rag floating on the water and thought, "A-ha! I can make paper!" But somehow the genius put two and two together and became China's hero, because they were fed up with drawing on silk.

Cut to the thirteenth century, when Arab traders—who'd wrangled the Chinese to get the secret paper formula—brought it to Venice. Italians went crazy over the discovery. "Alleluia! We're fed up with those stinky sheep skins!"

It was as amazing as the unveiling of the first PC. Europe rejoiced over the new paper world. Guttenberg really appreciated it, because the one Bible he wrote out the old way required skins from 300 sheep. "Let's put it on paper. I'll make a printing press," he said.

And so the Italians, many in Florence, became bookbinders. And being Italian, they wanted to make their books pretty. So they covered them in tooled leather or paper they decorated with wood-block stamps. And they didn't stop there. "What about those pages with all those words.... How about some designs!"

And that is why you'll be wowed by the designs on Italian paper that artisans reproduce to this day. Most of them come from Renaissance times, such as lilies, which are the symbol of Florence. All that marbled paper got popular around 1750, when a company in Bassano del Grappa, north of Venice, produced it and sent it all over Italy.

Here's where you can pick up beautiful handmade paper:

## Florence

* **Giulio Giannini & Figlio**, Piazza Pitti 37r (Oltrarno),
www.giuliogiannini.com
The Giannini family started out as bookbinders in 1856, then went on to become printers, publishers, and finally top decorative papermakers. This is a big shop with many varieties of designs, lots of marbled paper, and also classy leather desk sets. If you're interested in the secrets of the craft, they offer classes in papermaking.

* **Il Torchio**, Via dei Bardi 17 (San Niccolò),
www.legatoriailtorchio.com
Artisan Erin Ciulla owns this enchanting, tiny store and workshop, with a fabulous line of journals, frames, and gorgeous paper, that's lower priced than most others in town. She's also expert at customizing products to suit your desires.

## Venice

* **Il Pavone**, Fondamenta Venier dei Leoni 721 (Dorsoduro),
www.ilpavonevenezia.it
Here rich colors are blended as brilliantly as those on a *pavone's* (peacock's) tail, then hand stamped on to paper. You can buy sheets of paper (suitable for framing) stamped with patterns from geometric designs to gold-flecked floral prints. Their stationery, decorated with fancy lettered initials, makes for a great gift, as well as their textiles—from shopping bags to neckties.

* **Paolo Olbi**, Ponte di Ca Foscari 3253 (Dorsoduro)
Here's where you'll find the most classic Venetian designs. Olbi is a self-taught artisan, who makes such beautiful things

as journals covered with intricately hand tooled leather or Byzantine patterned paper, stationery decorated with etchings of Venetian landmarks, and pens made of Murano glass.

## Amalfi

The Valle dei Mulini, adjacent to the coastal town of Amalfi, was a major center of paper production from medieval times until the mid-twentieth century, when a flood wiped out the mills. Amalfi has a paper museum where you can walk through an old factory, get the scoop on how the whole production process went, and buy lovely stationery and journals in the gift shop.

**Museo Della Carta**: Via delle Cartiere 24, www.museodellacarta.it

You'll find **Fabriano Boutiques** (www.fabrianoboutique.com) in Rome (Via del Babuino 173, near Piazza del Popolo), and Italy's other major cities. This isn't handcrafted paper, but quality, chic stationery and journals designed by a company that's been in biz for hundreds of years. Fabriano is named after the town in Le Marche where one of Europe's first paper mills was founded in 1264. The watermark was invented there and now Fabriano's major work is printing out euros. I bless them for also having boutiques in the Rome airport—it's a great spot to pick up last minute souvenirs.

**Golden Day**: In Amalfi, visit the **Paper Museum**, see the **Amalfi Duomo,** and eat at **Trattoria Da Gemma** (Via Fra Gerardo Sasso 9, 089 871 345, www.trattoriadagemma.com).

# Milan

SHOPPING IN MILAN IS STEPPING INTO THE FUTURE. Newborn styles, fresh from the showrooms of megastar designers, fill the city's fabulous shop windows. It'll take a while for these fashions to appear in stores back home, so whatever you buy here will be sensational for a couple of seasons.

The city is a teeming cauldron of energy, a fashion kingdom that rose to power in the 1970s. Here Italy's old-time traditions of tailoring and craftsmanship are transformed into a spectacular industry.

And everybody looks so good! Women walk down the street as if they've just stepped off a fashion-show runway. And then there are all those handsome soccer players, as Milan is home to Italy's two top teams.

You'll inevitably begin your Milan explorations at **The Galleria**, the city's heart. It's the world's oldest mall, rising in neo-classical splendor between the **Duomo** and **La Scala** opera house. The very first **Prada** store is the highlight here. Though Milanese call it the "Tourist's Prada," it's still a beautiful place to peek into: two floors of exquisite stuff created from the vision of Miuccia Prada, the reigning Queen of Italian Designers.

Miuccia's grandfather founded Prada in 1913, making leather bags and suitcases. At first, Miuccia (born in 1949) couldn't care less about her family's old-fashioned business. She went to

university for a Ph.D. in Political Science and then on to theater
school for five years and performed mime in the streets. During
that phase, she was also an outspoken Communist and rallied hard
for women's rights.

In 1978 she inherited the company, which was on the financial
skids. The same year, she married Patrizio Bertelli. He took over
the marketing, while encouraging Miuccia to design. What she
ultimately came up with in 1985 turned Prada's fortunes around: a
simple, sleek, black nylon handbag. Since then, her runway shows
have been media sensations, with styles that range from austere to
outrageous. Always a lover of the avant garde, Miuccia spreads the
mega-fortunes of her company around, with a foundation that
supports and exhibits contemporary artists.

The Galleria is fun for a look at Prada and people watching, but
for a caffè, I say head to the nearby **Trussardi** (Piazza della Scala 5).
It's a sleek, ultra-modern place where you can blend in with the locals.

If you're pressed for time, the **Rinascente** department store
is right around the corner from the Galleria, with seven floors of
everything. Best of all is its rooftop food halls and **Obika** mozzarella bar, which has a terrace that puts you eye-to-eye with the top
of the nearby Duomo.

While all this is wonderful, be prepared to be blown away as
you head toward the **Quadrilatero della Moda**, the *zona* that's the
high-fashion heart of Milan. On the way, stop into the world's
first luxury department store, the **Excelsior Milano** (Galleria del
Corso 4). It feels more like visiting an art gallery than a department
store, with stunning designer displays and an array of deliciousness
offered in its vast basement food halls and restaurants.

Finally—ta da!—you'll reach the Golden Rectangle—Quadrilatero
della Moda. This is the Mount Olympus of Italian designers—Dolce
& Gabbana, Moschino, Versace, Armani, etc—all tucked into a
few blocks of scrubbed cobblestoned streets, centered around Via

Montenapoleone. I believe this is the world's best window shopping experience—complete with price tags in the stratosphere.

Heading a few blocks away you get to the **Brera** district, bordered by Via Manzoni, Via Fatebenefratelli, and Via Bonaparte. Here's where you'll find antique shops and boutique designers—such as the crisp looks of **Patrizia Pepe** and, a favorite, the romantic, flowing creations of **Luisa Beccaria** (Via Senato 18). Don't miss the **D Magazine Outlet** (Via Manzoni 44), to score 40 to 60 percent markdowns on top brands.

The place designers love most of all in Milan is **10 Corso Como**, owned by a former editor of Italian *Vogue*. It's about a ten-minute walk from Brera. When you get there, the mosaic sign up top and narrow entrance gives you the feeling that it's a private club. Then it opens up to this elegant courtyard where there's a garden restaurant/cafe, and upstairs photography galleries and a huge art bookshop. Best of all is the warehouse-sized dazzling store packed with designer goodies—from clothing to housewares. There's even a three-room B&B. Close by is the **Corso Como Outlet** (Via Tazzoli 3, open Friday-Sunday), where items from seasons past are discounted.

The best bargain you'll get in Milan will not be while you're shopping, but at the evening's 'Appy Hour. From six to nine every night, bars all over the place spread out lavish buffets. For the price of one cocktail, you can fill up on snacks that will add up to dinner.

**Golden Day:** Shop and stop for caffè where your desires lead you. Get to the roof of **Rinascente** (Piazza Duomo) at sunset, settle into the terrace of **Obikà** mozzarella bar. A good choice for 'Appy Hour is the **Hotel Sheraton Diana Majestic** (Viale Piave 42), that also puts on a fabulous Sunday brunch.

## TOURS

**Select Italy** (www.selectitaly.com) offers great guided shopping
tours of Milan that they can custom design to your tastes. They
also can arrange for special entrances to stores during sales
weeks, and private visits to ateliers.

# 69 *Antique Markets*

IT'S WORTH IT TO PLAN YOUR TRIP so you'll be in **Arezzo** the first Sunday of the month. That's when this Tuscan town's historic center overflows with Italy's biggest outdoor antique market. Five hundred vendors spread out an eclectic mix of treasures to satisfy your inner huntress. There are carved armoires, candelabras, and giant urns. And suitcase-friendly treasures from vintage linens to jewelry, cordial glasses, faded postcards, and comic books.

Besides Arezzo, loads of other small towns and cities regularly have weekend antique markets, that aren't as big as Arezzo's but still grand. No matter where you land, it's an entertaining shopping experience. There's the magic of being in a piazza that's transformed into looking like countless *nonnas* have snuck in before your arrival and dropped off their pretty possessions, each piece unique and holding memories of the past. The vendors are colorful characters—from antique fanatics to teenagers who'd rather be watching the soccer game and are easy to bargain with.

Most antique markets also have flea market-type set-ups at their borders, so if you need cheap socks, there you go.

A few suggestions among the many:

* **Arezzo Antique Market,** first Sunday of every month and preceding Saturday
Besides the best market, right here is Piero della Francesca's stunning *Legend of the True Cross* fresco cycle in the church of San Francesco. Or go on the *Life Is Beautiful* tour, which takes you to spots around town where the movie was shot.

* **Florence: Oltrarno Flea Market** in Piazza Santo Spirito, second Sunday of every month
The Brunelleschi-designed **Basilica di Santo Spirito** is a perfectly pure backdrop for this market. Along with antiques, there are stalls where Florentine artisans sell their latest creations.

* **Rome: Ponte Milvio Antique Market,** first Sunday of the month
The neighborhood surrounding Rome's oldest bridge is one of the city's hippest. Historically, it's where Emperor Constantine won the battle that began the Christian era. These days you'll see the bridge's lampposts adorned with padlocks. It's a craze begun in 2006 by the bestselling book *I Want You*, that's inspired lovers to write their names on padlocks that they chain to the bridge. Then they toss the keys into the Tiber, symbolizing their eternal devotion.

* **Near Padua: Piazzola sul Brenta,** last Sunday of every month
This is Italy's second biggest antique market, held in a piazza that fronts the splendid **Villa Contarini**, which you can tour while antiquing. En route take the opportunity to visit some Palladian villas.

❊ **Near Parma: Antique Trade Market of Fontanellato,** third
  Sunday of every month
  At this castle surrounded by a water-filled moat, along with 200
  vendors, you get a chance to see recently restored Parmigianino
  frescos. It's an 11-mile/18-km drive from Parma, and bus service from town is available.

❊ **Naples: Villa Comunale Antique Market,** select Saturdays and
  Sundays, check www.napoliunplugged.com for current schedule
  Surrounded by gardens, close to the picturesque bay, here's a
  place where you may find antique crèche figures and if you're
  lucky, an impromptu puppet show.

❊ **Sarzana, Liguria: National Antiquarian Exhibition,** every
  August for two weeks, evenings, www.leviedisarzana.it
  The August event transforms the pretty walled town of Sarzana
  into what's called "The Attic in the Street," with hundreds
  of stalls from international vendors, all curated to insure top
  quality. For the rest of the year, come here to enjoy wonderful
  antique shops, chic restaurants and bars.

❊ **Fossano, Piedmont: Città Antiquaria,** Monday-Saturday and
  fourth Sunday of the month
  Pros call this the best antique shopping spot in Italy. It's a huge
  indoor exhibition center, arranged to look like an old fortified
  town, where you'll find antiques, paintings, and crafts from all
  over the world.

❧

**Golden Day**: Get to the **Arezzo Antique Market** and see *The Legend of the True Cross* fresco cycle. Eat at **Buca di San Francesco** (Via San Francesco I, 0575 23271, closed Tuesday, www.bucadisanfrancesco. it), to enjoy delicious Tuscan classics in the charming atmosphere of what was once the wine cellar of a fourteenth-century palazzo.


## RECOMMENDED READING

*The Antique and Flea Markets of Italy* by Marina Seveso, translated by Oonagh Stransky

# VIII

*Active Adventures*

Mother Nature poured a heaping helping of beauty on Italy, then spread glorious days of sunshine on top of it. You could sit back on a terrace and admire its seas and lakes, rolling farmlands, volcanoes, and majestic mountains. But it's even better to get up and into it for a knock-out sensorama experience.

Outside the cities, you'll have the chance to be hiking in Italy's golden light that poets have praised. You'll stop and smell the lavender. Or maybe you'll be diving into cool waters off the coast of Ponza, in a cove you discovered as you were circling around it by boat. You could be in the Dolomites, warming up with a sip of fiery grappa after an exhilarating day on the ski slopes.

Inevitably, the countryside brings with it the chance to experience the natives' warmth and generosity. As in one May afternoon in Puglia when I was riding a bike past a cherry tree grove. I stopped to take pictures and a ninety-something-year-old farmer walked over, took two handfuls of just-picked cherries from his bucket, and put them in my bike basket.

That's just a for instance of the sweet surprises that will likely come at you when you get into exploring Italy as an active adventurer.

# 70 Biking

I GET AN "I'M FREE!" RUSH whenever I take off on a bike. That feeling, plus the Italian atmosphere, equals pure bliss. Italians bike with passion. You'll see everything from *nonnas* cycling through village markets to super athletes who compete in the *Giro d'Italia Feminile*, one of the world's most famous women's bike races.

There are loads of ways to blend in with Italy's cycling culture. You can be the chic *signorina* gliding into the piazza in **Ferrara**, nicknamed "The City of Bicycles," where about a third of the population gets around on two wheels.  You can take off for a day ride through the **Chianti** province, surrounded by vineyards. If you're feeling all woman warrior, you can get an endorphin rush mountain biking through the **Dolomites**.

* **For an easy, whimsical experience, go to Lucca, Tuscany:**
  Going to Lucca and not biking along the top of the town's old wall is like going to Paris and not visiting the Eiffel Tower. The thick wall took over one hundred years to build back in Renaissance days. After all that, Lucca was never attacked, and in the early 19th century, the wonderful female ruler Marie Luisa di Borbone had the great idea to beautify the top of this structure with landscaping.

Today this 3-mile/5-km loop, shaded by tall trees, is divine for a flat easy bike ride, with views of Lucca rooftops down below, backyards where the locals don't mind you clicking photos of their laundry waving in the breeze, and fields of wildflowers. It's perfect for families. Even my friend Cheryl's five-year-old did the ride with no problem.

❀ **If you're feeling more adventurous, Group Biking Trips:**
Choose your region, and take off for a week-long biking adventure. There are many companies out there offering trips for all levels of riders.

Not an experienced long-distance biker, I signed up with **Backroads** (www.backroads.com), to go to Puglia, attracted by the words: "Puglia is Italy's flattest region." I loved it so much I went back the next year to southern Sicily where there were more hills. Both were fantastic weeks. We were pampered by excellent guides, with ingenious routes that took us through farmlands and small towns for lunch and gelato breaks. Backroads supplied the bikes, great snacks, and a support van rode alongside so if we pooped out we could hop in. I had the freedom to lag behind and talk with the local farmers or speed up and join the more athletic of the group. Accommodations were in farmhouses or fortresses that had been converted to luxury hotels, with nightly feasts. There was loads of good eating, but with all the exercise, I didn't gain a pound.

Backroads also custom designs itineraries if you want to do something really fabulous like set up a private trip with your girlfriends for a reunion or big birthday.

Also, check out **Ciclismo Classico** (www.ciclismoclassico.com), which runs group bike tours all over Italy, with native guides, unique immersion experiences, and language lessons along the way.

* **If you're independent and up for a bigger challenge:**
Here you also have lots of choices of companies, such as
**Randotrek** (www.randotrek.com), that arrange self-guided
biking tours of Italy, providing bikes, maps, and a service to
move your luggage from hotel to hotel.

✣

**Golden Day:** In **Lucca**, rent a bike at **Antonio Poli Bicicletta**
(Piazza Santa Maria 42, www.biciclettepoli.com) to circle the town's
wall. Eat at **Buca di Sant'Antonio,** (Via Cervia, 0583 55881, www.
bucadisantantonio.com), an old tavern that serves excellent local
specialties, including farro soup, homemade pasta, and sliced beef
sauced with truffles.

## RECOMMENDED READING

*Lonely Planet Cycling Italy* by Ethan Gelber

# 71 *Hiking*

EXPERIENCING ITALY ON FOOT IS THE PERFECT WAY to savor every detail, get peace of mind, and a good fragrant hit of nature while you're at it.

You don't even have to be a gung-ho hiker to do it. In Rome you can get your endorphins going with a half-hour uphill walk from Trastevere to the **Janiculum Hill** or in Florence wind up to the **Piazzale Michelangelo** and beautiful San Miniato church. Both reward you with fabulous city views.

If you're up for more vigorous hiking, you can:

❂ **Enjoy the Coast**
The most popular hiking place in Italy for American travelers is the **Cinque Terre** on the northern Ligurian coast. There, the **Sentiero Azzuro** (Blue Path) connects five enchanting seaside villages. You can do the one-way walk (starting at Riomaggiore) in five to six hours, then take a ferry or train back to your starting point. But a better idea is to settle in for at least a few nights for beach and boating time.

Two of my gal friends who have lots of Cinque Terre experience call **Manarola** the best village of the five to stay in. "I thought I was over hostels," Lauren told me. But she makes an exception for **Hostel Cinque Terre** (0187 92039, www.hostel5terre.com, reservations a must), which has a fantastic rooftop terrace and rooms with private baths. Hope (a girlfriend of many exclamation points) sings the praises!!! of **Trattoria dal Billy** (018 792 0628, www.trattoriabilly.com, reservations a must), a seven-table restaurant where Billy's mamma cooks up such great things as fried shrimp or pesto. By the way, pesto is absolutely what to order in these parts, where it was invented.

Guidebook writer Rick Steves made the Cinque Terre famous so these days it's best to avoid it in summer high-tourist season, and no matter when you come, reserve your digs well in advance and be prepared to pay a fee to get on the hiking trail. As far as how challenging a hike it is, the first leg (from Riomaggiore to Manarola) is flat enough to be done with a baby stroller, and then things get progressively steeper and harder as you go along. It's all glorious.

My favorite coastal hike is the **Sentiero degli Dei** (Path of the Gods) above the Amalfi Coast. Here steep paths, that were once used for mules to bring goods to the mountain villages, take you through lemon groves, forests, and vineyards. You get great views of the candy-colored villages below that stretch out to the tantalizing sea horizon.

A well-marked three- to four-hour hike on this path starts in **Agerola (Bomerano)**, and leads you along cliffs and vineyards to **Nocelle**, where you have a choice to walk down over 1,700 steps to Positano, or take a bus from the Nocelle village center. For guided tours with fun natives, check out Carto Trekking (www.cartotrekking.com).

❋ **Mountain Towns**
Umbria and Tuscany have loads of well-marked trails, with good maps available at small town tourist offices. A favorite starts in **Spoleto**, leading you up to where Saint Francis gave his famous Sermon to the Birds.

❋ **National Parks** (www.parks.it)
There are over a hundred to choose from, including the **Gran Paradiso** (in northern Piedmont and Valle d'Aosta) that has everything from glacier walking to paths specially designed for the disabled. A two-hour drive east from Rome takes you to **Abruzzo**, where wolves and bears are kept in ingeniously designed zoo reserves. My friend Maria loves hiking **Lo Zingaro**, in Western Sicily, a park with trails along rocky seaside cliffs that lead to quiet pebbly beaches.

❋ **Group Hikes**
If you're up for a week of hiking with a group in a particular region, **Country Walkers** (www.countrywalkers.com) offers choices up and down the boot, with excellent native guides, accommodations, and meals included. I loved a week in Sicily with them, where we hiked the range of terrains—from the flat Vendicari bird reserve to the top of Mount Etna's volcano.

Another Country Walkers veteran, Jill Clark, went along with her sportier husband through Tuscany and loved that there were side trips to wineries and artisan workshops. "It was my first time in Tuscany, and it was wonderful to get into places we never would have seen if we were traveling on our own."

These are perfect trips for families. With everything so well taken care of, nobody can whine to Mommy, and bonding goes on among the different generations, often leading to life-long friendships that began on the shared adventure.

**TIP:** *Club Alpino Italiano is a good resource for hiking maps for Italy (www.cai.it).*

৯৬

**Golden Day:** From **Bomerano**, hike the **Sentiero degli Dei** to **Nocelle** and continue on to **Montepertuso**. Have a delicious lunch at **Il Ritrovo** (89 812 005, www.ilritrovo.com), where Salvatore cooks up dishes such as ravioli with tomatoes and basil that come straight from his garden. Sleep in Positano at **La Rosa Dei Venti** (www.larosadeiventi.net), where you can relax on your balcony after all that hiking.

## RECOMMENDED READING

*Walking in Italy* by Sandra Bardwell

*Walking on the Amalfi Coast* by Gillian Price

*Songbirds, Truffles, and Wolves* by Gary Paul Nabhan

# Skiing

FOR THE MOST DELICIOUS AND LEISURELY SKI EXPERIENCE, you've got to come to Italy. The day typically begins around ten-ish, with a stop at a caffè, and then along your ski path you can stop at restaurants and *refugios* (wooden huts) where for lunch you could go gourmet (lobster) or rustic (pizza from a wood-burning oven). Top it off with the best of the region's wines or prosecco, and then you're back on the slopes until late afternoon. Why push it when the après ski scene—spas, shopping, and evening jazz or disco—is such fun?

You can score a bargain package of this routine by going in for a *settimana bianca* (white week), which Italy's ski resorts regularly offer.

Where? With all the mountains and volcanoes, there is skiing in every region. Doing Sicily's Mount Etna could be exciting or you could take off on the slopes of Abruzzo's national parks. But the best is on those glorious mountains at the top of the boot, where you can ski from November to mid-April.

## Bormio, Lombardy

When Sara Chamberlin, from Milan, had to pick the perfect place for her girlfriend's bachelorette party, she chose Bormio. This place near the Swiss border in the western Dolomites is not only great for skiing, but has an equally *splendido* attraction: natural thermal springs. Picture it: outdoor steaming pools you can relax in after ski time, right in the midst of snow-covered mountains.

The **Hotel Bagni Vecchi** (www.bagnidibormio.it) is the place to be based to get the best of them. "There's nothing else like it in the world," Sara said. The twelve-room converted convent is built right into the mountain. Its spa has thirty areas, some that incorporate original Roman bath structures and others that are tiny natural caves. You can even go into one that's built into the mountain, directly where the water springs from.

The skiing is fab, with a 5,000-foot vertical drop and twenty-four lifts. Runs are good for beginners and intermediates, without many super-challenging ones, so head to nearby Santa Caterina and Livigno if that's what you're looking for. Lots of fun is to be had on Thursday nights, when Bormio lights up the slopes until 11p.m., with music and entertainment.

For dinner, head to **Baita de Mario** (www.baitademariobormio. com) for specialties like *pizzoccheri* (buckwheat pasta with cabbage and fontina cheese), *bresaola*, and the rustic red wine of the region: Valtellina Superiore.

The town of Bormio has a chic pedestrian-only center of zigzag cobblestoned streets filled with fun shops and both Romanesque and Renaissance architecture. And how about a grappa tasting? You'll have much more than a skiing vacation here in Bormio.

## Alta Badia, Alto Adige (www.altabadia.org)

Here's a Tyrolean Italy. You'll hear German, Italian, and Ladin—a language that's existed since before the Romans came, which about twenty thousand natives still speak. The area originally belonged to Austria until after World War I, so much of the architecture is chalet-style—old farm huts, which blend in with the green meadows and rugged Dolomite Mountains. On menus you'll find unusual dishes like venison carpaccio, and a full-bodied, bright red wine called Lagrein.

What's wonderful about Alta Badia is that there is so much ski area. It's made up of six rural hamlets, so you can ski from place to place, with hundreds of runs to choose from. It's perfect for families-with a renowned ski school, a nursery to take care of the little ones while you're getting snow time, and cross-country paths. There are also sleigh rides and horse shows. This all sounds very folksy, but there's a sophisticated edge-three Michelin starred restaurants in the area.

"And you should see the men! They have beautiful blue eyes.... I even saw George Clooney there, at Rosa Alpina (www.rosalpina. it), playing cards and drinking wine with the hotel people," says my friend Marzia, who comes here from Rome. Marzia e-mailed me a photo to prove it, full of many exclamations!

### Sauze d'Oulx, Piedmont

Of the five *Via Lattea* (Milky Way) towns in this alpine area that borders France, Sauze d'Oulx is the liveliest, beloved by British and French skiers for its great variety of 140 runs as well as its pubs and discos where partying goes on til the wee hours. I loved dining at **l'Ortiche** (0122 850 329, www.ortiche.com) that serves delicious seasonal specialties, such as tagliatelle with shaved truffles and a divine panna cotta. The **Grand Hotel Besson** (www. grandhotelbesson.it) is a choice 4-star to settle into a friendly, woodsy atmosphere, and relax in its big spa with a saltwater pool.

※

**Golden Day:** In **Alta Badia** (www.altabadia.org), base yourself in the village of **Corvara** at the **Hotel Posta Zirm** (www.postazirm. com), which has a Feng Shui-designed spa with a huge pool. Eat at **Club Moritzino** (Piazza La Ila, 0471 847 403, www.moritzino. it), where Marzia recommends the five-course dinner with fresh lobster: "Eating seafood up there at 4,000 meters is amazing!"

# *73 Boating*

WITH 4,536 MILES/7,300 KM OF COASTLINE, gorgeous lakes, and all
those enchanting islands, Italy has opportunities
*amundo* for boating adventures. Getting out on
the water gives you a chance to change your perspective and take in the landscape like an old-
time explorer. Rentals of everything from canoes
to 40hp boats can be arranged without a license,
but if you'd rather not boat on your own, there
are plenty of natives available who will take you
around—stopping at choice spots for swimming,
fishing, and snorkeling. You can even take a
*barchetto* (old-fashioned gondola-style boat) ride down the Arno
River in Florence, which comes with prosecco for sunset excursions
(www.viator.com).

Here's a few primo boating ideas:

### Row Venice (www.rowvenice.org)

One of the most extraordinary experiences to be had in Venice is to
take a lesson to learn how to row like a gondolier. I'm still amazed
when I look at the photo that was snapped of me, standing on the
stern of the boat, oar in hand, rocking with the current in the sunset light of the lagoon...

Row Venice is the organization that offers such an adventure. It was created by a team of women, among them Nan McElroy, an American who fell in love with Venice and now lives near the dock in Cannaregio where we started our lesson. The boat used is called a *batellina code de gambero*, shrimp's tail, because of its curved shape. It's just like what you see in the eighteenth-century paintings of Canaletto.

The lesson begins with a demo, but learning comes more as you row along. First there is gliding through back waterways, flanked by lines of laundry, and boats delivering groceries, getting an insider's look at Venetian life, as Nan calls out to her neighbors who wave from their windows. Then you're out in the lagoon, a speck in the splendid expanse, with glorious palazzos in the distance.

Lessons are offered all year long, are great for families, and especially wonderful at sunset. For an added treat, there's an option to take a *cichetti* row, stopping at various *bacari* (wine bars).

### Kayak Tours in Italy (www.barbarakossy.com)

Californian Barbara Kossy combines her passion for Italy and kayaking by organizing trips to Sardinia, Sicily, and the island of Elba. It's what she calls, "Soft adventures, the cross-country skiing of kayaking. We sleep in hotels every night and get to wash the salt out of our hair before dinner."

On these leisurely tours, travelers get to explore a different part of the coast by kayak each day. "It's a great social experience," Barbara said, "not only within the group, but lots of times we're joined by kayakers from Italy and other parts of the world as we go along." There's also fun to be had swimming, at group dinners, exploring enchanting small towns, and hiking through olive groves, vineyards, and, on the Sicily trip, around Mount Etna.

Best of all, you get to experience the island as the natives do. Leading the trips are expert guides, such as Gaudenzio Coltelli, who grew up on Elba and knows every inch of the island, or Francesco Petralia, a Sicilian volcanologist, who adds dramatic entertainment along the way, as he tells stories of ancient myths.

## Ponza, Lazio

The remote island of Ponza, aka the Roman Capri, has its share of spicy, dark history: Homer wrote that Circe lived here and seduced Odysseus to stay for a year, Pontius Pilot bred moray eels in the island's caves, and it was a place of exile for naughty empresses and Fascists, including Mussolini.

Its heaven for boating, with a coastline that's an enticing mix of chalk-white cliffs, emerald grottoes, and mysterious tunnels, surrounded by clear, deep turquoise waters. Rock formations make each of its beaches unique, and most can only be reached by boat. It's easy to hop a small ferry from the harbor to get around, or to rent a *gozzo* (small fisherman's boat).

Except for weekends in July and August, when it gets mobbed with tourists, Ponza is the perfect spot for an idyllic getaway—at least three days. The harbor town has a wonderful mix of restaurants, bars, and gelaterias. It's also great for hiking in the hills to the **Antiche Cantine Migliaccio** winery (www.antichecantinemigliaccio.it), or Ponza's cemetery—a terraced complex of mausoleums and chapels, set on the rocks, that's one of the most beautiful cemeteries in Italy.

**To Get There:** Take a ferry from the coastal towns of Formia, Anzio, or Terracina. Travel times range from 50 minutes to 2-1/2 hours, depending on departure point and type of ferry (www.laziomar.it).

※

**Golden Day:** In Ponza, take an excursion from the harbor with **Cooperativa Barcaioli** (www.barcaioliponza.it) that circles the island, with a swimming break at the beach on the island of Palmarola. The boat captain doubles as chef, and serves a delicious pasta lunch on board. Stay at **Piccolo Hotel Luisa** (www.piccolohoteluisa.it), an adorable family run 3-star, with spacious rooms and balconies.

# 74 *Yoga*

IMAGINE IF INSTEAD OF RUSHING BACK into traffic after your yoga class, you're in bell'Italia strolling through a baroque Sicilian village...or walking along the River Arno...or staring out into an olive grove...

The yoga retreat scene in Italy is growing, with masterful minds from the United States and United Kingdom setting up programs that cover all the bases when it comes to combining yoga with the pleasures of Italy's peaceful surroundings, including English-speaking instructors. There are also many good day classes available in cities and towns, where classes are, of course, in Italian, but if you have some yoga experience, it's easy to follow along.

Each of the suggestions below are open to beginners or long-time practitioners, classes are small so there's lots of individual attention, and prices are affordable.

* **It's Yoga,** Via de Bardi 121, Oltrarno, Florence, www.itsyogafirenze.it
  This light-filled loft with arched ceilings and shiny wooden floors is well located in the historical center, with three to four classes a day, making it a convenient stop for travelers who want to keep their yoga practice going when they're away from their home studios. The atmosphere is welcoming, with mats provided, and an international mix of students.

◉ **Sunflower Retreats Holidays,** Casperia, Lazio,
www.sunflowerretreats.com
Casperia is an idyllic, un-touristed medieval village (population
350) in the Sabine hills north of Rome. Here you'll discover
Sunflower Retreats, created by Hatha yoga teacher and holistic
practitioner Lucy Bremner, and her husband Alan Scheda,
a Casperia native. In the eighteen years they've run the yoga
programs, they have revitalized Casperia—renovating homes,
employing locals, and promoting eco-tourism

Along with morning yoga classes, their packages include
B&B accommodations in houses scattered around the village, a
swimming pool, a guided walk in the mountains, and bikes for
the week. You can add on excellent massages and holistic treatments, go horseback riding, head to hot springs for a soak, or
take a cooking class at a nearby agriturismo. They also have some
weeks with Pilates instruction and offer retreats in Sperlonga, a
beautiful seaside town.

The freedom to create your retreat however you want it to
be is what makes this so appealing. When I got there and checked
into my attic room, with a skylight directly over the bed so I
could see the stars, I felt heavenly. The morning yoga classes
were sublime. Highlights of my stay were afternoon classes on
the outdoor deck with a soft breeze blowing and birds twitter-
ing, buying some of the best olive oil in Italy from the old signor
photographer in town who filled up a bottle for me out of his
work shed vat, and best of all meeting Lucy, Alan, and their
children, who bring true heart and soul to the scene. They've set
it up so everything is easy-—whether you want to add on private
yoga and meditation classes, go to a nearby village for dinner,
or get a lift to the train station to head out for a day in Rome
or Assisi.

Adrienne Storey, who has been here six times, tells me she cries every time she leaves and goes back to London. "From the first time I went to Casperia it felt like coming home. It's like one big happy family," she says.

* **Yoga in Sicily,** www.yoga-escapes.com
Yoga-Escapes—which also offers holidays in Greece and Egypt— is the successful passion project of Laura Bianchini. Born and raised in Rome, Laura left her corporate career working in London and New York to pursue her love of travel and yoga. The holiday week in Sicily combines yoga, culture, art, great food, and relaxation in an ideal seaside location, just outside Siracusa, Sicily. It's a yoga vacation, not a retreat—meaning drinking wine, sleeping in, and experiencing the surroundings according to your desires is the way things are set up to flow.

Alice Johnson, a documentary filmmaker from London, raves to me about her trip: "It was so well organized, so you can get to the authentic heart of the culture. Laura, brought a great personal touch to the week, taking us off the beaten track to hidden beaches and local restaurants."

The program attracts an international mix—British, American, German, and Italian travelers—and it's great for solo travelers. Along with morning and sunset yoga, there are options for biking, wine tasting, visiting the baroque towns of Noto and Taormina, and exploring the breathtaking archaeological sites of Siracusa and enchanting Ortygia island. Guests stay in a 5-star hotel, where spa treatments, a private beach and pool make for a luxurious base. It's the perfect escape to recharge the body and mind.

# IX

*Cooking Classes*

Taking a cooking class in Italy is getting a backstage pass to the country's soul. Everything comes together in the kitchen: a cook's passion, the freshest flavors of the season, enticing aromas, sounds of garlic sizzling, and wine glasses clinking.

Each class will give you an opportunity to experience a different type of cuisine, depending on what region you land. In Rome you may be stuffing artichokes, in Naples kneading pizza dough. You can sign up for a one-day class or join in on the many week-long programs offered, where the itinerary typically includes visits to wineries and food artisans. Whether you're an experienced cook eager to learn every detail or more the type who wants to sit back and watch some culinary magic, Italian kitchens welcome you.

Often classes revolve around recipes that were taught to your teachers by their *nonnas*. You follow along, becoming part of the tradition, by watching and learning through your senses of touch and smell. It's an experience that takes you far beyond what you'd get if you were creating a dish from a written recipe.

It's a joy to get swept up in a cook's enthusiasm. That could mean prowling the Rialto market in Venice, intensely focused on the color of fish eyes or swooning over the smell of just-picked basil in Ravello.

Whatever form your class takes, there will be that glorious moment, when you sit down at the table to enjoy the fruits of your labor and toast, *"Buon appetito!"*

## RECOMMENDED READING

*The World Is a Kitchen: Cooking Your Way Through Culture* edited by Michele Anna Jordan and Susan Brady

# 75

## Cooking in Rome

**Daniela's Cooking School** (www.danielascookingschool.com)

The divine aroma of peppers cooking in olive oil and garlic fills Daniela del Balzo's kitchen. Six of us American travelers in Rome are hovering around her stove, sipping prosecco, nibbling bruschetta, stirring and chopping, under Daniela's enthusiastic guidance. Her one-day cooking class is a lovely respite from the tourist treadmill of the Eternal City. We're slowing down and immersing ourselves in the culinary traditions of Rome.

Daniela is a mamma-to-all type signora, who sets up her class as though she's taking us along with her for a typical Roman day: shopping at the local market and cooking in her apartment. Her passion for cooking is boundless. She learned the traditional way—from her mother, grandmother, and great-grandmother, during her childhood in Naples. Then, after a twenty-year career working for Alitalia, she went back to school to focus on her love for cooking. She studied at Italy's renowned Gambero Rosso Cooking School, the French Culinary Arts School & Le Cordon Bleu, and the International Cooking School of Naples.

Now she teaches from her home on Rome's Aventine Hill. She's married to a Roman, has a mother-in-law who lives two floors above her, and two twenty-something sons—one who has also become a chef, following in her footsteps. Putting all these work and life experiences together, Daniela has created a program where she teaches Roman classics with professional flair, always adding a Neapolitan touch from her ancestors. As her classes are so popular, she's added a three-day course for those who wish to go deeper into learning about Roman cuisine. She also is a private chef, and prepares elegant dinners in her home for travelers or can even cook meals for them at their apartment rentals.

Our class begins in the bustling Testaccio market. Rome's slaughterhouse was once located nearby, and Testaccio became famous for restaurants that featured quality meat dishes and Roman specialties from the *quinto quarto* (fifth quarter), meaning what's left of the animal after butchering—oxtails, tripe, *pajata* (calf intestines), etc.

The neighborhood has become, as the Italians say, "trendy," with clubs and hot spots, but discovering it with Daniela is the ideal way to connect with its roots. Everywhere we go it feels like we're tagging along with her on a family visit. Vendors ask about her sons, she tells them her cooking plans for the day, then there's serious teamwork to pick out the best peppers. Next there's an intense discussion with her handsomest of butchers, Daniele Sartor, about the right amount of veal for lunch. The excursion is a sensory treat— we're surrounded by abundant displays of deep green chicory, glistening anchovies, the first strawberries of spring.

We move on to Daniela's apartment—a sophisticated, sunlit place, with cozy family antiques. Fun begins in the kitchen, where we learn as we go, to Daniela's free-flowing teaching style. Her recipes are simple, but by watching her, we learn subtle techniques for bringing out the best flavors of the market's ingredients. There's the way to jiggle the pan to cook up *saltimbocca*—which translates to "jump in your mouth," because the taste of the veal/ prosciutto/sage combo is so lively. There's an extra step in her peperonata recipe—covering the pan with a domed lid after sautéing, just before baking, so the result is a perfectly soft, creamy dish. "It's how my grandmother taught me," Daniela says, smiling as she shares this memory. And so each of us slips into a long line of Italian tradition—learning the secrets behind the country's delicious dishes, thanks to the abundant, generous spirit of its cooks.

## TOURS

**Context Travel** (www.contexttravel.com): For Cooking with Daniela in Rome and classes in Florence, Venice, and Naples.

**Eating Italy** (www.eatingitalyfoodtours.com): Offers cooking classes with Roman nonnas and food walking tours. I loved their Trastevere Twilight Food Tour, led by a native, who guides you to local specialty shops (for such Roman specialties as *porchetta*, *suppli*, biscotti, and gelato), a wine cellar, and restaurants. It's a perfect activity to orient you to Rome's culinary scene.

**The Gioia of Cooking:** Rome native Gioia (pronounced JOY-A) Acon teaches classic Roman cooking with exuberance and detailed instruction, and is also available as a private chef.

## RECOMMENDED READING

*Williams-Sonoma Rome* by Maureen Fant

*Flavors of Rome* by Carol Coviello-Malzone

# 76 *Morning at the Market—Florence*

THE **MERCATO CENTRALE DI SAN LORENZO** is a place so revered by the Florentines that it's overseen by the same art commission who looks after the Uffizi galleries. The vast glass-and-cast-iron structure from 1865 is one of the oldest and biggest markets in Italy. Its top floor was recently renovated into a blockbuster food court, and throughout you're surrounded by mouth-watering temptations: wheels of fragrant pecorino cheese, tubs of grapes, shelves glowing with bottles of olive oil, stuffed pig heads.

The market is as overwhelming as a Florentine gallery, which is why I signed up with an expert foodie guide, Judy Witts-Francini, to delve deeper into the finest treasures to be found here.

Judy's been shopping at the Mercato Centrale since 1984. That was the year she left her job as a pastry chef in San Francisco and moved to Florence. She arrived not knowing a soul and didn't speak a word of Italian. It was at the market where she learned the language—talking to the vendors, hearing their recipes, eavesdropping on conversations. Falling in love and marrying a Florentine, Andrea Francini, soon followed.

Though she's studied professionally and is a member of top international chef associations, Judy tells me her best teacher was her Florentine mother-in-law. "She taught me the most important thing about Italian cooking: *Spend more time shopping and less time cooking.* It's not the recipe or the hours you spend in the kitchen that makes good food. It's the quality of the ingredients. In Italian they say: *"La materia prima."*

And ah, the materials at the market are *divina!* "Taste this," Judy says, as we stand in front of the counter of one of her friend's shops. It's twelve-year-old balsamic vinegar that wakes up every taste bud. That's just the beginning of the flavor-filled tour. There's aged pecorino, olive oil fresh from the press, and *lampredotto* (the specialty tripe of Florence). Judy knows all the artisans in the glamorous upstairs stands, so we easily navigate the crowds, stopping to smell the truffles, sip Chianti, savor the chocolate, meet the award-winning pizza maker.

Judy's passion for the details is infectious, and she's an absolutely delightful person to be with. Though she's lived in Florence most of her life, her drive and spirit are a reflection of her California roots. She was part of the first wave of expats setting up travel businesses and websites in Italy (in the 1990s), and has expanded her successful company, **Divina Cucina,** to offer cooking classes in the Tuscan countryside as well as Sicily, has written a cookbook and a wonderful travel app for Chianti.

Heading out of the market, we make a final stop at **Pork's,** one of the restaurant stalls on the lower level. This one has been run by a Sicilian family for over twenty years.

"Meet my market Mamma," Judy says, introducing me to Benita—Pork's matriarch—a seventy-something signora with a jet-black bouffant hairdo.

Benita proudly shows off her case of food: *eggplant caponata, arancine.* Within minutes, she's insisted on sitting us down for tastings, though we protest that we're absolutely full. Without Judy, I would have passed this place by, thinking: *Why a Sicilian restaurant in Florence?* The answer comes after one bite: because the flavors are out of this world.

Pork's is now my go-to lunch spot at the market. Benita is always there to welcome me back with a kiss and a *caponata*. I toast Judy for the bonus I got from her backstage tour: a little piece of family at the Mercato Centrale for many visits to come.

## TOURS

**Divina Cucina** (www.divinacucina.com) offers Florence Market Tours, Culinary Adventures in Tuscany and Beyond, and restaurant advice. Check out her website, blog, and Chianti App, a wonderful guide to the region.

**Florence Urban Adventure** (www.florenceurbanadventures.com) offers Foodie Walks and Wine Tours, led by entertaining local guides, that are great introductions to family run specialty food stores, bakeries, gelaterias and wine bars in the historic center. Recommended for early in your Florence trip, so you can become well oriented to the culinary scene.

## RECOMMENDED READING

*Secrets from My Tuscan Kitchen* by Judy Witts-Francini

# 77 Cooking with Chef Patrizia—Venice

"I'LL MAKE YOU A SPRITZ!" SAYS CHEF PATRIZIA, the moment I enter her apartment. I barely have my coat off when this darling sprite-of-a-signora hands me the classic Venetian refreshment: a sparkling glass of Campari mixed with prosecco, garnished with an orange slice. Chef Patrizia, her assistant/translator Silvia, and Lisa, another student, toast: *"Cin cin!"* The vibe is set for a happy party/cooking class.

School began earlier that morning, when I met assistant Silvia and Lisa at the Rialto market. This bustling spot by the famous bridge has been The Venetian Food Shopping Center since 1097. It's a great scene of curious tourists like me and natives, strolling through the fish stalls, that glisten with the bounty from the lagoon and beyond—from squirming live crabs, to shrimp, octopus, tiny clams, and sea bream. Next to the fish market are vibrant stands of fruits and vegetables, overflowing with goodies such as bright purple Treviso cabbage and ripe, orange *kaki*—a variety of persimmon that's a popular dessert fruit.

With our bags full, we wove through narrow *calle*, along canals, over little bridges, and past the massive Santa Maria Formosa church. Along the way, Silvia turns out to be an excellent guide—showing me the top cheese shop near the market *("Casa del Parmigiano—I saw Mario Batali there!")*, a good pizza place *("Cip Ciap—my husband is Neapolitan and he loves this pizza!)*, and pointing out the variations in the winged lion sculptures found all over Venice: *"If the lion is holding an open book in its paw, that means Venice was at peace, and if the book is closed, it was made when the city-state was at war."*

Finally, we land in front of a palazzo in the Castello *sestiere*, and zigzag upstairs to Patrizia's apartment. Patrizia is in her sixties, but has the energy of an eight-year-old girl, flitting around in a black mini-skirt and vest that's embroidered with flowers, Alpine style. Her airy apartment is decorated with folksy touches: marionettes, framed needlework pieces, and a wood burning stove. Right off the kitchen is a terrace, where students dine in warmer months, enjoying a lovely view, with the steeple of San Marco in the background.

Patrizia typically designs the menu herself, based on what's in season, but when I booked the class I asked if I could learn to make one of my favorite Venetian specialties: *sarde in saor*. It's a traditional dish of fried sardines marinated in onions, vinegar, and sugar, resulting in an intense, savory flavor. Marinating it for at least a few days is essential to the recipe.

Chef Patrizia pulls out a surprise: A *sarde in saor* she made a few days ago, so I could taste her proper rendition, and then shows me another version she's made: *verdure in saor*, where sardines are replaced with sautéed zucchini, potatoes, eggplant, and peppers.

"We make both so you learn, but first we start with my dessert— my invention!" Patrizia says. It's a brilliant mix of mascarpone, sugar, cocoa, and raisins soaked in grappa (the signature liqueur of the Veneto region). We set it aside to chill in the refrigerator before the Saor lesson begins.

With four of us women in the kitchen plus spritz refills, talk inevitably turns to men and *amore*, along with lots of laughs.

I get busy gutting sardines and chopping onions, as Patrizia stands by and tells me the *sarde in saor* story: How it originated centuries ago when fisherman would be at sea for weeks at a time and since there was no refrigeration, fisherman's wives invented a way of preserving fish so it would last for their husband's time away from home. In the Renaissance, pine nuts and raisins were added to the recipe, to aid digestion and sweeten the breath.

The kitchen fills with the homey perfume of onions slowly cooking in oil. Patrizia hands me toothpaste to wash my hands, her clever way to take away the fishy smell.

Our work done, we gather at the table set with pretty lace placemats and floral-patterned china. The taste of Patrizia's pre-prepared *sarde in saor* is so much richer and more satisfying than the one I just made. We toast with Venetian wine, a lively, white Tocai. The lunch ends sweetly with Patrizia's dessert invention, then caffe, "corrected," as the Italians say, with a few drops of grappa.

We linger at the table, in a delightful, well-fed haze, as the afternoon light fades...

**Cooking with Chef Patrizia**: Contact The International Kitchen (www.theinternationalkitchen.com), a company that offers classes all over Italy.

## RECOMMENDED READING

*Polpo, A Venetian Cookbook (Of Sorts)* by Russell Norman

# 78 Cooking in Milano

IT'S A CHILLY GRAY MORNING IN MILAN, but the moment teacher/chef Clara Raimondi opens her apartment door, my world warms up. There's Clara's welcoming smile and one of life's most comforting aromas: meat broth cooking. Thus, the lesson begins: "That broth is one of the secrets of risotto," Clara says, "I started making it at seven this morning."

This friendly, easy-going, yet precise manner is the signature style of **Cook in Milano**, Clara's company that offers cooking classes and wine seminars in her gracious home near Milan's city center. Clara is a classic Milanese woman—exuding elegance even in a simple chef's jacket and slacks. Her English is perfect, which she credits to spending a year in New York as a high school exchange student. Now she's in her forties, married, and the mother of two teenage boys, happy to be sharing her culinary passions and expertise with students from all over the world, who are either visiting or living in her native city.

The class seamlessly blends her chic business-like manner with deeply rooted family traditions. "It all started with my nonna," she says, pointing out her kitchen window to a terrace nearby, where nonna lived. "She was a great cook, and I loved spending time with her in the kitchen." Though a variety of classes are offered, I've come to learn Milanese specialties—specifically the secrets of one of my favorite Italian dishes: Risotto alla Milanese.

"There are three essential rules to make a great risotto," Clara begins: "First is the meat broth, which must be made that morning or the day before. Second is the marrow, which you scoop from one of the shins, and melt with the butter to start the risotto process. And finally, you must use carnaroli rice." She explains how carnaroli has a higher starch content than other rices, so it can absorb more liquid, and its long grains remain separate when cooked—in contrast to such sticky rice varieties as those used for sushi.

Clara's hands-on class is delightful, with all of us assigned different tasks, which she oversees, pausing for coffee and prosecco breaks as we create a northern Italian meal. Along with the risotto, appetizers, and dessert, we make another Milanese classic—*ossibuchi* (braised veal shanks), which we sauce with *gremolada*—a savory anchovy/parsley/lemon mixture.

Halfway through stirring the risotto, we add saffron powder, and a distinctive yellow color emerges. The story goes that this Milanese touch was inspired by a sixteenth-century Belgian master glazer, who was working on the stained glass windows of the Duomo. He became famous for using saffron to create golden colors. When his daughter was married in 1574, as a joke, his apprentices made a dish of rice colored with saffron for the celebration. Apparently it was a hit with the wedding guests, and Milanese have loved it ever since.

As we take our final risotto step, *mantecatura*—swirling in butter and cheese after the risotto has been removed from the heat—it feels as though we're making magic.

We sit at the dining table, beautifully set with linens embroidered by Clara's mother. She pours Barolo wine, we toast, and there's a silence as we take our first bites…followed by sighs of pleasure. Together we've created a classic, delicious lunch…*alla Milanese*.

## TOURS

**Cook in Milano** (www.cookinmilano.com) offers one- and multiple-day cooking classes and wine seminars.

# 79 Tuscan Women Cook–Montefollonico, Tuscany

IF YOU ASK AN ITALIAN "WHO'S YOUR FAVORITE COOK?" the inevitable answer is: "My mamma." When Bill and Patty Sutherland, charming Texans, came to the village of Montefollonico in Tuscany's Val D'Orcia in the 1980s, they fell in love with the place, and discovered that the best cooking indeed was to be found in the homes of local mammas. This inspired them to create **Tuscan Women Cook** in 2001, a school where the mammas are the teachers. Guests learn family traditions from them, and are treated to visits to winemakers, artisans, nearby villages, and fabulous local restaurants. It adds up to a week that fulfills every aspect of a traveler's *Under the Tuscan Sun* fantasy.

Over the years, **Tuscan Women Cook** has flourished. I've returned many times, and so has Rhonda Vilardo, who now hosts the program with Coleen Kinan Friedmann, two women from Los Angeles who bring their passion for Tuscany and its *mammas* to continue what the Sutherlands began.

Local signora cooks range in style from the classic Isa, who teaches students how to roll *pici*, the thick spaghetti specialty of southern Tuscany, to Dania Masati, a flirty blonde who flits about in stiletto heels and Prada ensembles like an Italian movie starlet. Dania's a Michelin-starred chef and cookbook author who owns and operates **La Chiusa**, a luxury hotel and restaurant that was once an olive press. She takes you strolling through her herb garden and then back to her restaurant's kitchen where you'll learn to prepare her signature exquisite *ragu*. Rounding out the group are the Bernadini *signore*, three generations of women who run a nearby hilltop agriturismo, where just picked vegetables are used in class, and delicious pizzas are cooked in their outdoor wood burning ovens.

The Montefollonico location is ideal: smack in the middle of the Chiana Valley, where rolling hills of olive groves and vineyards present a landscape right out of the Florence galleries. Along with morning classes followed by lunch, there are visits to Pienza, Montepulciano, the spa town of Bagno Vignoni, a full-day excursion to Siena on its market day, and a tasting with Flavio Andreucci, one of the region's most good-looking winemakers.

Dinners are relaxed affairs that stretch late into the evenings, at restaurants where the bounty of the surrounding farmlands is transformed to flavorful dishes—from simple grilled Chiana beef to rich duck spiced with wild fennel.

You stay at **La Chiusa** (www.ristorantelachiusa.it), where each of the fifteen rooms is uniquely designed and furnished with antiques. Fragrant lavender borders the breakfast terrace, where you'll be mesmerized by the view of the hilltop town of Montepulciano in the distance.

The two-*via* village of Montefollonico (population 700), where the school is based, is so enchanting you may want to extend your stay after classes are over. This is the kind of place where faces become familiar after only a few days, *barista* Ernestina at the caffe will remember your morning order after just one visit, and you'll be greeted with cordial *buona seras* by the *signoras* who gossip on stone benches in the tiny village square.

## TOURS

**Tuscan Women Cook** (www.tuscanwomencook.com): Programs
run May–October.

## RECOMMENDED READING

*The English Patient* by Michael Ondaatje
*Under the Tuscan Sun* by Frances Mayes
*War in Val D'Orcia* by Iris Origo

# 80 Mamma Agata Cooking School—Ravello

IN ITALY I OFTEN FIND MYSELF GUSHING, "Life is beautiful!" But in Ravello, high above the Amalfi Coast, the gushing gets elevated to "Life is more beautiful!" The sky is bluer. The sea more sparkly. The horizon more hypnotic. The tomatoes more delicious.

It's fitting that in such a divine spot there lives a Goddess of Amalfi Coast Cooking: Mamma Agata. She's an irresistibly adorable woman—pleasingly plump, with twinkling, almond-shaped eyes. Her smile warms my heart. She's been cooking for most of her eighty-some years, and to watch her move around a stove is simply marvelous.

This one-day Mamma Agata Cooking Class takes place at her home: an eighteenth-century villa, surrounded by terraced gardens, perched on a cliff with a to-die-for view of the sea. Chiara Lima, Mamma's daughter, is the gracious mastermind behind the whole operation.

Chiara even turned my traveling pal Carol and me on to fantastic digs nearby at the **Villa Scarpariello** (www.villascarpariellorelais. it). It's an amazing mix of old buildings, and a tower from the twelfth century, hidden in a seaside nitch. It feels like a well-kept secret, but here I go blabbing about it, because that's the way I am. Each balconied suite of rooms is unique, and many have kitchens, so it's a temptation to check in for a week and just bliss out. One of the many zigzags of stone steps on the property took me right down to the water for a refreshing before-school swim.

Class at Mamma Agata's begins with lemon cake and coffee. "It was Humphrey Bogart's favorite," Chiara tells us. When Agata was thirteen, she began her pro-career working in the Ravello villa of a wealthy American woman who entertained star visitors. "Baby Agata" was what Bogey called her, and he wasn't the only one among the glitterati who was wowed by her cooking. Agata has great stories about making *pasta e fagioli* for Anita Ekberg, *spaghetti alla puttanesca* for Fred Astaire, and *insalata Caprese* for Jacqueline Kennedy. "Jackie was Mamma's favorite," Chiara says. "She always talks about how she was a real lady; so kind she'd even insist on washing her own coffee cup." The lemon cake is phenomenal. And eating it out on the terrace surrounded by the very trees where the lemons came from makes it all the more delicious.

The class is mostly demonstration. Twelve of us students are gathered in the tiny kitchen, with Agata at the stove, joined by Chiara's husband, sommelier Gennaro, who brings many years cooking at top kitchens to the mix, as Chiara narrates. Practically every ingredient is what's grown right here in the gardens. There's rolled eggplant appetizers, eggplant parmigiana, pappardelle with sausage and peppers, and lemon chicken. We get tastes of fresh tomato sauce, sniffs of just-picked basil, as Chiara tells us Mamma's "secret techniques." This is simple cooking—it's the details that make it divine. "Listen to the sound of that sizzle, that's when you know the garlic is ready, now's when you put in the tomatoes for the sauce" says Chiara. She's printed out all the recipes for us in a glossy handout and CD, so we don't even have to take notes. We can just sip wine and watch the master at work.

It's delicious fun. We take breaks to walk around the gardens with all of us *ooh*ing and *aah*ing over the paradise we are in.

After three hours, we take our places at a long, wooden table on the terrace. Lovely *signorine* magically appear with platters and pans of everything we've watched Mamma have her hands in. The sun streams through the pergola. More than one of us says, "This is the best lunch I've ever had."

For the grand finale, Agata comes out with her exquisite home-made limoncello. The day has gone along like a song.

I can't resist giving Agata a hug goodbye. My arms don't reach all the way around. She tilts her cheek to me for a kiss. "*Grazie, grazie, grazie,*" is all I can whisper to her smiling face, again and again and again. I don't hold back. I am in Ravello, after all, where everything is elevated.

## TOURS

**Mamma Agata Cooking School** (www.mammaagata.com) offers cooking classes, and can arrange private dinners or even a wedding party. Check the website for the shop that sells Mamma Agata's Signature Products, including pasta, olive oil, and limoncello.

## RECOMMENDED READING

*Simple and Genuine: Recipes of Mamma Agata* by Chiara Lima

# 81 Cooking in Tropea– Calabria

WITH HER MOM JEANS AND GOLD MADONNA on a chain swinging between her breasts, Marianna Giuditta reminds me of mothers I grew up around in my New Jersey neighborhood. It makes sense, since so many of them were descendants of folks from Calabria, this region in the toe of Italy's boot. Marianna even moves around the kitchen like they did—a tigress going in for the kill.

"The pig is the meat of Calabria," she tells me, hacking away at a chunk of pork and tossing big fatty pieces of it into a pot to start off her *sugo Calabrese*.

Cooking in Tropea is taking the straight shot into the rustic, generous spirit of the region, that's under the tourist radar.

The program was created by Tania Pascuzzi, an Australian-Italian whose parents were born in Calabria and then emigrated to Melbourne. Tania, who grew up around delicious Calabrian food, came to live in Tropea after fourteen years of high-pressure work as a New York stylist. She's a sophisticated woman in her forties, the type who looks chic even when she's wearing faded jeans.

Tropea is a beautiful school base. It juts out above the sea, a jumble of crumbling sandstone baroque buildings, tiny piazzas that look like opera sets. I'm staying in a seventeenth-century renovated palazzo, right off the main square. Inside is a modern surprise: a spacious suite, sleekly designed, with filmy taupe curtains and balconies where I can overlook the action in the piazza below.

The cooking program includes a food tour of Tropea, where with Tania by my side, everyone treats me like I'm part of *la famiglia*. This is hot red pepper territory. They're dried and tied up in garlands all over the place. They're minced up and made into *n'duja*, a spread that sizzles on the tongue or has me choking and gasping, depending on intensity.

"It's so much more than a cooking school," says Nicole Gait, a New Yorker, who went on the adventure with her husband. "The week was about becoming a part of this authentic community, an experience we never would have had without Tania's guidance."

Guests rave about how Tania customizes their experiences to match their desires and the changing seasons. Along with cooking classes, she can add mushroom hunts, visits to festivals or award winning wineries, guided hikes by the seaside or in the mountains, and painting classes. All is set up at a leisurely pace, so there's time to relax on Tropea's beaches, which are praised as some of the best in Italy. Tania also offers genealogy tours, so visitors can be escorted to villages where their ancestors came from, find their relatives names in record books, and visit hidden cemeteries.

The coastline offers beautiful opportunities for boating excursions with Tania's friend Francesco, who takes guests on fishing expeditions, dropping anchor at choice spots where they can swim or snorkel. Francesco doubles as a chef, and will cook up the catch-of-the-day right on board, for a memorable lunch.

Classes take place in home kitchens, with local bakers, butchers, and *mammas* who teach students how to make Calabria's specialty pasta—*fileja*—a shape similar to *cavatelli*, or what Calabrian Moms in New Jersey called *"gava-deels."*

An evening class at the agriturismo of Pepe and Vera is a beloved highlight, where the whole family, including their two children, join in. As the sun sets, students stroll around the farm, picking grapes from the vineyards, sample freshly pressed olive oils and honey, and make meals using Tropea's prized red onions, which thrive in the fields. The outdoor table amidst all this beauty is lit with candles, as course after course is served. And don't be surprised if strolling musicians appear to bring even more heart and soul to the delicious experience.

## TOUR

**In Italy Tours** (www.initalytours.com) offers cooking classes in Tropea, throughout Calabria, and on a private yacht while circling the Aeolian Islands. In addition are excellent classes in the **Castelli Romani**, hilltop villages near Rome.

## RECOMMENDED READING

*Cucina di Calabria: Treasured Recipes and Family Traditions from Southern Italy* by Mary A. Palmer

*My Calabria: Rustic Family Cooking from Italy's Undiscovered South* by Rosetta Costantino with Janet Fletcher

# X Learn Italian Crafts and Culture

Becoming a student instead of a tourist in Italy pulls you in closer to her. It gives you the chance to immerse yourself deeper into the culture and pursue a particular passion while you're at it.

While for decades there have been lots of language schools to choose from all over the country, these days more and more art workshops are being created. They are headed up by pros who teach using the age-old master-apprentice model. Here's where you can roll up your sleeves and take time to learn one of Italy's traditional handicrafts, such as mosaics or ceramics. Classes are open to beginners, who simply want to explore their creative side, or advanced artists, who want to get to the source—the place where the art form that's captured their enthusiasm all began.

You may be amazed at how relaxing these experiences are. Italy can be overwhelming, so when you focus on one of its aspects, it's less so. Instead of flitting from place to place with your guidebook and map, you are rooted in a fascinating environment, where your creative side can flow.

An additional wonderful thing about the workshops is that you'll be spending time in Italy with others who share your passion. The built-in creative community is perfect for a solo traveler and often leads to lifelong friendships.

Once you open the door to the idea, possibilities flow...

# 82 *Mosaics at Cassio Workshop—Rome*

I'M WEARING GOGGLES, AND HAVE A SHARP HAMMER poised in one hand, while the other steadies a small piece of white stone on a metal pedestal. I'm setting it up just right to strike and split the stone.

My teacher Uliana just demonstrated what looked like a simple move. She did it a few times, perfectly creating tiny tiles, what the Romans named *tesserae,* that are used to make mosaics. Now it's my turn to try. I feel the gut-clenching *I'm going to smash my thumb* fear, as I lower down the hammer. *Doh!* My move just chips the stone instead of splitting it. "Try again," Uliana says, smiling. More vain attempts follow until, miraculously, I hit with just the right stroke and force, and the stone cleanly breaks in two. It's a *ta-da* moment.

I'm feeling my way through this morning mosaic-making class at **Studio Cassio**, in Rome's Monti Rione. This area, between the Colosseum and Santa Maria Maggiore Basilica, is a working-class-turning-trendy neighborhood, with vintage stores, artisan workshops, and the lovely Piazza della Madonna Monti, where *mammas* hang out by the fountain with their baby strollers. Narrow cobblestoned *vias* flanked by ivy covered stone buildings create such a perfect atmosphere that Woody Allen chose it to film scenes from *To Rome With Love.*

The mosaics studio is run by the Cassio family, master mosaic artisans in Rome for three generations. It began a hundred years ago with Lorenzo, who directed the Vatican Mosaic Studio. Uliana tells me that Lorenzo was so passionate about the work, that he required his eight children to complete one mosaic every day while they were growing up.

Lorenzo's son Antonio founded this Monti workshop in 1945, and the business flourished as he and his crew decorated and restored hundreds of Rome's churches, private villas, and monumental sites such as Pompeii and the Baths of Caracalla. They also expanded their work to international projects, including the circular "Imagine" mosaic that's the centerpiece of John Lennon's memorial in Central Park, a place I visit on every trip to New York. It's a thrill to look through a photo album that Uliana pulls out, seeing Antonio in the 1980s standing over a circular patch of dirt in the park, and the mosaic being installed step-by-step.

I choose a decorative swirly pattern and with black and white *tesserae* begin my work with tweezer-like-tools, putting together the small puzzle with the stones I'd split. At the next table is a much more experienced *signora*, working on an intricate portrait of Pope Francis, with richly colored *tessarae*, as Uliana leans over, coaching her along.

It's about following lines, paying close attention to the subtle difference in the stones' shapes to choose which will make the best fit for the design. There are stones all around me—overflowing out of drawers and cloth bags and on my work table. Uliana tells me that restoration work was once done by bringing the pieces that were to be repaired to this studio, but now by law the restoration has to be done on site, using pieces of the original. The stones I'm using are from the stash left over from the old days—2,000-year-old pieces that were part of mosaics in Pompeii or the Vatican.

As my swirl begins to take shape, I'm imagining the crews that worked hundreds of years ago, decorating the Rome church interiors I love—the dazzling Santa Maria in Trastevere, circular patterned floors of Santa Maria in Cosmedin. My hands move as theirs did, breaking stones apart to carefully put them in a new order. There's a profound satisfaction in doing this *tesserae* by *tesserae* until the design emerges.

No thumbs were smashed during the making of my mosaic. Uliana boxes it up and I tuck it into my purse. I head out, enlightened, seeing every mosaic from this workshop on with a new appreciation of all those hands of the past, who broke stones to put them together and create awe-inspiring beauty.

**Studio Cassio:** Via Urbana, 98-98a, studiocassio.com
Courses range from half day (2.5 hours) to three-day immersions, with options to follow ancient patterns or make self-portraits.

# 83 *Florentine Crafts*

WITH SO MANY WONDERFUL ARTISANS IN FLORENCE, there are lots of opportunities for you to become an apprentice to a master, joining in on traditions of craftsmanship that have been practiced here for centuries. You can sign on for a few hours, immerse yourself in the hands-on experience for weeks, or as long as you wish.

Some suggestions:

## Leathermaking at Scuola del Cuoio

A morning at **Scuola del Cuoio** taught me the true meaning of "tough as leather." Compared to the journal cover I labored over at the *scuola* in the morning, a bad *bistecca* is a cinch to cut. The challenge of experiencing just a little of what it takes to make all these items marked **Handmade Leather** I see all over Florence gave me a whole new respect for the price tags. And I forever thank master Carlo, Papa Patience, who guided me every step of the way, through a class that ended with a souvenir journal that brings back fond memories of Florence.

The *scuola* is in a former Renaissance monastery, tucked behind the Santa Croce church, in an area where leathermaking in Florence began hundreds of years ago. In 1950, the Gori family established the property as an artisans' school for boys who'd been orphaned after World War II. The goal was to teach them a trade so they could earn a practical living. The Goris teamed up with Franciscan friars to create the *scuola*, turning the monk's dormitories, that were built by the Medici in the fifteenth century, into a workshop. The upstairs section, open to visitors, is a gorgeous fresco-lined hall, where senior artisans at old-fashioned wooden workstations turn out some of the best handcrafted leather to be found in Florence. The descendants of the founder—three elegant Gori daughters and a grandson—expertly run the place.

Downstairs is the *scuola*, where my lesson took place, amidst pros and some other students. Across the room from me were two happy American gals, here for a longer program, who were turning out adorable purses.

Once I got the slowed-down pace of the process, I fell into my hours there, with *pazienza, pazienza, pazienza*. Cutting the leather was the hardest, and then Carlo took me through each step that followed, with exacting instructions for folding, pressing, hammering holes along the border.

After the days I'd spent running around Florence, looking at stupendous masterpieces, this detailed work took me into another dimension. As I sat there, focused on pulling one thin strip of leather through tiny holes of the journal cover to make a braided edge, I gave into "leathercrafting" time. The room had an overwhelming scale of aromas—from the deep smell of leather to top notes of nose-tingling glue. Church bells rang. It was simply divine to be there.

Carlo filled my finished journal with fine blank Florentine paper, then escorted me to an upstairs workbench where Bosco, a venerable, bald-headed artisan, performed his magic over it—with egg white, a flame, and twenty-two-carat gold. He handed it back to me, transformed: with my embossed initials in gold—a lasting reward for hours of *pazienza, pazienza, pazienza*.

**Scuola del Cuoio**: Piazza di Santa Croce 16, 055 244 533, www. scuoladelcuoio.com. Half-day, full-day, three-month, and six-month courses.

## Jewel on the Arno/Jewelry Courses in Florence

Ken Scott, originally from New Zealand, is an artisan who has worked for major jewelry companies in Florence for fourteen years. He has also branched out on his own, creating an exquisite jewelry line, and teaches the craft at Florence's prestigious professional institutions. Recently he opened his own workshop/school, in a well-equipped studio, where students can come for programs of various lengths, learn about the history of jewelry making in Florence, and receive individual attention according to their level.

As Ken puts it: "The purpose is not to learn just how to make jewelry, but how to become a jeweler." He's praised by his students for his great sense of humor and expert guidance.

**Jewel on the Arno,** Via Guelfa 85, www.kenscottdesign.com. Two-week, four-week, and twelve-week courses are available for beginners, intermediate and advanced learners.

## Ceramic Workshop, Sbigoli Terrecotte

Right near the Duomo is my favorite Florence ceramic shop, which originated in 1857, and has been run by the Adami family for the past fifty years. Shelves display beautiful hand painted tableware and urns, with traditional Renaissance designs, countryside scenes, and contemporary patterns. The artistic force that began it all is Antonella Adami, now in her eighties, who followed in the footsteps of her famous ceramicist father, and continues to paint ceramics to this day. She inspired her daughter Lorenza to carry on the tradition, and you will find Lorenza (recently awarded Maestro Artigiano) in the shop's back workshop, where classes are held.

Spending time here is not only slipping into tradition, but also being surrounded by the graciousness of the Adami family. Daughter Chiara, who handles the shop business, also assists in the classes, and with Lorenza sets the tone for a relaxing, creative time. My women's tour in Florence includes a painting morning here, and it's a joy to don our smocks, choose a pattern for a plate, and get to work with brushes and pigments, learning as we go from the experts. The plates are fired and a few days later arrive shiny and bubble-wrapped at our hotel, to tuck into our luggage, and display proudly in our homes.

**Sbigoli Terrecotte,** Via Sant'Egidio 4/r, www.sbigoliterrecotte.it. Workshops for individuals or groups can be arranged by appointment.

# 84 *Maskmaking at Tragicomica—Venice*

AFTER DAYS OF MUSEUM-MUSEUM-MUSEUM, Sandy Osceola and her two daughters needed to step off the tourist treadmill. So they stepped into the **Tragicomica** workshop, spending a morning decorating masks. It turned out to be a highlight of their vacation. Not only was it great fun to be together painting and gluing on feathers and sequins, but they also got an entertaining art history lesson while they were at it.

Tragicomica is one of the finest spots in Venice to pick up traditional masks, and rent hats, sumptuous ball gowns and capes for Carnevale. The store is packed with these fantasy-inspiring goodies, and a wonderful place to browse even if you're not heading to the back for the workshop.

Gualtiero Dall'Osto is Tragicomica's master maskmaker, following in the footsteps of artists who began dressing up Venetian partiers in the thirteenth century. His creations have been exhibited internationally, and he's designed costumes and set pieces for theaters all over Italy, including La Scala in Milan.

In the 1970s Dall'Osto was one of a group who fought successfully to bring back the Venice Carnevale that Mussolini had put an end to in the 1930s. The traditional pre-Lent party began in Venice in the twelfth century. It was named Carnevale from the Latin for "Farewell meat!" because the forty days before Easter were days of abstinence.

Masks were initially worn only during Carnevale. But then came the wild eighteenth-century era. With rascally guys like Casanova running around, being in disguise all year long had its advantages. Fellas who were in debt could wear a mask to gambling rooms and play undiscovered by creditors. Married gals could slip away for romantic trysts without damaging their reputations. Ultimately the government stepped in and banned mask-wearing except for Carnevale, as they felt things with the citizenry were getting way out of control.

The Osceola's three-hour workshop kicked off with an entertaining demonstration by Dall'Osto's assistant, Alessandra. Putting on masks, she showed how each one has a story behind it, corresponding to a Commedia dell'Arte character or a bit of Venetian history. Next came a demonstration of how papier—mâché is molded on to forms for the first stage of the mask-making process.

Sandy and her daughters picked out blank masks to decorate and got to work in the backroom, right where expert artisans turn out the pretty things that fill the shop. Sandy chose a Medico della Peste, the Plague Doctor mold. That's the one you've seen in so many photos, with the long-beak-shaped nose and tiny eyeholes. It originated in the sixteenth century when doctors would stuff the nose with a sponge soaked in vinegar, so they could move plague victims around and be protected from the disease. Sandy's daughters, Jessica (21) and Marissa (12), went for styles that they decorated with paints and sequins to look as though they could be eighteenth-century ladies on their way to a Carnevale ball.

By lunchtime they had three one-of-a-kind souvenirs. Now back at home, the masks bring back great memories of the trip the Osceolas took to celebrate Jessica's graduation from college. Moreover, they'll always remind them of the entertaining spirit that pervades the unique city of Venice.

**Tragicomica:** Calle dei Nomboli, off Campo San Toma in San Polo, 041 721102, www.tragicomica.it.

---

### TOUR

**European Connection** (www.europeanconnection.com) arranges maskmaking classes and is an excellent company that custom-designs itineraries for trips throughout Italy.

# 85 *International School of Ceramic Art— Deruta, Umbria*

"EVEN SOMEONE WHO'S NEVER PICKED UP a paintbrush can spend a little time here and come away with something beautiful," Florence Welborn told me. She's a retired schoolteacher from Tacoma and self-described "arts and crafts person." Florence and her husband fell in love with Italy, bought a place in Umbria, and every time they have visitors, this Deruta school is on the itinerary. What great hosts.

The class set-up here is freeform and casual. Which is surprising, because the school building is also a major ceramics institution (opened in 2001), with lecture halls, galleries, a retail shop, and professional workshop. But as far as ceramic painting classes, anyone can just call or e-mail a day in advance, make a reservation for a few hours (at least four is good for a beginner), and get one-on-one tutoring to learn traditional techniques that have been going on here since the Renaissance.

If you're a beginner, you choose what design you'd like to paint from a selection of tiles, and then you're set up at a worktable with all the supplies you need, including a blank tile that's stamped with the design. It's like paint-by-number.

Well, not that easy. Which is where the one-on-one tutoring comes in and you're taught how to mix the paints, and hold the brush, which is different for ceramics than it is for painting on canvas.

Here's the important thing: when you make your reservation for class, if you don't speak Italian, be sure to confirm that there will be an English-speaking teacher on hand. A favorite English-speaking instructor is Nicola Boccini, an international art star, not only expert with traditional designs, but he also paints ceramics in a modern style that's critically acclaimed.

The school was founded by Romano Ranieri, a world-renowned ceramic painter and teacher, whose masterpieces sell for high prices and are in museums around the world. Despite his mega success, he's a humble sort who's been teaching and painting for fifty years. You'll definitely see him here—he's that artsy looking gentleman with the shoulder-length salt-and-pepper hair, passionately working on some incredible project. Inevitably, hawk-eyed teacher that he is, he'll break away from his painting to stand over your shoulder and give you advice if he sees you straying in the least.

You can also take classes in pottery making, like Ekta Nadeau did after she saw a You Tube video of Nicola working at a wheel. The video inspired her to travel from Vancouver to Deruta to learn his technique. She set her trip up so she spent a few days throwing pottery Italian style, then left to tour around for a week, so by the time she came back her pots and jars had been fired. Then, with the help of Maestro Ranieri, she chose a pattern that was just right for their shape and stayed a few days to learn ceramic painting. Recently the school added classes in porcelain jewelry, ceramic prototype and printing, and special ceramic techniques for designers and architects.

The big perk of being in Deruta is that right out the door are hundreds of artisan shops and a ceramics museum, so you get an education just walking around.

The school will give you lots of recommendations for accommodations nearby, from apartments to B&Bs. Gina Garner, who's been here twice for classes, usually stays at the **Hotel Melody**, a simple three-star, which she says is "Great, as long as you don't eat there!"

Deruta's a very relaxing place to stroll about, especially when you're feeling so artsy. The natives, accustomed to visitors, are warm and welcoming. The same goes for the staff at the school. Don't be surprised if Floriana Spaccini, the *scuola* president, stops by with a tray of *caffè* and *biscotti*. Yes, they're for you. Put down your paintbrush and take a little *pausa*.

**International School of Ceramic Art "Romano Ranieri,"** Via Tiberina Sud 330, Deruta, 075 972 383, www.scuoladarteceramica.com.

# 86 Landscape Painting— Buonconvento, Tuscany

IMAGINE STANDING ON A TUSCAN HILLSIDE, looking out over a vineyard, with that gorgeous golden light all around. Instead of gasping at the view for a few moments, you're at an easel for a couple of quiet hours, capturing it with your brush and paints. The light changes. A gentle breeze blows through carrying the smell of earth, lavender, grass. Birds twitter. There may be butterflies.

Landscape painters Maddine Insalaco and Joe Vinson run workshops where this is how it goes for a whole week. O.K., the reality is maybe it'll rain and they'll set up a tarp overhead to cover you. There will also be lunch breaks in the shade, where Maddine, who's an expert cook as well as painter, mixes up what she's got fresh from the local market into a delicious meal. You'll have a glass of wine and take a break with your fellow painters, then it's back to the easel, so you're painting as the sun sets.

The goal of these workshops is to give beginners to advanced painters a rigorous, focused experience of the open-air style of painting, called *plein air*. The tradition of artists coming to Italy to paint outdoors goes back to the eighteenth century, when painters from France and England traveled to Rome to see Renaissance masterpieces. They were amazed by the countryside surrounding the Eternal City—the light, rolling hills, and architectural ruins. They lugged their easels out there, developing new techniques to capture these scenes, working quickly and spontaneously. It was a liberating experience, in contrast to working in a studio. Camille Corot's landscape paintings from this time paved the way to Impressionism.

Maddine and Joe follow in the footsteps of this tradition and are passionate about the form. They've been landscape painters for thirty years and their work is shown in American and Italian galleries. They're also passionate about Italy, and divide their time between an apartment in New York and a place in Buonconvento (southern Tuscany). Workshops are based in Buonconvento for beginners, and advanced lessons are given in Murlo, (south of Siena), and Civita Castellana, (north of Rome). In each location, students get Maddine and Joe's enthusiastic, expert instruction as they paint, along with the joy of being integrated into the local scene.

"What was so wonderful is that everything was taken care of—the only decision I had to make all week was what to paint and what colors to use," said Voni Schaff, a student from Minnesota. Voni had studied art in college, then put it aside for thirty years while she brought up four children. The week in Tuscany was a kick start for her to pick up where she left off. It turned out to be amazingly productive—she went home with a suitcase full of paintings and liked it so much she returned for a second time.

"Spending a week there is equivalent to a semester in a college art course," said Rachel Newman, who went to her first workshop with no experience, hoping it would help heal a heartbreak. She's since returned every year. The heartbreak is long behind her, and she's had gallery shows of her paintings.

The program is an art-high week, where you'll be painting for a total of around fifty hours. Maddine and Joe intensely focus on giving detailed, basic instruction and encouragement for everyone to paint according to their own style. "They're not making clones of themselves," said Elizabeth Garat, an artist from Tennessee, who has worked as a studio painter for many years and loved learning new outdoor painting techniques.

The focus is all about being connected to nature and responding to it with your brush and colors. At the end of each day, students' paintings are displayed and a critiquing session follows. "It's not just patting on the back," said Elizabeth, "It's honest, specific, constructive, and encouraging."

An art teacher once told Maddine that landscape painters were the happiest people he knew. Maddine and her students understand why. There's something quite wonderful spending the day outside, especially in the Italian countryside. Add to that the great satisfaction of quick creation, learning something new, and the camaraderie that naturally evolves in the group.

In the evenings, you'll find yourself sitting in a cozy restaurant, still in your painting clothes, drinking wine and talking late into the night about art, naturally.

**Landscape Painting:** Workshops are held from May through October (www.landscapepainting.com). The program includes most materials, accommodations in beautiful locations, meals, slide-show lectures, museum visits, and canvases small enough to fit in your suitcase. Optional cooking classes are also available. Enrollment is limited to twelve students.

### RECOMMENDED READING

*Seasons in Basilicata: A Year in a Southern Italian Hill Village* (written and illustrated) by David Yeadon

# 87 Giuditta Brozzetti Weaving and Embroidery Workshop—Perugia, Umbria

I LOVE THE SOUNDS IN THIS CHURCH CLASSROOM. I'm not talking bells or heavenly choirs. It's the clickety-clack of wooden looms. It's a calm, rhythmic beat that echoes softly through the vast gothic **San Francesco delle Donne**, The Women's Church of Saint Francis. The building was turned from a holy place into a weaving workshop in the nineteenth century when 300 women had jobs here.

Now that craft tradition is beautifully preserved. Pale light filters through big curved gracious windows onto nine looms. In the space that was once an altar, round tables are draped with enticing creations for sale—royal blue, gold, and red patterned cloths. Their designs are callbacks to medieval times—grape leaves and that mythological griffon (half-bird, half-lion) that's the symbol of Perugia. On another table delicately embroidered pieces add a light, elegant touch.

This is an extraordinary place to stop by and browse around even if you aren't taking a class. You could even take a guided tour or spend some time at a simple loom to get a feel for how to work the threads as you pedal, like I did. *It's not easy!* Nearby is the **Perugia Duomo**, where the BVM's wedding ring is enshrined and from there you have the whole charming mix of Perugia's cobblestoned streets lined with designer and artisan's shops.

If you have a day or a week to sign up for a workshop, a step-back-in-time experience awaits. You'll be learning to weave on simple shaft looms and then Jacquard looms, all built over a hundred years ago, that are scrupulously maintained here.

"I was in awe to be experiencing this small part of Italy's history—to be a part of that continuity," said June Rogovin, a student from California who's been hand weaving for twenty years. "The teachers were so welcoming and patient, it was absolutely humbling at times."

The Brozzetti workshop began in 1921 when Giuditta Brozzetti, who was the headmaster of Perugia's elementary schools, was riding around in her horse and carriage and heard that clickety-clack sound coming from the looms of surrounding farmhouses. Weaving had begun in Perugia in the twelfth century, when the town became a textile-making center, turning out table coverings that were renowned all over Europe. Giuditta decided to open a workshop not only to preserve the handicraft that was dwindling away because of the Industrial Revolution, but also to give women jobs so they could become financially independent.

Now Giuditta's molto-chic great-granddaughter Marta teaches the weaving classes. Marta (also an interior designer) is the only one around who knows how to repair those antique looms. In addition, she's an extraordinary weaver, who recreates designs from medieval paintings, where those famous Perugia tablecloths are featured.

Marta's seminars and one-week classes include lectures on the history of hand-weaving and there is an option to visit the nearby Citta di Castello, for a look at the Tela Umbra studio, to see a different style of weaving. The studio was created from the same inspiration as Brozzetti, to preserve the tradition and give women jobs. And since those women had children, Maria Montessori was brought in to open up a classroom that became her first training ground for teachers.

If you'd like to learn lacemaking and embroidery, classes with Lina Montagnoli, who has been at it for fifty years, can be arranged. She is a maternal and meticulous teacher, who can go simple for beginners or teach intricate medieval designs to the more advanced. When local women show up to her classes, she says, "They see it as group anti-stress therapy."

**Giuditta Brozzetti**: Via Tiberio Berardi 5/6, 075 40236, www.brozzetti.com. Classes are held June through September, one-day seminars or one-week workshops.

## TOURS

**Bella Vista Tours** (www.bellavistatours.com) arranges group artisan workshops here and throughout Italy.

# 88 Art Restoration Workshops—Puglia

*"I am in Italy, working under a hot mid-day sun, in a subterranean world of Byzantine adorned frescos. I am lovingly and painstakingly restoring them to their former glory."*

Canadian artist Jennifer Bell tells me she imagines this would be the opening of her *Eat, Pray, Love*-style memoir. In 1994 she heard about a volunteer restoration project in Puglia. It sounded like the perfect adventure for a solo traveler—a chance to really immerse herself with the locals, learn a new skill, plus she'd be doing some good by taking part in conserving the artistic heritage of the area. Jennifer never imagined that the adventure would unfold into a romance. Twenty years later she's married to the man who founded the project, Tonio Creanza. Together they've grown the organization, running full programs of art restoration workshops that attract international travelers.

"Ninety percent of our participants are women," Jennifer tells me. Time here gives them a chance to connect with the southern Italian culture much more easily than if they were traveling on their own in this under-touristed area. Two- and three-week programs are based at Masseria La Selva, a former eighteenth-century hunting lodge that once belonged to the Roman Orsini family. The property is now a working farm, an hours' drive southwest of Bari. It sits on 500 acres of rolling green hills and olive groves, with sheep, pigs, geese, cows, and a *caseificio* where cheese is made every morning.

The program's founder and director Tonio, along with guest lecturers, expert restorers, and local university students give hands-on instruction at a relaxed pace, and there are no artistic requirements to join in. Participants can spend time restoring frescos in one of the area's many underground natural caves that were used as private places for worship in the fourteenth to sixteenth centuries. In the lab adjoining the *masseria*, students create their own frescos, learning the full process, from making the plaster to crafting natural pigments. Art works from the seventeenth to nineteenth centuries, found in local homes and churches, are also restored in this lab, where participants focus on intricate tasks with scalpels and Q-tips. They are living with history and becoming a part of it.

Combined with these activities and lectures are field trips where they're introduced to archaeologists and restorers in Pompeii, the UNESCO World Heritage Site of Matera, and Frances Ford Coppola's Palazzo Margherita Hotel in Bernalda (Basilicata), which Tonio restored.

Rounding out the rich experience, there's full immersion in Puglia's culinary culture. Wendy Keller, from Los Angeles, tells me how she enjoyed making mozzarella, tasting fresh-pressed olive oil, baking focaccia in a 600-year-old oven in the nearby town of Altamura, and even going out into the fields with a scythe to harvest wheat.

For Michelle Jones, the experience was transformational. She came to the workshop at a point in her life when she was searching for a new career path. She'd worked in the travel business in Canada, then her software engineer husband was transferred to California's Silicon Valley, where she found herself in a holding pattern, waiting for working papers to clear. It was time to try something different, and this workshop beckoned. In the lab making frescos and restoring a 200-year-old painting, her artistic side was reawakened. She's now at Stanford University, working toward a BA in Art History and MA in Museum Studies.

Michelle also fondly recalls the spontaneous, Italian style with which the program was run: "There was a day when we took off to go the beach, and on the way pulled off the road when we saw a tree ripe with apricots, and picked them to have with our lasagna picnic. We built a big bonfire on the beach and Tonio got out his guitar and improvised verses of songs about each of us. That was a while back, and I'm still in contact with the women who were with me on that beach."

Sounds to me like Golden Days await for those who join in.

**Messors, Italy Workshops** (www.messors.com): Offers art restoration, culinary, and shepherding workshops.

# 89 *Italian Language Classes*

"GET AN ITALIAN BOYFRIEND," is what girlfriends tell me is the best way to learn the language. Learning to speak Italian while falling in love is a lot like how a baby makes its first attempts. First it's all about *amore*, then it moves on to basic necessities where you're like a demanding two-year-old, and if things go farther you'll inevitably be expressing feelings, which could lead to anything from a tearful breakup or, in the case of my friend Lisa, a happy marriage and two adorable bi-lingual children.

Going another route, you could follow my friend Louise's lead. She's a card-carrying Italophile and has taken lots of language classes in Italy. For her it's been a good way to take a trip that feels "rooted" and gets her more deeply immersed into the culture. And since she's past the backpacking days of meeting fellow travelers in youth hostels, the classes have the perk of a built-in social scene for those times when she's traveling solo.

If you do an internet search, you'll find schools all over Italy—from Elba to every major city. Most are reasonably priced and have sliding scales of accommodations, so you can stay in a low-priced dorm or private apartment. Italians have become professional in setting these schools up all over, as so many people from all over the world want to learn Italian. As far as accreditation, you may want to check with your local Italian teachers to see if they have any recommendations.

So the question is: *Where to study?* Since it's Italy, every place where there's a school has its charms.

You could break the question down to, "Do I want a village or city school experience?" If you choose a city, as Louise says, "It's like going to a commuter college in America. There's the advantage of having so much interesting culture around you in a place like Rome, but it's going to be a bit more expensive than a village school. And most likely the other students will be running off after class to do their own thing."

If you choose a village, it's like going to college in a small town. There's camaraderie with the other students, and since you'll be in a place where most of the natives don't speak English, it's a good "sink or swim" situation when you're not in class. A middle ground choice would be a town like Siena or Perugia, where you have a lot of cultural activities, but it's a more closely knit community than a major city.

Taking Louise's advice, years ago I went to **Ciao Italia** (www. ciao-italia.it), a small school in Rome, near the Colosseum. They fixed me up with budget accommodations (my own bedroom and bath) in a huge Trastevere apartment, where I was hosted by Antoinella, a half-deaf, seventy-something widow. She insisted on feeding me and I got a kick out of hanging out and watching blaring TV with her just like I'd done back in Jersey with my nana.

My classmates were a writer from Edinburgh who was working on translating Belli (his favorite Roman poet), a thirty-something Venezuelan gal who'd married an Italian and was on a job hunt, and a Japanese chef who worked in an Italian restaurant in Tokyo. This mix of nationalities is typical. "Most of the time I'm the only American at the school," Louise says.

At Ciao Italia the instructors were enthusiastic types, who rode Vespas to work and looked like fashionistas even when they were just wearing jeans and zip-up jackets. The classes were excellent and structured as most schools are: three-hour morning sessions, broken up into grammar and conversation classes, and optional afternoon activities that ranged from cooking classes to a walking tour of the Jewish Ghetto, or watching *Cinema Paradiso* without subtitles.

I loved the two weeks. It was rigorous classwork, but fun. At the same time, there were distractions, like my American-Roman friends who I'd have dinner with and break my "only speak Italian rule." And then the endless sights I'd want to get to or re-visit from past trips, which cut into what I could've gotten from the afternoon programs.

One of Louise's favorite language school experiences was in the small port town of Milazzo, Sicily, where she signed up for a few weeks at **LaboLing** (www.laboling.com). The classes were small, the school had sailboat excursions to the nearby Aeolian Islands, there was a beach to hang out on, and a historic town center that wasn't touristy. Louise now speaks excellent Italian, and she says taking this class really helped to improve it.

Wherever you choose to go, you should have basic Italian 101 under your belt, as most schools teach using the "direct method," with classes totally in Italian. And though there is fun to be had, keep in mind there will be homework.

What's best about taking classes in Italy rather than back home is that the learning curve is speedy. All of a sudden you'll be out in the street, overhearing conversations you can actually understand or having interactions with Italians, using what you've just learned. Ah—those "Eureka!" moments.

# XI

## Be Entertained

While you're often surrounded by tourists in museums and restaurants, if you venture out to a jazz club, puppet show, or concert, you'll be blending in with Italian life. How fantastic to be in the midst of elegantly dressed patrons of the opera, or adorable children cheering at a puppet show. Where's Fellini's camera?

You may want to plan your entertainment in advance (recommended for opera), or there's sure to be something wonderful going on you could just happen upon during your travels.

Italy is also world renowned for its **summer festivals**, which attract international artists and audiences. Here's a chance to stay in one place and enjoy a variety of entertainments: theater, symphony orchestras, ballet, and film. Two of my favorite festivals:

❀ **The Ravello Festival, Amalfi Coast**
Summer, www.ravellofestival.com
An outdoor stage is set up on a cliff overlooking the sea at the Villa Rufolo, where Richard Wagner came in 1880 and was inspired to write *Parsifal*. To be there on a moonlit night to hear an orchestra under the stars is an experience of a lifetime. The festival also includes dance, film, and art exhibitions.

⚙ **Festival of Two Worlds (Festival dei Due Mondi), Spoleto**
Late June to Mid-July, www.festivaldispoleto.com
A showcase for new and insightful theater and music, here you'll
find exciting events such as a play directed by Robert Wilson or
opera directed by Woody Allen.

## FOR WHAT-WHERE-WHEN IN ENGLISH

**Rome:** www.inromenow.com
**Florence:** www.theflorentine.net
**Venice:** www.aguestinvenice.com

# 90 Opera

ITALIAN OPERA IS A SPECTACULAR MIX of so many things I love about Italy: rich emotional expression, splendid music and scenery, and gorgeous theaters that bring on transcendent states. It's well worth the splurge and advance planning to reserve your seat and immerse yourself in this cultural tradition.

Opera began in Italy when a group of radical academics and musicians (the *Camerata Fiorentina*) got together in Renaissance Florence with a vision to create a new kind of performance, unlike the stiff style of the day. Inspired by the spectacles of ancient Greece, they invented an art form where the focus was the human voice expressing emotion through music, telling high-stakes, dramatic stories.

At first opera was "only for royalty" entertainment, but by early eighteenth-century Venice, regular folks had become avid fans. The shows were as popular as the Broadway musicals of our day. Seventeen Venice opera houses would be filled to the rafters with courtesans, merchants, and noblemen. Though women's roles were first performed by *castrati*, soon composers realized they needed real female voices, so out onto the stage stepped Italy's first divas.

When it comes to opera in Italy, Fred Plotkin is who I go to for advice. He's a modern-day Renaissance man—an expert on Italian food and wine, classical music, and opera. A native New Yorker, he's studied and traveled extensively in Italy, and was recently awarded the title of *Cavaliere* by Italy's president, in recognition of his outstanding service to Italian culture through his writing and public lectures.

According to Fred...

🌣 **Three Top Destinations for Italian Opera:**
**La Scala, Milan** (www.teatroallascala.org)
We have Empress Maria Theresa, Duchess of Milan, to thank for the construction of this theater in 1778. La Scala is the world's most famous opera house, where many of Verdi's operas premiered, and legendary Maria Callas first took the stage in 1950. Today it presents a rich season of popular and lesser-known operas, with international stars.

🌣 **Teatro Regio, Turin**
(www.teatroregio.torino.it)
Director Gianandrea Noseda, a brilliant young musician of world-class stature, has turned this theater into a mecca for opera lovers. Teatro Regio was built in 1740 and its shell still exists, but it's been renovated due to fires, so inside you'll find a contemporary design. The Regio is surrounded by great restaurants and caffès for a fun social opera scene during its September through June season.

🌣 **La Fenice, Venice** (www.teatrolafenice.it)
*Fenice* means phoenix—the mythological bird that rose from the ashes—as the theater was built in 1792 over one that had burned. After another fire in 1996, the building was restored to its original splendor and presents an opera season of classics. Lesser known works can be seen at **Teatro Malibran**, an elegant 900-seat theater, named after diva Maria Malibran who found the theater in such shoddy shape when she sang there in 1835, that she donated her fee for its restoration.

## Other notable opera venues:

❀ **Rome**

It's worth it to venture outside the historic center to the **Auditorium Parco della Musica of Roma** (www.auditorium. com), a marvelous modern theater complex, designed by superstar architect Renzo Piano. Since 2005, musical director Antonio Pappano has made the resident orchestra, **Accademia Nazionale di Santa Cecilia** (named after the Trastevere saint), a hot destination for classical music and opera. "If I see Pappano is doing anything in Rome, I'll plan my life around it," says Plotkin.

Also, there's the memorable summer experience of seeing popular operas at Rome's **Baths of Caracalla** (www.operaroma.it).

❀ **Naples**

**San Carlo** (www.sancarlo.it) is the oldest opera house in the world, founded in 1737. "I love the passion of the audiences here," says Plotkin. "Even the intermissions are entertaining. Often in the lobby caffe or garden, chorus members and orchestra musicians join in for the break, so you may find yourself mingling with a violin player or a performer who just played an Ethiopian slave."

❀ **Verona**

The **Arena Opera Festival, Verona** (www.arena.it) is a beautiful summertime experience for tourists to enjoy popular operas in a first-century Roman amphitheater.

❀ **Lombardy**

Every autumn **Opera Lombardia** (www.operalombardia.it) presents five operas that tour five provincial towns in the Lombardy region: Brescia, Bergamo, Como, Cremona, and Pavia. "It's a chance to see the Triple-A teams of opera in wonderful small eighteenth-century theaters, an old-world experience," Plotkin says.

## The Marches

The seaside and mountain towns in this central coast region are home to over seventy *teatri storici* (historic theaters)—from jewel boxes to arenas, built between the seventeenth and nineteenth centuries—giving audiences high quality opera in beautiful settings, such as:

* **Pesaro**, the birthplace of Rossini, of *The Barber of Seville* fame. This is a lovely beach town that's home to an annual August **Rossini Opera Festival**. Three theaters are involved, one from 1637 and two other modern spaces.

* **Macerata** is a quintessential Italian hill town, loaded with Romanesque, Renaissance, and Baroque architecture. In July and August operas are staged outdoors at its **Arena Sferisterio**, a huge neoclassical structure that was built in 1820 for handball games.

So go and cheer *Brava!* to the Divas. Join in with the natives and call out, "*Bis! Bis!*" for an encore. Hopefully you won't hear whistles, which in Italian is the sound that means "Boo!"

### RECOMMENDED READING

*Opera 101: A Complete Guide to Learning and Loving Opera* by Fred Plotkin
Also check out Fred's Operavore blog at www.wqxr.org, where he writes excellent posts on the subject matter.

# 91 *Classical Music*

YOU MAY BE WALKING ALONG AND HEAR VIOLINS. The music is coming out of a church. Take a peek inside: a chamber ensemble is at the altar, surrounded by luscious baroque architecture. Heavenly.

You're in Italy where this kind of thing isn't rare, especially in the major cities. Yes, there are impressive symphony halls, opera houses, and outdoor summer festivals where you can go to hear excellent classical music. But there's something about the intimacy of the church setting, where the music is often not miked, the surroundings pull you back to gentler times when the pieces were composed, and there you are up close to a handsome fella soulfully playing a cello...

Many chamber ensemble concerts are free; none are very expensive. This is an experience you could plan ahead for, but you're bound to just be walking along and see a banner announcing the event and decide to go that evening. There's no set seating, so get there early if you'd like to be up front. If you or your beloved traveling partner grumbles "Classical music, not me," try an "It'll only be an hour or two tops" nudge. This will probably become one of the most memorable experiences of your trip, and theirs.

## Venice—Home of Vivaldi

Venice reveres Vivaldi, that romantic baroque musician of *Four Seasons (Quattro Stagioni)* fame, who was born here in 1678. He was a revolutionary composer, boldly bringing emotion to the violin and its sister string instruments—from heights of joy to depths of melancholy. His ornate music matches the Venetian spirit.

All over Venice you'll see posters for chamber ensemble performances where Vivaldi is the headliner. And there will often be other greats such as Corelli, Rossini, and Mozart on the bill. You'll also be approached by beaming costumed folks who are putting on Vivaldi shows. To put it as nicely as possible, the costumed folks are not who I mean when I'm talking great Vivaldi in Venice, so don't confuse them with the authentic chamber ensembles.

Tickets are easy to get online, at tourist kiosks, or through your hotel; I've also done fine off-season just showing up right before the concert. Performance nights vary and most starting times are 8:30ish.

❁ **Interpreti Veneziani—Chiesa San Vidal, San Marco**
(www.interpretiveneziani.com)
The very best! A young, exuberant ensemble that's received critical raves since they came onto the scene in 1987. The seventeenth-century church setting is enriched with paintings from Carpaccio and other Venetian masters.

❁ **Ensemble Antonio Vivaldi—Chiesa di San Giacometto, Rialto** (www.ensembleantoniovivaldi.com)
The cherry red interior of one of Venice's oldest churches makes for an especially romantic experience. This is also an exceptionally well-heated venue, perfect for a chilly night.

❁ **Collegium Ducale—Palazzo delle Prigioni, San Marco**
(www.collegiumducale.com)
This ensemble is composed of the best musicians from Venetian orchestras, performing classical repertory in rooms of the Doges Palace prison, where the notorious Casanova once had a stay.

## Rome

* **Concerts in the Sacristy of Borromini–Piazza Navona** (www.santagneseinagone.org)

Right off Piazza Navona, in the back of the Church of Saint Agnes in Agony, is this jewel box, designed by the baroque master Borromini. Here guest artists—from award-winning young players to musicians of international fame—bring in a varied repertoire. Your program may include Schubert, Paganini, Debussy, Mozart, Brahms, or Chopin. Evening performances usually start around 6 P.M.

## Florence

* **Concerts in Chiesa di Santa Monaca–Oltrarno** (www.classictic.com)

This fifteenth-century church, close to the Piazza Santo Spirito, hosts small ensembles that excellently play baroque classics with great passion.

* **Orchestra da Camera Fiorentina** (www.orcafi.it)

Critically acclaimed as the best chamber orchestra in Europe, this forty-piece ensemble performs chamber music and symphonic concerts, from such composers as Pergolesi, Schubert, Beethoven, and Haydn. Star guest musicians often add flash to the bill. It's on a grander scale than most "music in churches" experiences, and performances take place in various beautiful venues in Florence, including the Museo di Orsanmichele and the Courtyard of the Bargello Museum.

# 92

*Jazz*

ITALY GAVE AMERICA PIZZA. AMERICA GAVE ITALY JAZZ.

Just like there's pizza in even the smallest American burb, the same goes for jazz in Italy. Italians went gaga over the style in 1904, when a Creole group, hailed as "the creators of the catwalk," performed in Milan. With great enthusiasm, orchestras were formed. Over the decades star players emerged, bringing Italian twists to this American form.

From the start, American jazz musicians who came to Italy were welcomed and revered. Louis Armstrong toured through in the thirties, Chet Baker lived in Turin for a while, Ella Fitzgerald celebrated her fortieth birthday (really her forty-first, she was tricky about it) with a concert in Rome that's one of her best recordings.

These days in Italy you'll find top American players on the bills, along with legendary natives such as trumpeteer Enrico Rava. As far as Italian jazz gals to look out for, there are vocalists Tiziana Ghiglioni (called Italy's "First Lady of Jazz"), and Maria Pia de Vito, a Naples native whose take on Joni Mitchell tunes is wonderful.

As a backdrop to the cool players, the varied performance venues are exquisite. You may find yourself at one of Italy's many jazz festivals, mostly held in summer, when an entire small town is filled with music and you can see shows in baroque theaters, chic clubs where the food is fantastic, or in amazing outdoor settings, where often the performances are free.

Like pizza in America, jazz in Italy varies greatly in quality. As in, you wouldn't want to spend a euro to hear the sour saxophonist who played "Strangers in the Night" outside my Rome apartment again and again.

Here are some outstanding venues:

### Clubs, reservations necessary

### Rome

❀ **Gregory's Jazz Club**

A cozy spot near the Spanish Steps that hosts top of the line players, offering dinner downstairs, and a whiskey tasting bar with over a hundred varieties. (Via Gregoriana 54/a, 06 679 6386, Closed Monday, dinner reservations essential, shows start around 10:00 P.M., www.gregorysjazz.com)

❀ **Casa del Jazz**

Praised as one of the best jazz venues in Europe, this former villa of a Roman crime boss was confiscated by the government and turned into a jazz cultural center that opened in 2005, with a theater, library, restaurant, and outdoor performance spaces. (Viale di Porta Ardeatina 55, 06 704 731, www.casajazz.it)

### Ferrara

❀ **Jazz Club Ferrara**

Chic, intimate spot to see headliners, with fantastic food of the Emilia-Romagna region. (Torrione San Giovanni, Via 167, Rampari di Belfiore, 167, 339 788 6261, shows on Monday, Friday, Saturday, www.jazzclubferrara.com)

## Torino

* **Jazz Club Torino**
  In the heart of this elegant town is this cozy club, featuring jam sessions, headliners, and it transforms to a dance club after 11 P.M. (Via S. Francesco Da Paola, 011 882 939, closed Monday, www.jazzclubtorino.it)

### Festivals

* **Umbria Jazz Festival** (www.umbriajazz.com)
  The largest jazz festival in Italy, which takes over the town of Perugia for ten days in July. Two hundred thousand fans flock in to see what's been called the best in the world. The more low-key **Umbria Jazz Winter** takes place in December in Orvieto, in venues such as Teatro Mancinelli (built in 1886) and the Palazzo del Popolo, from the eleventh century.

* **Ancona Jazz Festival—Le Marche** (www.anconajazz.com)
  The seaside town on the northern Adriatic is filled with jazz all year long and every July with this festival, featuring performances at the historic Teatro delle Muse and beautiful gardens.

* **Lucca Jazz Donna—Tuscany** (www.luccajazzdonna.it)
  In early autumn, top female players and vocalists reign here. The event includes gallery shows and films, and often performances that pay homage to a particular legend, such as Billie Holiday or Ella Fitzgerald.

### *Also*

* **The Brass Group—Palermo** (www.thebrassgroup.it)
  All year long, this non-profit jazz foundation hosts performances at various Palermo venues. The most beautiful is **Santa Maria dello Spasimo**, a roofless former Gothic church.

**TIP:** *For complete listings of jazz performances all over Italy by dates and regions: www.jazzitalia.net or www.italiajazz.it*

# 93 *Puppet Shows*

WHEN I WAS A KID, PUPPET SHOWS CREEPED ME OUT. I'd make a run from the birthday party as soon as a scary grownup got up to hide behind a dark curtain. So I never sought out Italian puppet shows. But there I was in Naples, in a great mood because I'd just eaten a *sfogliatelle*, the seashell-shaped pastry the city is deservedly famous for.

Timing is everything. A dinky portable puppet stage appeared right on the Via Toledo route that led to the apartment I'd rented. *Mammas* and *bambini* crowded around it, clapping and laughing. I stopped and saw Pulcinella, the rascal clown who's the mascot of Naples, get whacked in the head by a *signorina* puppet. I laughed. I was cured. And hooked.

 Italian puppet shows are hysterical spectacles that have a Warner Brother's cartoon-like style. They're great fun even if you aren't a kid and don't know a word of Italian. They'll pop up spontaneously in parks or can be found elaborately produced in theaters, with locals of all ages making up a rapt audience.

The puppet tradition in Italy goes back thousands of years, and though the shows are full of laughs, creating them is taken very seriously, with artists crafting characters, sets, costumes and music to make enchantment.

The characters and stories you'll see will depend on the region you visit. In Naples, you'll always find Pulcinella, whose name translates to "little chicken." He's the hook-nosed guy in the baggy white costume who's always causing trouble. Sometimes he's making a play for the perky servant gal, Colombina, who's traditionally dressed showing lots of cleavage and typically turns the story around by saving the day with some tricky smart move. Tambourines rattle, there is much whacking with sticks—its rhythm blends with the mercurial Neapolitan spirit.

In Palermo, right across from the Cattedrale, you can see grand puppet opera created by the Argento family that's been in the biz since 1893. Their shows tell stories of the Knights of Charlemagne battling the Saracens, with marionettes dressed in fancy armor saving damsels in distress. I'll never forget watching one of their action packed finales: Knights charged a king, split his head open with their swords, each head-half plonked to the stage, and then in rushed a clown marionette to cheer the happy ending.

Puppet Theater worth checking out:

## Rome

❀ **I Burattini di Carlo Piantadosi**, Janiculum Hill (behind Garibaldi's statue), 06 582 7767. Though the great master Piantadosi passed away in 2012, his traditional puppet shows carry on, enjoyed by generations of Romans on this outdoor hilltop. Show times may vary: Monday-Friday at 4 & 7, Saturday-Sunday at 10 & 3. Free.

❀ **Teatro Verde,** Trastevere, www.teatroverde.it. Founded in 1947 by acclaimed puppet master Maria Signorelli, and now under the artistic direction of Veronica Olmi, this lively venue and *scuola* presents classic fairytales.

* **San Carlino**, Borghese Gardens, www.sancarlino.it. This charming, 100-seat theater in the Borghese Gardens presents traditional *Pulcinella* puppet shows, along with fairytales, such as *Pinocchio* and *Little Red Riding Hood.*

## Sicily

* **Palermo: Opera dei Pupi di Vincenzo Argento e figli**, Via Pietro Novelli 4A, near the Cathedral, 445, 091 611 3680, www.pupisicilianoargento.it.

* **Siracusa: Teatro dei Pupi**, Via della Giudecca, www.teatro-deipupisiracusa.it. The Vaccaro-Mauceri family has run these shows for over one hundred years. Tours of their workshop are also available.

## Milan

* **Teatro Colla,** Teatro La Crete, Via dell'allodola 5 and Theatre Silvestrianum, Via Andrea Maffei 19, www.teatrocolla. org. Originated in 1835, here stunning marionettes perform children's favorites—from *Alice in Wonderland* to *Tom Sawyer.*

# XII

## Advice from Writers

I love to read books that take place in Italy. They fling me around through its history; give me a chance to see the country through a different lens. They take me beyond guidebooks, bringing another layer to my experience of a destination.

Sometimes I'll get caught up with historical fiction—delving into the lives of cloistered nuns in Renaissance Ferrara with Sarah Dunant's *Sacred Hearts*. Or on my last trip to Rome, I reread Tennessee Williams' *The Roman Spring of Mrs. Stone*, a hoot of a melodrama, which brings *La Dolce Vita* days back to life. What was there to do after I finished it, but get myself to the Rosati in Piazza del Popolo and order a Negroni.

When I'm not in Italy, reading one of the many memoirs that's come out over the past decades has been an excellent way to hold me over until my next trip. I've gone along, vicariously restoring several farmhouses and getting over various heartbreaks. Wondrously, there's that "reading as communion" thing that happens when these writers pour their passion for Italy on the page. That's me on the couch, sighing.

While writing this book, I've been thinking about some of my favorite female writers who've taken me around "their" Italy. So I checked in with them to talk about Italian travel. Each generously shared with me some of their favorite places, so now I share them with you…

## RECOMMENDED READING

*Desiring Italy: Women Writers Celebrate the Passions of a Country and Culture*
edited by Susan Cahill

# 94 *Frances Mayes*

*"I came to Italy expecting adventure. What I never anticipated is the absolute sweet joy of everyday life—la dolce vita."*
-FRANCES MAYES, *Bella Tuscany*

WITH VIVID WRITING THAT CAPTURES sensual moment by moment details, Frances Mayes has turned readers all over the world on to the joys of life in Italy. For any of you who missed it, she's the author of *Under the Tuscan Sun, Bella Tuscany, A Year In the World, Every Day in Tuscany,* and *The Tuscan Sun Cookbook.*

Her books have taken me along with her—hacking away at weeds in her Cortona garden, discovering Saturnia's thermal springs, and temples in Sicily. It's engrossing writing that gets me daydreaming about my next trip. Plus her recipes are wonderful.

Always, she connects the experience of her outer journey to the fascinating, ever-changing inward journey. "In Italy you can find the place that corresponds to your soul more easily than any other place in the world," she says.

Frances first traveled to Italy after studying its art and architecture in college. She remembers landing in Bologna one autumn morning:

"It was staggering. I was sitting under one of those big arcades... all around there were people drinking coffee and smoking, and I remember thinking...*Ah! this is really fun.* That's when I started getting

intrigued by the vivacity of the Italians. I have that great attraction
us pale-faced people have to it, like a moth to a light bulb."

That great attraction led Frances to find her "soul" place: rural
Tuscany. As much as I love reading about her life there in Cortona,
I also get thrilled by her writing when she takes off to explore other
parts of Italy. She brings such a great spirit of whimsy, curiosity,
and passion to her traveling.

I spoke to her by phone during a busy time. She and her husband
Ed were in the midst of the second renovation of Villa Bramasole
in Cortona, plus she was writing two more books—one fiction and
another that centers around undiscovered places in Italy. Still, this
generous woman, with her charming southern accent, took time to
share her advice about destinations in Italy she loves.

"When we think of the coast, most travelers go to the
Mediterranean, but we've been enjoying the Adriatic, and have
loved spending time in **Senigalia**," she said. This seaside town in
**Le Marche** is a popular spot for Italian tourists, with a wide, white
sandy beach and grand Liberty-style architecture in its historic
center. On Thursdays, there's a big market that takes over the
central *vias*—a tradition that harkens back to the thirteenth century
when Senigalia's trade fair attracted crowds from all over Europe.
"And the fish restaurants are extraordinary," Frances adds, "from
shacks on the beach where you eat with the locals to the more
elegant Uliassi (www.uliassi.it) and Madonnina del Pescatore (www.
morenocedroni.it), which both have Michelin-starred chefs."

She and her husband Ed also keep going back to **Friuli-
Venezia Giulia**, the northeastern region that's world-renowned
for its wines. "It's a beautiful junction of Slavic, Austrian, and
Italian culture," Frances says. "You can visit so many small towns
by car, including **Cormons**, and discover small wineries where you
just pull up to a vineyard, and out comes the owner to show you
around, then you sit under a pergola for wine tastings."

"Now for women traveling solo, I would always go back to Venice," is her advice. "You can just wander around on your own steam, completely relaxed, though of course you'll get lost!"

I could feel her poet's soul through the lines as she told me about her springtime stay on the Venetian island of Torcello: "After the last ferry left, we had the whole island to ourselves, it got so quiet, stars came out, and we could walk all over in the silence..."

## RECOMMENDED READING

All of Frances Mayes' books, including:

*Bella Tuscany*

*Under the Tuscan Sun*

*A Year in the World*

*Every Day in Tuscany*

*The Tuscan Sun Cookbook*

*Under Magnolia*

# 95 *Sarah Dunant*

*"The city was filled with the smell of paint and the scratch of ink on contracts...you couldn't walk the streets for fear of falling into a pit or mire left by constant building.... What I hear described even now as a golden age was then simply the fashion of the day."*
—SARAH DUNANT, *Birth of Venus*

SARAH DUNANT'S ENTHRALLING HISTORICAL FICTION has kept me up at night turning pages. I fall back hundreds of years to scents and sensations of Renaissance Florence, Venetian canals crowded with gondolas, and a convent in Ferrara where cloistered nuns sing heavenly harmonies. Women are the central characters in her captivating stories that burst with rich emotion and such fascinating details, that I've learned more about Italian history through these reads than any class or non-fiction book has ever taught me.

"It all began with a crisis," Sarah tells me, from her home in London. "Number one, a relationship had broken down, and number two, I'd been writing thrillers and was ready to move on to something else, but I had no idea what that was. Now, if you're in a crisis, it's very important to choose the right place to have your breakdown. I chose Florence."

Living in Florence for months, Sarah let herself get lost, to no longer be a tourist. And in her wanderings, came the questions: "What the hell really happened here five hundred years ago? What was it like to actually be walking the streets as Brunelleschi's dome was being built? *And* what was it like to be *female* during that time?"

Sarah had loved reading historical fiction as a teenager, and went on to study history at Cambridge, when in her words, "it centered around dead white males." But decades later, she realized there had been "a kind of revolution in history." Women historians had begun to write about their discoveries, tapping a deep vein, uncovering court records, letters, and diaries that told stories of courtesans, nuns, married women, teenagers. Pouring over documents in the British Library, and living part-time in Florence set Sarah off on a new path.

"I'm now living in 1503," she joked, when I reached her as she had just finished up another book about the Borgias, a follow-up to the critically acclaimed *Blood and Beauty*.

Sarah's advice for "off the beaten track" Florence, where she set *Birth of Venus* is to visit the **Museo San Marco** (see details in Chapter 8). "Here's where you can wander through the labyrinth of frescoed monk's cells and truly get in touch with what that life was like for them, their method of meditation, surrounded by this great art." And for a fabulous eating experience, she loves **Rocco's** in the **Sant'Ambrogio market** (near Santa Croce). "Take a seat at the counter for a delicious homemade Florentine lunch, with the owner himself, seventy-something Rocco, whizzing around serving everyone."

Sarah's *Sacred Hearts* is set in Ferrara, an under-touristed town in the Emilia Romagna region, perfectly preserved with medieval and Renaissance architecture. Going beyond the major sights, such as the d'Este Castle, Sarah's advice is to visit the convent where her story is based: **Sant' Antonio** in **Polesine**. It belonged to Beatrice d'Este and was beautifully embellished by her noble family's fortunes. Sarah tells me with a knock on the door you'll be greeted by a nun of the order who is designated to greet guests, who will show you around to the huge courtyard. The highlight is inside the nun's choir, where you'll discover unique frescos from the school of Giotto, painted in the thirteenth and fourteenth centuries. "They are images I've never seen anywhere else," she tells me. "One is Christ climbing a ladder to the crucifix, and another is Mary and Joseph on a donkey, leaving Bethlehem, with Joseph carrying Jesus on his shoulders."

"Discovering this place is an *adventure*," Sarah says, "which is what I believe *all* travel should be."

**Monastery of Sant'Antonio in Polesine** (www.ferraraterraeacqua. it). Check website for visiting hours. Vespers are sung at five every evening by the remaining cloistered nuns—you can listen to them through the grill. It's not the same experience as during the Renaissance, when this convent was renowned for its choir. Nowadays only fifteen cloistered nuns are in residence, though their aged voices will give you a glimmer of the convent's former glory.

---

### RECOMMENDED READING

All Sarah Dunant's historical fiction:

*Birth of Venus*
*In the Company of the Courtesan*
*Sacred Hearts*
*Blood and Beauty*

# 96 *Marcella Hazan*

*"Eating in Italy is one more manifestation of the
Italian's age-old gift of making art out of life."*
—MARCELLA HAZAN, *The Classic Italian Cook Book*

MARCELLA HAZAN, THE QUEEN OF ITALIAN CUISINE, wrote inspiring, award-winning cookbooks. I will always treasure the phone conversation we had while I was writing the first edition of this book, from her home where she spent her final years, in Longboat Key, Florida. Marcella and her husband Victor had lived and taught cooking classes in Venice in the 1980s and '90s, and she was passionate about sharing her thoughts with me about her beloved Serenissima. Sadly, Marcella passed away in 2013, but her advice about enjoying the food there is timeless.

"Order *canocchie*," she told me, "It's a type of spider shrimp that you can only find in Venice and Japan. It's very soft, very sweet, very delicate." She also recommended *moleche* (soft shell crab) when it's in season, which is usually April and November. Then there is sole: "For Americans, Maine has the lobster, but Venice has the sole," she said. It's much smaller than American sole and served as *sole in saor*, where the fried fish is put in a sauce with vinegar, pine nuts, and raisins.

As far as shopping for food at the **Rialto Market**, she sighed, "I'd like to shop there every day of my life." And, "You should notice how each item is marked to tell where it came from. What's local is more expensive than what's imported, like asparagus from

Sant'Erasmo or fish marked *nostrane*. It's the freshness that costs much more," she explained. "Salmon is cheaper, it's not Italian."

When it came to restaurant recommendations, **Fiaschetteria Toscana** was her immediate response. "It doesn't have anything to do with Tuscany, that was its name from the beginning and now Mariuccia who cooks there is very good, it's very Venetian, and she makes wonderful desserts."

If you mention "Victor and Marcella Hazan sent me" to the owners of any of the restaurants listed below, they will give you a warm welcome.

The woman whose voice that came across so strict and uncompromising through the pages of her cookbooks, got soft and nostalgic talking about Venice: "Every corner you turn is unbelievable. Have you ever seen it in the snow? It looks like embroidery on the Ca' d'Oro, like it came from Burano. And the light...the fog... when you can see Venice coming out little by little and you wait and it is coming to life...Venice..."

### Places to say "Marcella sent me..."

- **Fiaschetteria Toscana,** ask for Mariuccia. Salizada S. Giovanni Grisostomo, Cannaregio 041 528 5281, closed all Tuesday and Wednesday for lunch.

- **Da Ivo**, ask for Giovanni. Calle dei Fuseri, San Marco, 041 528 5004, closed Sunday.

- **Da Fiore**, ask for Maurizio. Calle del Scaleter, San Polo, 041 721 308, closed Sunday and Monday.

### RECOMMENDED READING

All Marcella Hazan's cookbooks and *Amarcord: Marcella Remembers*

# 97 *Mary Taylor Simeti*

*"Sicily is a fun-house mirror in which Italy can behold her
national traits and faults distorted and exaggerated."*
—MARY TAYLOR SIMETI, *On Persephone's Island: A Sicilian Journal*

AT JUST THE MENTION OF FEMALES IN SICILY, Mary Taylor Simeti comes
out with: "There's that pre-Greek ancient sculpture in the archaeological museum in Syracuse. A large seated woman, with two infants,
each suckling a breast. And her head's been lopped off. Such an
image of the Great Mother! And of motherhood in general!" That's
typical of Mary's wry, personal take on the island's legends.

Mary's writing—whether it's memoir, travel story, or cookbook—
weaves together her expatriate-in-Sicily experience with her extensive knowledge of mythology, history, and culinary traditions. It's
a rich mix that really prepared me for my first trip to the island—
giving an honest picture of Sicily's light and dark sides.

Mary arrived in Sicily in 1962, a New Yorker who'd just gradu-
ated with a degree in Medieval History from Radcliffe. Her plan was
to spend a year volunteering at a community development center in
Partinico, west of Palermo. In the prologue of *On Persephone's Island*,
Mary's self-deprecating look back at her naïve but determined
younger self hooked me. I won't spoil it. Pick up the book.

Mary's year in Sicily turned out to be much longer. While
working at the center, she met an agronomist, Tonino Simeti.
They married, had two children, lived in Palermo and then rebuilt

Tonino's family farm. Now, over fifty years after she first set foot in Sicily, Mary lives on that farm, called Bosco Falconeria.

"It was all accidental," she laughs. These days, part of Bosco is converted into a B&B. So if you drive to Alcamo, forty miles west of Palermo, you could stop by and get a taste of those white mulberries Mary writes about, or whatever delicious thing happens to be growing in their organic fields and orchards.

When we spoke more about women and Sicily, Mary focused on **Erice,** about an hour's drive west of her farm: "A fascinating place, laden with Venus myths."

Erice is dramatically set overlooking the coast, on a mountain so high that there's often a haze shrouding the view. It's a tiny town of narrow cobblestoned lanes, hidden courtyards, medieval architecture, with sprinklings of baroque.

Venus worship here goes back to the Carthaginians, who worshipped her as Astarte, Goddess of fertility. Every spring, priestesses would release a flock of white birds from the Erice promontory to fly off to Astarte's temple in Carthage. The birds would return nine days later with a red dove leading them, symbolizing nature's renewal.

Greeks, who came later, claimed that the goddess (as Aphrodite) rose from the sea below Erice in a cockleshell chariot, making the mountain her sacred spot. It was where Aphrodite's ancestor—the primordial God of the Sky Uranus, and his Titan son Cronus—clashed. Cronus sliced off Uranus's balls with a sickle, then threw that sickle (where the name Sicily comes from) into the sea, along with his father's balls. Up splashed Aphrodite! Once on her mountain, she bedded the Argonaut Butes, and gave birth to a son, who she named Eryx.

During Roman times, a huge Venus Erycina cult swept the Mediterranean. She was worshipped not only as Goddess of Beauty, but also of Sacred Prostitution. Romans would come to Erice to lay (in the Biblical sense) with Venus Erycina's priestesses.

"Venus worship continued in Erice well into Christian times, all the way into the Middle Ages," Mary said. "So the main church (**The Matrice**), was purposely built right at the city gate. The idea was the Madonna would catch the women before they could get to Venus, on the opposite side of town. It was a ploy by the Roman Catholics to put an end to pagan practices."

Now the **Castello di Venere,** built by the Normans in the thirteenth century, stands where Venus's temple once was. It's a grand spot for amazing views. Also, as Mary writes, take a good look at the succulents growing out of the castle walls. The ones with smooth circular leaves, dented in the middle, are called Venus's navelwort— or *ombelico di Venere* in Italian.

"And definitely stop by Maria's for the pastries," Mary said. That would be **Pasticceria Maria Grammatico,** a shop run by a woman who grew up in a convent orphanage, where she learned to make these traditional sweets. Maria is a sort of Erice celebrity, thanks to the book, *Bitter Almonds,* which tells her life story. It was co-written by her friend, Mary Taylor Simeti.

**In Alcamo:** Taylor Simeti's Agriturismo: Bosco Falconeria (www.boscofalconeria.it).

**In Erice:** Pasticceria Maria Grammatico, Via Vittorio Emanuele 14 (www.mariagrammatico.it). Check the website for information about pastry making classes with Maria.

## RECOMMENDED READING

*On Persephone's Island* by Mary Taylor Simeti
*Travels with a Medieval Queen* by Mary Taylor Simeti
*Pomp and Sustenance* by Mary Taylor Simeti
*Bitter Almonds* by Mary Taylor Simeti and Maria Grammatico

# XIII

## La Famiglia
## Experiences

These are the places you go where everlasting memories are made; trips that will live on for generations. And as welcoming as Italy is to any traveller, when you arrive with children, or for a wedding, or to visit your Italian relatives, the heart of Italy expands even more for you.

These trips may begin as daydreams. Find a way to make them come true. Especially when it comes to taking children or visiting family over there, don't delay. There will always be reasons to stay home and put off going until next year or the next. But keep in mind the obvious: children grow up fast, grandparents don't live forever. *Carpe diem.*

And take lots of pictures.

# 98 *Places for Children*

MANY CALL ITALY THE MOST WELCOMING COUNTRY in the world to children. Italians adore their own children and will roll out the red carpet for yours on sight.

If you take a baby through a city market, I'm warning you, you're going to have a slow go of it. Inevitably, *signoras* will be leaning down to pinch their cheeks. You may even have the shock of seeing Roman waiters, notorious for their rudeness, drop their "I'm-a-very-important-person—too-busy-to-deal-with-you-attitude" and bending over backwards to bring treats.

Along with its welcoming spirit, Italy has an infinite number of places children will love. Little ones are awestruck by its fountains and castles. School-age kids get to see their history books come alive and will get giggles and thrills from all the nude statues. There are parks or beaches to frolic off the energy. Then there's pizza and gelato. Winning combinations all around.

If you'd rather leave the planning to others, group adventure trips (with companies such as **Backroads** or **Country Walkers**) are there to take the pressure off, and they offer family trips so the kids can make new friends during the week. Also, if you're thinking of bringing the kids to one of the major archaeological sites like the Roman Forum or Pompeii, save yourself and get a children's guide.

For expert help setting things up, check out **Ciao Bambino** (www.ciaobambino.com). The company was created by Amie O'Shaughnessy, a mom herself, who's traveled to Italy often, and along with her staff, checks out properties and chooses the best of the child-friendly. You can go to the website and find them rated according to what age ranges they're best for, from "Baby Ready" to "Cool for Teens." The company can also help you find kid-friendly restaurants and sites, guides, playgrounds, and English speaking babysitters in any region.

Amy's advice for one of the best places to land if you're traveling with young children is a rural resort in Tuscany. These are converted villa or farmhouse estates, which are well set up with cribs, laundry, and a pool for older kids to mingle with travelers their own age. They're well located for day trips to charming towns nearby, but you may just find yourself staying put for at least one idyllic restful day at what will feel like your Italian home.

Some fun places for kids:

## Rome

⚘ **Borghese Gardens,** www.turismoroma.it
Sixty-five acres of manicured green, shadowed by umbrella pines. In the Porta Pinciana area, you can rent surrey-style pedal carts, roller skates, plain ol' bikes, or even give your child a pony ride treat. There are paddleboats available at the park pond, a mini-cinema (www.cinemadeipiccoli.it), a puppet theater (www.sancarlino.it), and a tiny tram that takes you to the Bioparco, a huge zoo. That about covers it.

## Florence

⚘ **Museo dei Ragazzi–Palazzo Vecchio,** www.musefirenze.it
Costumed characters lead kids through this palace where the Medici lived, for entertaining adventures that may include shadow shows, dressing up in sixteenth-century costumes, and

fresco workshops. There are a few programs to choose from, for children ages four and up. Reservations necessary.

## Venice

❁ **Lion Hunt with Context Travel,** www.contexttravel.com
Children easily slip into the fairytale aspect of Venice (Walt Disney's favorite city), and all the boating makes for easy entertainment. For more focused fun, Context Travel offers **Lion Hunt tours**, which begin at Piazza San Marco and take families on an interactive walking tour, as children enjoy discovering all the different lions, the symbol of Venice, and much more. Itineraries are custom-designed according to ages and interests.

If you're in Venice for more than a few days, and with kids that like biking, vaporetto to **Sant'Erasmo**, an island that lies between Burano and Murano. It's covered with vegetable gardens and orchards that have supplied Venice markets for centuries. If you get there in June, lucky you: there will be fields of purple artichokes in bloom. The bike loop around the island is 3.5 miles/5.5 km, and you may want to join Venetian families at the tiny beach for a swim—this is where the natives come to escape the Lido crowds.

❧

**Golden Day:** Take Vaporetto 13 to the Capannone stop at Sant'Erasmo—it's about a thirty-minute ride. For bike rentals, walk up Via Forti to **Lato Azzurro** (Via Forti 13, 041 523 0642, www.latoazzurro.it). Eat at **Ristorante Ca'Vignotto** (Via Forti 71, 041 244 4000, www.vignotto.com). Lunch Tuesday-Sunday, dinner Thursday-Saturday, reservations essential). It's a treasured family-run place that serves just-picked deliciousness grown on the island.

## RECOMMENDED READING

*Florence and Tuscany with Kids* by Ariela Bankier

*This is Rome* and *This is Venice* by Miroslav Sasek

# 99 An Italian Wedding

IF YOU GET AN INVITATION TO AN ITALIAN WEDDING, don't waffle about how you're going to pay for airfare or take time off work. Go for a once-in-a-lifetime unforgettable event. Prepare yourself for an extravaganza of delicious food and dancing until the wee hours.

It'll be a rare invitation. These days Italians say it's not practical to get married, so most are shacking up together for years, and the statistics for Italian marriages are at a historic low. Along with that, there's the trend of "*mammoni*" or mamma's boys, that is, men living at home and having their mothers cook for them and do their laundry until they're well into their thirties.

Still, if you're in Italy, especially in June (thanks to Juno, Goddess of Marriage), you'll run into Italian weddings in churches. I spent a week in Palermo one June where almost every church I peeked into had a marriage ceremony going on, with wonderful music and stunning get-ups from the bride on down. You'll never see a real Italian wedding on a Tuesday or Friday, as that's considered not a good day to begin any venture. Which is why when I visited Ravello's Villa Cimbrone on a Friday, the wedding party posing for pictures were Americans from Massachusetts.

Speaking of which, you may be considering getting married in Italy. It's naturally a great place for a wedding, completely romantic, with locations from castles to vineyards to cliffs overlooking the sea that can satisfy every bride-to-be's fantasy.

A major advantage to getting married in Italy is that you can cut your guest list down to a core group of dearest family and friends, who'll be thrilled to be in on the adventure. Plus, what better place is there for a jumping off point for a honeymoon?

As far as the nitty-gritty, it's better to have a symbolic wedding in Italy rather than an official one, as the paperwork to make things official is complex and time consuming. To help get things set up, here are some companies that specialize in Italian weddings:

* **Doorways, Ltd.,** www.villavacations.com
  One of this company's top "I Do" spots is a sixteenth-century villa on the outskirts of Lucca, which sits on 300 acres of vineyards, olive groves, and woodlands.

  There's a fantastic frescoed bridal suite at the villa, and it's perfectly located for day trips before the big event, such as a boat ride to the Cinque Terre. Another option is Villa Laura, the luxurious property that was featured in the movie, *Under the Tuscan Sun*, that's located within walking distance from Cortona.

  Along with beautiful villas in Tuscany, the Doorways wedding collection also includes Lake Como, the Amalfi Coast, and the Veneto.

* **Italy 4 Real,** www.italy4real.com
  Intimate country weddings in Tuscan and Umbrian agriturismos, are Italy 4 Real's specialty. The company's philosophy is for clients to fully experience the environment they're in, so they bring in local expert chefs and musicians and it's all very traditional. Marriage ceremonies feature stunning backdrops of

vineyards and olive groves. Brides and grooms are whisked off to nearby picturesque hill towns such as San Gimignano or Assisi for photo shoots.

The company also offers custom-designed honeymoons, believing "it's the most important trip a couple will take." They meet with the bride and groom and really get to know their traveling styles, working within any budget to ensure it's a vacation that perfectly suits their desires.

* **Perillo Tours,** www.perillotours.com

This company, that's been creating group tours to Italy for over seventy years, has branched out to wedding planning. Experts can create packages in any location, including Tuscany and the Amalfi Coast. Every detail is covered—from English speaking celebrants, to photographers, local hair stylists, and makeup artists. Their honeymoon planning services offer top accommodations at gorgeous properties, such as Hotel Luna Convento in Capri or the boutique Eden Roc in Positano.

## RECOMMENDED READING

*Italy, a Love Story* edited by Camille Cusumano
*In Love in Italy* by Monica Larner

# 100 *Go Find Your Mammas*

LIKE MANY ITALIAN AMERICANS, as soon as I land in Italy, a deep, powerful connection to the *mammas* of my past takes hold of me. It's more than just seeing those look-a-like faces from my maternal line. It's a sensational hit to the core, a feeling of belonging, joining into the continuity of *la famiglia*. Even when I'm not with my relatives face-to-face, when I'm in Italy, I feel those roots. For many that feeling will be enough, but to travel to your ancestor's hometown and maybe even connect with long lost Italian relatives can be life changing.

Meeting my Italian cousins and eating together (which takes up most of our time) is one of the gifts I'm most grateful for in my life. If your family is still in touch with your relatives over there, you're lucky. The door is open. Plan your trip so you'll have time for a visit, even if they live off your tourist track, which is most likely the case.

It took me a few visits to Italy before I got my sister to come along with me to Vinchiaturo, a postage-stamp-sized town in the region of Molise, where my nana grew up. How can I begin to tell you about our times together in their twenty-room villa (which they only live in part of), left to them by my great-great-uncle, the wealthy Monsignor? Let's leave it at absolutely extraordinary, full of affection, and a salt-encrusted baked fish.

There are many of you whose families have lost touch with their roots. Over 4 million Italians immigrated to the United States between 1820 and 1920, most from the impoverished south, never to return to their homeland. They became Americans, worked hard, and didn't pass on much family history. Often "somewhere near Naples" or "a town in Calabria" are the only answers families have to "Where was nana from?"

There are lots of ways to get the facts to help you reconnect and the research can be fun from home. **Ancestry.com** is a good starting point, where you can be guided to create family trees, hire a pro to dig deep and find long-lost relatives, or even get DNA analysis to trace your roots back thousands of years. And the Mormons have their **Family History Center** (www.familysearch.org), which has a free extensive database of records.

I enjoyed researching my grandparents on the **Statue of Liberty-Ellis Island Foundation's** site (www.libertyellisfoundation.org). Two million Italians immigrated to the United States between 1900 and 1914, and many came through there. A search got me to a ship manifesto with nana's name along with her siblings, mother, and father—who was bringing in $120. It listed that they were from Vinchiaturo and headed to a church address in Newark—coincidentally the one that rich great-great Monsignor Uncle had built—good move! It's a cool site that even has photos of the ship your ancestors came in on, along with lots of info about genealogy research.

To travel to the place where your ancestors came from, meet relatives, or look up their names in record books is something that takes advance planning and a helpful pro, especially if you don't know Italian. There are fairytale stories of an American showing up in a little town, flashing a passport with their Italian surname on it, and the next thing they know there's a spontaneous welcome banquet. But in reality, when we're talking small Italian towns, that's rare. *La famiglia* is a sacred and private thing, and just like here, Italians aren't going to open their doors to a stranger. That said, once the preliminaries are done, and that door is open, you are in for smotherin-lovin.

A great resource to assist you with finding your roots is **My Italian Family** (www.myitalianfamily.com). Founder Bianca Ottone is a native of Genoa who left her career in finance to create this company in 2000. "We have researchers on site, natives all over Italy, and that's what really brings value to the search," she told me. Ottone's staff goes to town halls or church offices, and as locals they know the intricacies of how to connect with just the right people, and (very importantly) the dialect. They find details that can combine to create a whole story—the house where a grandparent was born, occupations of relatives, sometimes even photos.

My Italian Family can organize a day for you to visit your ancestral village with a local interpreter, look at records, explore the *vias* and perhaps discover the house where your relatives lived. As the towns are often so small, and everybody knows everybody, it's common to find residents who may have memories of your family, or even distant family members. A tour highlight is a meal at a local restaurant and the day often finishes up at the town cemetery. Ottone describes this ending as "a mystical and silent place where one is reunited with their family past and can seal this unforgettable experience, creating a legacy for generations to come."

෨෬

**Golden Day:** Sit down at the table with your Italian relatives. That'll take up the whole day.

# Appendix 1
## Tips for Italian Travel

1. **Lie about when you're leaving and returning.** Tell yourself and those in your world you'll be away the day before and the day after whatever it says on your airplane ticket. It's not really lying. Mentally you're in Italy those pre- and post-travel days. This helps me to not leave packing until the last minute, and spares those around me from being with getting-on-the-plane-to-Italy-obsessed Suz. The day after you return, you'll be on an Italy high, unpacking, and will get no sympathy with your "I'm jet-lagged, just got back from Italy" spiel. Consider these border days gifts to yourself, to ease in and out of the journey. If you do tell anyone your *real* return date, have it be a masseuse.

2. **Get psyched.** Your destination has probably been featured in movies or *You Tube* videos to watch and books to read to enhance your experience. Before you get on the plane, use them to familiarize yourself with your chosen region's history, art, and cuisine. And though the natives you'll encounter in the major cities will most likely speak English, learn at least some words of the beautiful language—*buon giorno, buona sera, grazie*. You'll be thrilled with the Italians' cheerful reaction to your efforts to speak even a little bit of their language.

3. **Spread the Word.** Tell your friends through your social media circles where you'll be traveling, and inevitably they'll have a friend, someone they met when they were going to school in Florence, or a kind cousin once removed who lives in your destination. Make contact in advance and enjoy time with a local. It'll be a treasured part of your trip.

4. **Go Solo.** Italy is a fantastic place to wander solo, following your very own desires. As Italians are such wonderfully social people, you'll rarely find yourself feeling lonely. Even when I'm traveling with my husband or girlfriends, I love having time on my own during the day to explore at my own pace—it makes dinner times more fun, when we join together to share our separate adventures. If you are on your own and would like to break up your solo time, join a day tour in your destination. Or log on to Connecting Solo Travelers Network (www.cstn.org) to find out who else is around that you could meet up with, CouchSurfing, (www.couchsurfing.com), which lists events for travelers in various destinations, or join Women Welcome Women (www.womenwelcomewomen.uk), an organization that provides hosting and companionship for women travelers. You could also join a group tour that's focused on an active adventure, sightseeing, or a workshop that focuses on your interests. In other words, "I have no one to go with," doesn't have to be an obstacle to your Italian travel dreams.

5. **Flirting.** There's a shrink in New York who prescribes a trip to Italy for women who need a boost to their self-esteem. Italian men have mastered the art of flirting—it's one of the country's masterpieces. Females of all ages are adored here. Enjoy, without taking it too seriously. It's all in the spirit of: *You are women, we are men. We are alive! And what a fun game we play!* If you get harassment rather than flirting, a loud *"Vai Via"* ("Go Away") is the age-old stopper, and it usually works.

6. **Take a Guided Tour.** I resisted this for many trips, with visions of traipsing behind a screaming person hoisting an umbrella. At the same time, I had the frustrating experiences of waiting in line for the Sistine Chapel while tour groups were ushered through in front of me, being baffled in the Forum where nothing is marked, and so on. It's great to join a *small* tour group—two of my favorites are Context Travel (www.contexttravel.com) and Walks of Italy (www.walksofitaly.com). Also, in Rome, if you can get any time with the exquisite guide, Iris Carulli (www.imcarulli.tumblr.com), you'll have a golden time.

7. **Stay Healthy.** You'll inevitably be in crowds of coughers, so starting with the airplane, take Airborne or loads of Vitamin C and bring along anti-bacterial hand wash. And (God forbid), know the number to dial for an ambulance is 118.

8. **Bidets** are found in almost every hotel room. Even in a simple convent where I stayed, there was a spigot gizmo attached to the toilet to serve the bidet purpose. Answers to most frequently asked questions: (1) you can sit either facing the faucet or not, (2) Use after your normal toilet routine. To avoid surprises, test it out to see if it's the basin type or has squirting jets.

9. **Keep an Eye on Your Stuff.** Please don't become a paranoid traveler, but the truth is, as in all cities worldwide, there are expert purse-snatchers out there, who target tourists in places of major distraction: public transportation, outdoor markets, and crowded sights. Get your offensive style down, so it becomes second nature, and then you can roam around comfortably. While some prefer a secret money belt, neck pouch, or bra stuffing, I copy the native's style. Stand back and observe for a moment, and you'll catch on. I carry a shoulder bag tucked under my arm, always closed, on my inside-of-the-street arm, to avoid whizzing *motorini* thieves. At sidewalk

restaurants, keep it hooked to you or your seat. You'll get extra warnings regarding the fantastic city of Naples—warnings that made me feel like I'd be robbed the minute I stepped off the train. Instead I met the kindest people I've ever met on earth in Naples and fell in love with the city. So don't miss Naples, but like anywhere you travel, use common sense, don't flaunt expensive jewelry or large bills, and leave what you don't need back at the hotel.

10. **Experience *Il Dolce Far Niente*—The Sweetness of Doing Nothing.** Though you'll have "must sees" on your itinerary, take time to escape from an agenda and simply be in the moment in Italy. It may be sleeping late with the sound of church bells in the distance, lingering at a caffè while beautiful-people-watching, or meandering around a vineyard—such bliss! Ideally, plan a "vacation from your vacation"—at least a day or two outside a city where *Il Dolce Far Niente* peacefully awaits.

# Appendix 2
## Budget Travel Tips

**When to Go:**

**November to Easter is Low Season (roughly),** meaning that's when you'll find the lowest-priced airfares and accommodations. This excludes Christmas week, ski season in northern resorts, and Carnevale in Venice.

**Planning:**

❀ **Staying in one place obviously cuts down transportation costs,** and makes for a more tranquil vacation. For example, you may consider basing yourself in Rome and taking a day trip to Florence (one-and-a-half-hour train ride)—See masterpieces, have a *bistecca* for lunch, watch an awesome sunset over the Arno, and be back in Rome for a nightcap.

❀ **Consider a Tour Package.** There are loads to choose from that offer low prices for airfare and hotels. Check out offerings from Perillo Tours (www.perillotours.com), and Trafalgar Tours (www.trafalgar.com).

**Airfare:**

❀ **Flexibility is key to finding bargains.** Flying mid-week will save money, and you may consider flying into London, Paris, Amsterdam, or Frankfurt and then switching to a low-cost

European carrier, using www.whichbudget.com to search for the best deal. Just be sure to check for added fees (such as checked luggage) on the European carriers.

* **Good Websites to Check for Good Deals:**
www.johnnyjet.com
www.googleflights.com
www.kayak.com

* **Sign Up for Airfare Alerts:** You can put in your route (for example JFK-Rome) on websites such as www.airfarewatchdog.com and you'll be notified about sales.

* **Follow airlines on Twitter:** For up-to-the-minute notices on sales.

* **Use a travel agent:** It sounds old fashioned, and you'll probably be charged a fee (around $25), but these pros are up on fare fluctuations and have access to inventories that can save you money.

### Airport Transfers:

* **Plan ahead, so you don't get stuck with a big taxi bill upon arrival.** Major cities have low-cost, suitcase-friendly transportation that runs regularly to and from their airports. In Rome, the **Leonardo Express Train**, (www.trenitalia.it) or bus (www.terravision.eu or www.sitabusshuttle.com), in Milan, the **Malpensa Express Train** (www.malpensaexpress.it). My favorite in Venice is the **Alilaguna** waterbus (www.alilaguna.it), cheaper and less scenic is the bus to the train station (www.atvo.it, www.actv.it), and in Florence there is the **Vola in Bus** (www.ataf.net).

## Traveling within Italy

* **Discounts on train travel** are available if you plan ahead. Check **TrenItalia** Promotions and Offers (www.trenitalia.it). I prefer the newer train service **Italo Treno** (www.itaolotreno.it), which also offers promotions and features comfortable seating, free WiFi, a cinema car, and food by Eataly.

* **Buses are sometimes a more inexpensive way to go.** And in the case of getting to Siena from Rome or Florence, that's your best option. Check SENA Autolinee (www.sena.it) and SITA (www.sitabus.it) for information.

* **Flying from city to city** on a low-cost carrier can save money and time. Check www.whichbudget.com to compare fares, and be sure to read the fine print for added fees.

* **For low cost car rentals,** go with Auto Europe (www.autoeurope.com).

## Accommodations

* **For hotel discounts,** check www.hotelscombined.com, www.trivago.com, www.booking.com, or the hotel website for promotional deals.

* **There are lots of hotel alternatives** where you can save money. B&Bs (with private bathrooms) and apartment rentals are great options. Villas, when shared with a group, are also budget-friendly.

Some of my favorite sites are:

* **For B&Bs, apartments, villas, and farmhouses**: www.bbitalia.it, www.bed-and-breakfast.it, www.venere.com, www.airbnb.com, www.sabbaticalhomes.com, www.flipkey.com, www.homeaway.com, www.vrbo.com

* **Apartments and B&Bs in Rome:** www.romarentals.net, www.rentalinrome.com
* **Agriturismos** (a great way to experience the Italian countryside): www.agriturismo.it
* **Convent or monastery stays:** www.monasterystays.com
* **Hostels** (these vary from dorm-style to family-friendly apartment set-ups): www.hostelworld.com, www.italian-hostels.com

## Eating

You can eat well in Italy without spending a bundle. Do some restaurant research (check out my Resource suggestions), avoid the obvious tourist spots near the major sights, and you'll be on the delicious track. Often one major sit-down meal a day will be satisfying, with lunch being the best choice for fancier eateries. House wine is generally good and inexpensive. As far as tipping, 10 per cent is fine—unless a *"servizio"* charge has already been added to your bill, in which case the tip has been included in your bill.

* **Follow the locals to tavola caldas** (cafeteria-style places), **pizzerias** for dinner, or **wine bars** where you can fill up on delicious small plates of local specialties. Many cities, particularly in the north, have **'Appy Hours**, where an antipasti buffet is spread out between 6 and 9 P.M., so for the price of a drink you can enjoy such goodies as focaccia, cheeses, and salumi.
* **Italian picnics are divine.** Buy cheeses, breads, olives, sweets, and wine, then enjoy lunch in a park or in the evening back in your hotel room, watching hilarious Italian TV. And don't miss the marvelous street food opportunities—such as *arancini* in Sicily or *focaccia* in Genoa.

## Sightseeing

It's amazing how many masterpieces you can see for free in Italy. In Rome, the Pantheon, Florence, the Duomo, Saint Mark's in Venice, and all the great art in the churches. Cities offer combined tourist ticket deals for sights and public transportation, so check out their websites or stop in at tourist kiosks to see if this will save you money, according to the time you have. You can also find info there for free museum days. For Rome: www.romapass.it, Florence: www.firenzecard.it, Venice: www.veneziaunica.it

## Souvenirs

Though it's worth it to spend money on the high-quality artisan treasures each city offers, you can also pick up mementos that are not that expensive. It may sound corny, but I love having a towel from a Rome market with a Piazza Navona fountain on it in my Los Angeles kitchen, to bring back memories of my time there, and it's fun to bring something like that to friends back home as a hostess gift, wrapped around the neck of a wine bottle. Food is also always a good choice—from vacuum-packed cheeses, to chocolates, spices, or specialty sweets. Other ideas that are lightweight and budget friendly: rosaries, artisan stationery, soaps from the *farmacias*, Murano glass wine stoppers, or scarves from the outdoor markets.

# Appendix 3
## *Packing*

**What am I going to wear?** This will undoubtedly be at the top of your thoughts once you book your trip.

**Think simple:** Italian women dress stylishly without a lot of fuss. Color coordinate, be neat, and all shall be well. Over-packing will end up being a drag on your trip. You can always hand wash, or get to a laundry or dry cleaner while you're there. Plus, what's the hardship in *having* to buy extra clothes or shoes in Italy?

**Check the weather forecast:** Ten-day forecasts (found online) can be a big help in wardrobe planning.

**Tag your luggage:** Include the phone number of your destination on a tag outside and inside, on the top layer of your packed suitcase, just in case your luggage gets misplaced.

### Don't pack:

* **Your hairdryer:** Even budget hotels have them.
* **Spike heels:** They get stuck in the cobblestones.
* **Shorts:** You'll feel odd unless you're biking or on a beach.
* **Sneakers:** Meaning your gym shoes or white sneakers. That said, comfortable shoes are important as you'll be doing lots of walking. Check out Ecco, Arches, and Aerosoles for good styles. Rubber soles are best for hill towns, where leather slips on the slopes.

**Do pack:**

* **Umbrella:** To always carry with you on "iffy" weather days. You'll regret having to buy one from eager street vendors who jack up the price the moment the sky opens.

* **Tissues:** To double as toilet paper. There will inevitably be places that are lacking.

* **Band Aids and moleskin:** In case of foot blisters.

* **Travel-sized toiletries:** This is the stuff that can really add weight, so bring only what you need. Dry shampoo is a great invention for traveling—lightweight and time-saving. Hotels generally supply shampoo, conditioner, and body lotion.

* **Bathing suit:** Even for non-beach vacations, so you're prepared for a spontaneous spa visit or a pool. And consider a bikini, even if you feel you're past bikini days. You'll see Italian women of every age, shape, and size wearing them. Go ahead and join in on the pleasure.

* **Crossbody bag:** I find the crossbody style the most comfortable and convenient for those days of lots of walking.

* **Lightweight duffel bag:** To fill with souvenirs for your return trip.

* **Copy of your passport, credit card numbers, and toll-free numbers to call in case of credit card loss.** Give another copy and your itinerary to someone who can easily be reached, so they can be sent to you if necessary. Before you go, call your bank and credit card companies to give them a heads up, as in these days of high security, they may block your card if they aren't forewarned about your foreign spending.

* **Tablet and smartphone:** Loaded up with the guides and apps about where you're going. If you must take a guidebook, rip out

and pack only the pages that apply to your destination, or scan the pages into a document for your device—don't take the whole heavy book.

* **Streetwise Maps** for the cities you'll be visiting. These laminated, purse-friendly, well-indexed maps are far superior to the ones hotels and tourist kiosks hand out. Even if you're using GPS on your device, these are great to have in your hotel room as you plan your day. You can buy them in U.S. bookstores or online (www.streetwisemaps.com).

## Packing à la Susan:

* **Use Wire Hangers:** I know Joan Crawford would be horrified, but putting all your clothes on wire hangers, which you then roll up in plastic to prevent wrinkling and then whoosh into your hotel closet when you arrive, cuts down on unpacking time, which gives you more time for Italy.

* **Have a Dress Rehearsal:** Here I go confessing my corny secret packing ritual: I take my inspiration from Cher in *Moonstruck*—the scene where she gets ready for her date with Nicholas Cage. To get psyched for my date with Italy, I put my mirror center stage, have a glass of white wine nearby, Andrea Bocelli blaring in the background, and all the wardrobe possibilities on the bed, including jewelry and scarves. Then I dress for the plane, for that day I know I'll be touring a museum, for that special dinner, etc. Inevitably, this is where I'll figure out what to mix and match, what shoes won't work, and cut out half of what's on that bed. And so the light, lovely adventure begins…

# Favorite Restaurants

I could fill another book, but keeping it simple with these classics, where I've enjoyed many memorable meals (Reservations essential for all).

* **Armando al Pantheon, Rome**
  Salita de Crescenzi 31, 06 6880 3034, Closed Saturday night and Sunday, www.armandoalpantheon.it

* **Sostanza, Florence**
  Via Porcellana 25r, 055 212 692, closed Saturday and Sunday

* **Antiche Carampane, Venice**
  Rio Tera delle Carampane, Rialto, near Ponte delle Tette, 041 524 0165, closed Sunday and Monday, www.antichecarampane.com

* **Ristorante Da Dora, Naples**
  Via Ferdinando Palasciano 30, 081 680519, www.ristorantedora.it

* **Antica Trattoria della Pesa, Milan**
  Viale Pasubio, 10, 02 655 5741, www.anticatrattoriadellapesa.com

* **da Gelsomina, Anacapri**
  Via Migliara 72, 081 837 1499, www.dagelsomina.com

* **Osteria La Porta, Montichiello, Tuscany**
  Via del Piano, 3, 0578 755 163, www.osterialaporta.it

# Calendar of Madonna Holidays and Female Saints' Feast Days

No matter when you visit Italy, you're bound to come upon a celebration of the Madonna or a Saint. Which means colorful processions and great food.

The saints are traditionally honored in their home towns with big celebrations on their feast days. There are also less elaborate *festas* in other parts of Italy held simultaneously. For example, in Catania, where Saint Agatha lived and worked her miracles, an extravaganza (one of the largest religious processions in the world) takes place February 5 and the days surrounding it. Also on February 5 in Massa Lubrense, a coastal town in Campania, there's a smaller Santa Agata *festa*.

| | |
|---|---|
| JANUARY 21 | Saint Agnes of Rome |
| FEBRUARY 5 | Saint Agatha of Catania, Sicily |
| FEBRUARY 22 | Saint Margaret of Cortona, Tuscany |
| MARCH 8 | *Festa della Donna,* International Women's Day *Italian women are given yellow mimosas by their admirers* |
| MARCH 25 | The Annunciation *Big celebrations in Florence and Venice to celebrate The Angel Gabriel's announcement to the BVM* |
| APRIL 27 | Saint Zita of Lucca, Tuscany |
| APRIL 29 | Saint Catherine of Siena, Tuscany |

| | |
|---|---|
| MAY | The Month of Mary |
| | *Celebrations honoring the Madonna all over Italy* |
| MAY 4 | Saint Monica (entombed in Rome) |
| MAY 22 | Saint Rita of Cascia, Umbria |
| JULY 15 | Santa Rosalia of Palermo, Sicily |
| JULY 26 | Saint Ann, Mother of Mary |
| | *Celebrations in many Italian towns* |
| AUGUST 11 | Saint Claire of Assisi, Umbria |
| AUGUST 15 | Feast of the Assumption—*Ferragosto* |
| | *Biggest holiday in Italy after Christmas and Easter, celebrating the BVM's rise into heaven.* |
| SEPTEMBER 8 | Nativity of the BVM, Prato, Tuscany |
| NOVEMBER 21 | Madonna della Salute, Venice |
| NOVEMBER 22 | Saint Cecilia of Rome |
| DECEMBER 8 | Feast of the Immaculate Conception |
| | *The celebration of the BVM's purity is the start of Christmas festivities.* |
| DECEMBER 13 | Saint Lucy of Syracuse, Sicily |

# Online Resources

Websites and blogs continue to be created about all things Italian, so as you plan, search for sites that cover your destination. Don't overlook the official tourism sites for the places you are visiting, which can be relied on for general information as well as calendars of events which you can plan your itineraries around.

Here are some of my favorites:

## All Italy

❀ Italian Government Tourist Board, www.italia.it

## Up to Date Travel Advice

❀ Art Trav: www.arttrav.com

❀ Browsing Italy: www.browsingitaly.com

❀ Dream of Italy: www.dreamofitaly.com

❀ Gillian's Lists: www.gillianslists.com

❀ Go Italy: www.goitaly.about.com

❀ Italian Notebook: www.italiannotebook.com

❀ Italofile: www.italofile.com

❀ Italy Magazine: www.italymagazine.com

❀ Select Italy: www.selectitaly.com

- Slow Travel: www.slowtrav.com
- Spotted by Locals: www.spottedbylocals.com
- Walks of Italy: www.walksofitaly.com
- Wandering Italy: www.wanderingitaly.com

### Tour Consultation and Travel Arrangement Services

- Italian Concierge: www.italianconcierge.com
- Italy Beyond the Obvious: www.italybeyondtheobvious.com + great travel posts
- La Dolce Via Travel: www.ladolceviatravel.com

### And

- Becoming Italian Word by Word: www.becomingitalianwordbyword.typepad.com, for insights into Italian language and culture
- Karen Brown's World of Travel: www.karenbrown.com, wonderful accommodation recommendations

## BLOGS AND WEBSITES BY REGION

### Abruzzo

- About Abruzzo: www.aboutabruzzo.com
- Life in Abruzzo: www.lifeinabruzzo.com

### Basilicata

- My Bella Basilicata: www.mybellabasilicata.com

## Calabria

* My BellaVita: www.mybellavita.com
* Bleeding Espresso: www.bleedingespresso.com

## Campania (including Amalfi)

* Ciao Amalfi: www.ciaoamalfi.com
* Napoli Unplugged: www.napoliunplugged.com

## Lazio (including Rome)

* Aglio, Olio e Peperoncino: www.aglioolioepeperoncino.com
* Browsing Rome: www.browsingrome.com
* Elizabeth Minchilli in Rome: www.elizabethminchilliinrome.com
* Heart Rome: www.heartrome.com
* Parla Food: www.parlafood.com
* Revealed Rome: www.revealedrome.com

## Liguria

* Beautiful Liguria: www.beautifuliguria.com
* Come To Liguria: www.come-to-liguria.com

## Lombardy (including Milan)

* Rubber Slippers in Italy: www.rubberslippersinitaly.wordpress.com

## Piedmont

* Bella Baita: www.bellabaitaview.blogspot.com

## Sicily

* Passage to Sicily: www.passagetosicily.com, Cultural Tours and Travel Planning
* Sicily Scene: www.sicilyscene.blogspot.com
* Soul of Sicily: www.soulofsicily.com, Cooking Holidays

## Tuscany (including Florence)

* At Home in Tuscany: www.athomeintuscany.org
* Ciao Lunigiana: www.ciaolunigiana.com
* Divina Cucina: www.divinacucina.com
* Freya's Florence: www.freyasflorence.com
* Girl in Florence: www.girlinflorence.com
* One Step Closer: www.onestepcloser.net
* Tuscan Traveler: www.tuscantraveler.com
* Un Prosecchino: www.unprosecchino.blogspot.co.uk
* Wishversilia: www.wishversilia.com

## Umbria

* Brigolante: www.brigolante.com/blog
* Madonna del Piatto: www.madonnadelpiatto.com

## Venice

* I Am Not Making This Up: www.iamnotmakingthisup.net
* Monica Cesarato: www.monicacesarato.com
* Venice Experience: www.theveniceexperience.blogspot.com
* Venezia Blog: www.veneziablog.blogspot.com

# Index

10 Corso Como  273

Abano  195
Abruzzo  248, 288
Accademia Nazionale di Santa
   Cecilia  361
accommodations
  Baglio Fontana  87
  Bagni di Pisa  194
  Belmond Villa San Michele  145
  Casa di Santa Brigida
    guesthouse  25
  Casa Guidi  104
  Casa Poli Hotel  119
  Castello di Procopio  51
  Castello di Santa Maria  140
  Domus Mariae  85
  Fonteverde Spa  193
  Grand Hotel Abano Terme  195
  Grand Hotel Besson  292
  Grand Hotel des Iles
    Borromees  158
  Grand Hotel et des Palmes  82
  Grand Hotel Ortigia Siracusa  85
  Grotta Giusti  193
  Hostel Cinque Terre  286
  Hotel Augustus  170
  Hotel Bagni Vecchi  291
  Hotel Campo Marzio  116
  Hotel Corallo  168
  Hotel Da Sauro  267
  Hotel de Russie  185
  Hotel La Palma  158
  Hotel Melody  341
  Hotel Posta Marcucci  192
  Hotel Posta Zirm  292
  Hotel Relais Ducale  251
  Il Falconiere  58
  I Sensi della Terra  190
  La Chiusa  316, 317
  L'Albergo della Regina
    Isabella  199
  La Libellula del Conero  172
  La Rosa Dei Venti  289
  Maliosa di Arienzo  174
  Masseria Torre Maizza  202
  Mezzatorre Resort and Spa  200
  Palazzo Ravizza  55
  Pellicano Hotel  149
  Pensione Tranchina  180
  Piccolo Hotel Luisa  296
  Pira & Figli Estate  232
  Ristorante Vittoria  172
  Stresa Apartments  158
  Terme dei Papi  189
  Terme Manzi Hotel and Spa  200
  Villa Brunella  260
  Villa Cimbrone  152
  Villa Scarpariello  319
Acqua Pazza  112
Ada's  174
Agerola  287
Ai Gondolieri  109
Ai Monasteri  257
Albergo Ristorante Garden  152
Alcamo  386

All' Arco 227
Alta Badia 291
Altamura 349
Alto Adige 291
Al Travato 51
Amalfi 270
Amalfi Coast 150, 160, 173, 250,
    270, 287, 357
Amedei 220
Ancona Jazz Festival 368
Andrea Palladio 113
Andrea Slitti 220
Angela Caputi 254
Antica Focacceria San Francesco 82
Antica Osteria ai Ranari 119
Antica Pizzeria Vicolo della
    Neve 161
Antiche Cantine Migliaccio 295
Antiche Carampane 65
Antico Caffè della Pace 212
Antico Caffè Greco 212
Antico Ristorante Sibilla 137
antique market 275
Antique Trade Market of
    Fontanellato 277
Aqua Flor 258
Arena Opera Festival 361
Arena Sferisterio 362
Arezzo 50, 275
Arezzo Antique Market 276
Arienzo 173
Armando al Pantheon 20, 256
Arnoldo e Battois 245
art restoration workshops 348
Auditorium Parco della Musica of
    Roma 361

Bacco e Arianna 126
Baci 221

Baglio Fontana 87
Bagni di Pisa 194
Bagni Medusa Genova 155
Bagno Vignoni 192
Baita de Mario 291
Baratti & Milano 214
Basilica dei Frari 65
Basilica di San Francesco 50
Basilica Santa Maria Maggiore 15
Bassano del Grappa 248
Baths of Caracalla 361
Bauer Palladio Spa 187
beaches
    Arienzo 173
    Beach of the Black Pebbles 172
    Fornillo 173
    Forte dei Marmi 169
    Grotta Urbani 171
    Le Due Sorelle 171
    Lido Grotta dei Delifini 167
    Rena Bianca 177
    San Michele 171
    Santa Maria 170
    Sassi Neri 172
    Scopello 179
    Spiaggia di Michelino 175
    Spiaggia Grande 173
Beach of the Black Pebbles 172
Belmond Villa San Michele 145
Bettini Germano 249
biking 283–285, 395
bird watching 180
boating 293–295
Boboli Gardens 101
Bomarzo 138
Bonajuto 222
Borghese Chapel 15
Borghese Gardens 30, 394
Bormio 290

Bramante Cloister 19
Brass Group, The 369
Brenta Canal 113
Brera 273
Brighenti 262
Buca di San Francesco 278
Buca di Sant'Antonio 285
Buonconvento 342
Burano 265

Caffarel 223
Caffè al Bicerin 214
Caffè del Doge 214
Caffè Farnese 25
Caffè Florian 213
Caffè Gilli 212
Caffè Pedrocchi 68
Caffè Reale 123
Caffè Sant'Eustachio 212
caffès
    Antico Caffè della Pace 212
    Antico Caffè Greco 212
    Baratti & Milano 214
    Caffè al Bicerin 214
    Caffè del Doge 214
    Caffè Farnese 25
    Caffè Florian 213
    Caffè Gilli 212
    Caffè Pedrocchi 68
    Caffè Reale 123
    Caffè Sant'Eustachio 212
    Ditta Artigianale 213
    Evaluna Libreria Café 72, 214
    Gran Caffè Gambrinus 214
    Gran Caffè Giubbe Rosse 213
    Lavazza 215
    Rosa Salva 213
    Tazza D'Oro 212
    Trussardi 272

Calcata 190
Caldogno 116
Caltagirone 249
Calzature Francesco da Firenze 241
Campo 54
Cantinetta dei Verrazzano 226
Cantinone Già Schiavi 109, 227
Capitoline Museums 7
Cappella Sansevero 74
Cappella Tornabuoni 37
Capri 259
Carapina 218
Carmagnola 263
Carrara 170
Carthusia 259, 260
Casa del Jazz 367
Casa del Vino 225
Casa di Livia 9
Casa di Santa Brigida guesthouse 25
Casa Don Puglisi 222
Casa Guidi 102, 104
Casa Poli Hotel 119
Casato Prime Donne 229
Cascate del Mulino 191
Castelli 248
Castello di Procopio 51
Castello di Santa Maria 140
Castello di Venere 387
Cave of the Cumaean Sibyl 76
Ceramica Artistica Solimene 250
Ceramicarte 250
Ceramiche d'Arte Pascal 251
ceramic painting classes 339
ceramics 247
Ceramic Workshop 334
Cetaria Dive Center 179
Chiesa di Santa Margherita 56
Chiesa di Santa Monaca 365
chocolate 219–223

chocolate festival 223
Chocolate Valley, The 220
chocolatiers
    Amedei 220
    Andrea Slitti 220
    Baci 221
    Bonajuto 222
    Caffarel 223
    Casa Don Puglisi 222
    Moriondo & Gariglio 220
    Paul De Bondt 220
    Peyrano 223
    Roberto Catinari 220
    Simone de Castro 220
    Vestri 220
    Vizio Virtù 221
Church of Santa Brigida a Campo
    de' Fiori 24
Church of Santa Maria dei
    Miracoli 61
Church of the Madonna
    dell'Arena 66
Church of the Most Holy
    Annunciation 42
Church of the New Saint Mary 37
churches
    Basilica di San Francesco 50
    Basilica Santa Maria Maggiore 15
    Borghese Chapel 15
    Cappella Sansevero 74
    Chiesa di Santa Monaca 365
    Church of Santa Brigida a
        Campo de' Fiori 24
    Church of Santa Maria dei
        Miracoli 61
    Church of the Madonna
        dell'Arena 66
    Church of the Most Holy
        Annunciation 42
    Church of the New Saint

    Mary 37
    Duomo Fresco 45
    Duomo (Ortygia) 84
    La Martorana 80
    Pio Monte della Misericordia 74
    Sacristy of Borromini–Piazza
        Navona 365
    Saint Agnes 23
    Saint Cecilia 21
    San Domenico Basilica 52
    San Francesco delle Donne 345
    Santa Maria and the Martyrs 16
    Santa Maria dell'Ammiraglio 80
    Santa Maria della Pace 18
    Santa Maria della Salute 60
    Santa Maria dello Spasimo 81
    Santa Maria in Cosmedin 17
    Santa Maria in Trastevere 18
    Santa Maria Novella 37
    Santa Maria Sopra Minerva
        17, 54
    Santissima Annunziata 42
    Scrovegni Chapel 66
    The Frari 63
Cinque Terre 286
Città Antiquaria 277
classical music 363–365
Cloister of Santa Chiara 73
Club Moritzino 292
Coast of the Gods 175
Coccaro Beach Club 204
COI Spa 254
Collegium Ducale 364
Colline Emiliane 95
Conero Regional Park 172
Contesta Rock Hair 186
Context Tours 227
cooking classes 230–231, 303–324
Cormons 378
Corso Como Outlet 273

Cortona 56
Costume Gallery 99
Cristina Linassi 263
Cul de Sac 225
Cumae 76
cycling 283–285, 395

Da Benito e Gilberto 13
Da Dora 78
Da Fiore 384
Da Gildo 98
Da Ivo 384
Daniela's Cooking School 305
Del Cambio 123
Deruta 249, 339
designer outlets 237
Diego Percossi Papi 253
Ditta Artigianale 213
diving 179
D Magazine Outlet 273
Domus Mariae 85
Dorsoduro 109
Duomo Fresco 45
Duomo (Ortygia) 84

Elena Abet 263
Emilia-Romagna 248
Emilio Gandolfi 267
Enna 127
Ensemble Antonio Vivaldi 364
Erice 386
Eurochocolate 223
Evaluna Libreria Café 72, 214
Excelsior Milano 272

Fabriano Boutiques 270
Faenza 248
Fanny 245
Fatamorgana 217

Fattoria Resta 230
Ferragamo Museum 240
Ferrara 367
Festival of Two Worlds 358
festivals 368
Fiaschetteria Toscana 62, 384
Fiesole 141
Flora Lastraioli 261
Florence 31, 37, 42, 102, 134,
    186, 212, 217, 220, 225, 241,
    243, 253, 258, 262, 266, 269,
    276, 297, 365
Flower Art Festival 134
Fonte Arethusa 83
Fonteverde Spa 193
Forio 198
Fornillo 173
Forte dei Marmi 169
Fossano 277
Fosso Bianco 192
Four Seasons Hotel Spa 187
Fra Angelico 56
Frari, The 63
Fratelli Piccini 253

Galleria Borghese 28
Galleria Regionale 81
Galleria, The 271
Gallery of Modern Art 101
Gardens at La Foce 143
Gardens of Augustus 260
Gelateria del Teatro 217
gelaterias
    Alaska 218
    Carapina 218
    Fatamorgana 217
    Gelateria del Teatro 217
    Il Doge 218
    Il Gelato Claudio Torce 217

La Carraia 218
La Mela Verde 218
Vivoli 217
gelato 216–218
Genzano 134
Ghirlandaio 38
Giachi Grazia Ricami 262
Giambattista Tiepolo 114
Giardino della Minerva 160
Giardino dell'Iris 134
Gilda Ristorante 170
GiNa 30
Giotto 37, 66
Giovanna Zanella Atelier 241
Giovanni Ascione e Figlio 255
Giulio Giannini & Figlio 269
Gli Ulivi 201
Gloria Astolfo 254
Gran Caffè Gambrinus 214
Gran Caffè Giubbe Rosse 213
Grand Hotel Abano Terme 195
Grand Hotel Besson 292
Grand Hotel des Iles Borromees 158
Grand Hotel et des Palmes 82
Grand Hotel Ortigia Siracusa 85
Gran Paradiso 288
Grazia Giachi 266
Gregory's Jazz Club 367
Grotta Giusti 193
Grotta Urbani 171
Group Biking Trips 284
group hikes 288
Gubbio 249, 251

Hadrian's Villa 137
Halloween 155
hiking 179, 286–289, 295
Hostel Cinque Terre 286
Hotel Augustus 170

Hotel Bagni Vecchi 291
Hotel Campo Marzio 116
Hotel Corallo 168
Hotel Da Sauro 267
Hotel de Russie 185
Hotel La Palma 158
Hotel Melody 341
Hotel Posta Marcucci 192
Hotel Posta Zirm 292
Hotel Relais Ducale 251
Hotel Sheraton Diana Majestic 273
House of Augustus 9

Ibiz 244
I Burattini di Carlo Piantadosi 371
Il Doge 218
Il Falconiere 58
Il Gabinetto Segreto 71
Il Gelato Claudio Torce 217
Il Gioiello 266
Il Goccetto 225
Il Mosaico 201
Il Pavone 269
Il Ritrovo 289
Il Santo Bevitore 101
Il Torchio 269
International School of Ceramic
    Art 339
Interpreti Veneziani 364
Intimissimi 261
Ischia 198
I Sensi della Terra 190
Isola Bella 156
Isola dei Pescatori 156, 157
Isola di Caprera 68
Isola Isabella 156
Isola Madre 156
Isola Maggiore 267
Italian Language Classes 351

Janiculum Hill 153
jazz 366–368
Jazz Club Ferrara 367
Jazz Club Torino 368
Jewel on the Arno 334
jewelry 252–256
jewelry making 334
Jolanda Artigianato 250

kayaking 294
Key Largo 55

La Botteguccia 242
La Cantina 227
La Cantina della Sapienza 75
La Carraia 218
lacemaking 264–267
Lace Museum 267
La Chiusa 316, 317
La Fenice 360
La Foce 143
La Fornace del Bucchero 250
La Grotta dei Germogli 190
La Kalsa 80
Lake Maggiore 156
La Libellula del Conero 172
La Martorana 80
La Mortella 198
landscape painting 342
L'Angolo Divino 224
La Perla 261
La Piccola Rosticceria 176
La Rosa Dei Venti 289
La Scala 360
La Sostanza 36
La Tiseneria 161
Laura Tonatto 257
Lavazza 215

La Vecchia Cucina di Soldano 48
Lazio 298
leather goods 243
leathermaking 332
Le Due Sorelle 171
Le Marche 368
Le Volpi e L'Uva 226
Lido Grotta dei Delifini 167
Liguria 153
L'Infiorata 134
lingerie 261
L'Ingerie D'Elia 262
Lippi 33
Lombardy 361
Loretta Caponi 262, 266
l'Ortiche 292
Lo Zingaro 288
Lo Zingaro National Park 179
Lucca 283
Lucca Jazz Donna 368
Luisa Beccaria 273

Macerata 362
Madonnina del Pescatore 378
Madova 244
Magnanelli 250
Maliosa di Arienzo 174
Mall, The 238
Mamma Agata Cooking Class 319
Manarola 286
Mantua 117
Marchesi di Barolo 231
Marches, The 362
Mariano Fortuny 110
Martina Vidal 265
Maskmaking 336
Massacio 37
Masseria Torre Maizza 202
Massimo Maria Melis 253

Mediterraneo 174
Mercato Centrale di San
    Lorenzo 308
Merchant of Venice, The 259
Mexico 214
Mezzatorre Resort and Spa 200
Michelangelo 12, 34
Michele Doardo Hair Stylist 187
Miele Gioielli 255
Milan 271, 314, 360, 372
Modica 222
Monsummano Terme 220
Montecatini Terme 192
Monte Conero 171
Montefollonico 316
Montepulciano 143
Monterchi 49
Montopoli 220
Moriondo & Gariglio 220
mosaic-making class 329
Museo Archeologico di
    Sperlonga 168
Museo Archeologico Nazionale 69
Museo Bottega del Maestro
    Alessandro Dari 254
Museo dei Ragazzi–Palazzo
    Vecchio 394
Museo Della Carta 270
Museo dell'Opera dell Duomo 47
Museo dell'Opera Metropolitana 52
Museo del Merletto 265
Museo Diocesano 56
Museo Regionale di Arte
    Mediovale 85
Museo San Marco 42, 381
Museum of the Madonna del
    Parto 49
museums
    Capitoline Museums 7
    Casa Guidi 102

Costume Gallery 99
Ferragamo Museum 240
Galleria Borghese 28
Galleria Regionale 81
Gallery of Modern Art 101
Lace Museum 267
Museo Archeologico di
    Sperlonga 168
Museo Archeologico
    Nazionale 69
Museo dei Ragazzi–Palazzo
    Vecchio 394
Museo Della Carta 270
Museo dell'Opera dell
    Duomo 47
Museo dell'Opera
    Metropolitana 52
Museo del Merletto 265
Museo Diocesano 56
Museo Regionale di Arte
    Mediovale 85
Museo San Marco 42, 381
Museum of the Madonna del
    Parto 49
National Gallery of Art 93
Palatine Gallery 101
Palazzo Abatellis 81
Palazzo Barberini 93
Palazzo Bellomo 85
Palazzo Fortuny 110
Palazzo Massimo alle Terme 10
Palazzo Nuovo 7
Palazzo Venier dei Leoni 107
Pitti Palace 99
Porcelain Museum 101
Silver Museum 101
Uffizi 31
Villa Farnesina 96
My Italian Family 402

Nannini 54
Naples 69, 73, 255, 277, 361, 370
National Antiquarian
Exhibition 277
National Gallery of Art 93
National Parks 288
Nervi 155
Nocelle 287
Noto 134

Obika 272
Officina Profumo Farmaceutica di
Santa Maria Novella 258
Offida 266
Oltrarno 101, 102, 365
Oltrarno Flea Market 276
opera 359–362
Opera dei Pupi di Vincenzo
Argento e figli 372
Opera Lombardia 361
Oplontis 124
Orchestra da Camera
Fiorentina 365
Ortygia 83
Orvieto 250
Osteria Belle Donne 41
Osteria Dedicato a Mio Padre 161
Osteria del Cinghiale Bianco 105

Palatine Gallery 101
Palatine Hill 9
Palazzina della Meridiana 99
Palazzo Abatellis 81
Palazzo Barberini 93
Palazzo Bellomo 85
Palazzo Ducale 117
Palazzo Fendi 245
Palazzo Fortuny 110
Palazzo Massimo alle Terme 10

Palazzo Nuovo 7
Palazzo Ravizza 55
Palazzo Reale 120
Palazzo Venier dei Leoni 107
Palermo 79, 205, 369, 372
Panificio di Stabile e Anselmo 180
Pantheon 16
Paolo Olbi 269
papermaking 268
Pape Satàn 178
Parchi di Nervi 153
Parco Villa Grimaldi 154
Parghelia 175
Park of the Monsters 138
Pasticceria Maria Grammatico 387
Patrizia Pepe 273
Peggy Guggenheim Collection 106
Pellicano Hotel 149
Pensione Tranchina 180
perfume 257–259
Perugia 221, 345
Perugia Duomo 345
Perugino 118
Pesaro 362
Petrocchi 241
Peyrano 223
Phlegrean Fields 76
Piazza Archimede 83
Piazza Armerina 129
Piazza Bellini 69
Piazza del Campo 52
Piazza Farnese 25
Piazza Pretoria 79
Piazzola sul Brenta 276
Piccolo Hotel Luisa 296
Piedmont 231
Piero della Francesca 49, 50
Pietrasanta 170
Pietro da Cortona 93

Pietro Lombardo 61
Pio Monte della Misericordia 74
Pira & Figli Estate 232
Pisa 220
Piscine Carletti 188
Pistoia 220
Pitti Palace 99
Pizzeria Bellini 72
Pompeii 126
Pontedera 220
Ponte Milvio Antique Market 276
Ponza 295
Porcelain Museum 101
Pork's 309
Porta Margherita 57
Positano 173, 242
Prada 271
Prato 45
Procacci 242
Puglia 202, 348
puppet shows 370–371

Quadrilatero della Moda 272

Rapallo 267
Raphael 34, 94, 97
Ravello 150, 251, 319
Ravello Festival 357
Rena Bianca 177
restaurants
    Acqua Pazza 112
    Ada's 174
    Ai Gondolieri 109
    Albergo Ristorante Garden 152
    Al Travato 51
    Antica Focacceria San
        Francesco 82
    Antica Osteria ai Ranari 119
    Antica Pizzeria Vicolo della

Neve 161
Antiche Carampane 65
Antico Ristorante Sibilla 137
Armando al Pantheon 20, 256
Bacco e Arianna 126
Bagni Medusa Genova 155
Baita de Mario 291
Belmond Villa San Michele 145
Buca di San Francesco 278
Buca di Sant'Antonio 285
Club Moritzino 292
Colline Emiliane 95
Da Benito e Gilberto 13
Da Dora 78
Da Fiore 384
Da Gildo 98
Da Ivo 384
Del Cambio 123
Fiaschetteria Toscana 62, 384
Gilda Ristorante 170
GiNa 30
Gli Ulivi 201
Halloween 155
Hotel Da Sauro 267
Hotel Sheraton Diana
    Majestic 273
Il Mosaico 201
Il Ritrovo 289
Il Santo Bevitore 101
Isola di Caprera 68
La Cantina della Sapienza 75
La Grotta dei Germogli 190
La Piccola Rosticceria 176
La Sostanza 36
La Vecchia Cucina di Soldano 48
l'Ortiche 292
Madonnina del Pescatore 378
Marchesi di Barolo 231
Mediterraneo 174

Nannini 54
Obika 272
Osteria Belle Donne 41
Osteria Dedicato a Mio
    Padre 161
Osteria del Cinghiale Bianco 105
Pape Satàn 178
Pizzeria Bellini 72
Pork's 309
Ristorante Al Fogher 129
Ristorante Belvedere 158
Ristorante Ca'Vignotto 395
Ristorante Federico da
    Montefeltro 251
Ristorante Guidoriccio 55
Ristorante L'Ancora 85
Ristorante Museo Canova
    Tadolini 263
Ristorante President 126
Ristorante Villa Brunella 260
Rocco's 381
Roscioli 25, 30
Scaturchio 75
Sorbillo 75
Terre e Domus Enoteca della
    Provincia 11
Tramonto Bistrot 168
Trattoria Cibreo 246
Trattoria Da Gemma 270
Trattoria dal Billy 287
Trattoria Mario 44
Trattoria Molin Vecio 116
Uliassi 378
Vineria Le Potazzine 231
Rialto 364
Rialto Bridge 59
Rialto Market 383
Rinascente 272
Ristorante Al Fogher 129

Ristorante Belvedere 158
Ristorante Ca'Vignotto 395
Ristorante Federico da
    Montefeltro 251
Ristorante Guidoriccio 55
Ristorante L'Ancora 85
Ristorante Museo Canova
    Tadolini 263
Ristorante President 126
Ristorante Villa Brunella 260
Ristorante Vittoria 172
Riviera del Conero 171
Roberto Catinari 220
Rocco's 381
Roman Forum 8
Rome 7, 12, 15, 20, 21, 93, 96,
    134, 185, 212, 217, 220, 224,
    241, 244, 252, 257, 262, 276,
    305, 329, 361, 365, 367, 371
Rosa Salva 213
Roscioli 25, 30
Roseto di Roma Capitale 134
Rossini Opera Festival 362
Row Venice 293
Rucellai Chapel 40

Sacred Grove 138
Sacristy of Borromini–Piazza
    Navona 365
Saint Agnes 23
Saint Cecilia 21
Salerno 160
Salvador Dali 139
Salvatore Ferragamo 239
San Carlino 372
San Carlo 361
Sancesario Bijoux 253
San Domenico Basilica 52
San Filippo 191

San Francesco delle Donne  345
San Lorenzo market  44
San Marco  364
San Michele  171
Santa Caterina Chapel  52
Santa Croce  246
Santa Felicitá  42
Santa Maria  170
Santa Maria and the Martyrs  16
Santa Maria dell'Ammiraglio  80
Santa Maria della Pace  18
Santa Maria della Salute  60
Santa Maria dello Spasimo  81
Santa Maria in Cosmedin  17
Santa Maria in Trastevere  18
Santa Maria Novella  37
Santa Maria Sopra Minerva  17, 54
Sant' Antonio in Polesine  381
Santa Teresa di Gallura  177
Sant'Erasmo  395
Santissima Annunziata  42
Santuario e Casa di Santa
    Caterina  52
Sarzana  277
Sassi Neri  172
Saturnia Terme  191
Sauze d'Oulx  292
Sbigoli Terrecotte  334
Scaturchio  75
Scissor Staircase  121
Scopello  179
Scrovegni Chapel  66
Scuola del Cuoio  243, 332
Scuola San Rocco  64
Secret Cabinet, The  71
Segesta  86
Segesta Temple  87
Segreta Malizia  262
Senigalia  378
Sentiero Azzuro  286

Sentiero degli Dei  287
Settignano  143
shopping
    10 Corso Como  273
    Ai Monasteri  257
    Angela Caputi  254
    antique market  275
    Antique Trade Market of
        Fontanellato  277
    Aqua Flor  258
    Arnoldo e Battois  245
    Bettini Germano  249
    Brighenti  262
    Calzature Francesco da
        Firenze  241
    Carmagnola  263
    Carthusia  259
    Ceramica Artistica Solimene  250
    Ceramicarte  250
    Ceramiche d'Arte Pascal  251
    Città Antiquaria  277
    COI Spa  254
    Corso Como Outlet  273
    Cristina Linassi  263
    designer outlets  237
    Diego Percossi Papi  253
    D Magazine Outlet  273
    Elena Abet  263
    Emilio Gandolfi  267
    Excelsior Milano  272
    Fabriano Boutiques  270
    Fanny  245
    Ferragamo  241
    Fratelli Piccini  253
    Giachi Grazia Ricami  262
    Giovanna Zanella Atelier  241
    Giovanni Ascione e Figlio  255
    Giulio Giannini & Figlio  269
    Gloria Astolfo  254
    Grazia Giachi  266

Ibiz 244
Il Gioiello 266
Il Pavone 269
Il Torchio 269
Jolanda Artigianato 250
Lace Museum 267
La Fornace del Bucchero 250
Laura Tonatto 257
L'Ingerie D'Elia 262
Loretta Caponi 262, 266
Luisa Beccaria 273
Madova 244
Magnanelli 250
Martina Vidal 265
Massimo Maria Melis 253
Mercato Centrale di San
  Lorenzo 308
Miele Gioielli 255
Museo Bottega del Maestro
  Alessandro Dari 254
Museo del Merletto 265
National Antiquarian
  Exhibition 277
Officina Profumo Farmaceutica
  di Santa Maria Novella 258
Oltrarno Flea Market 276
Palazzo Fendi 245
Paolo Olbi 269
Patrizia Pepe 273
Petrocchi 241
Piazzola sul Brenta 276
Ponte Milvio Antique
  Market 276
Prada 271
Rialto Market 383
Rinascente 272
Sancesario Bijoux 253
San Lorenzo market 44
Scuola del Cuoio 243
Segreta Malizia 262

Sirni 244
Stellini 262
Studio Gioielleria R.
  Quattrocolo 252
The Galleria 271
The Mall 238
The Merchant of Venice 259
Tragicomica 336
Ubaldo Grazia 249
Venetian Dreams 255
Venetian Food Shopping
  Center 311
Venetia Studium 112
Villa Comunale Antique
  Market 277
Sicily 247, 249, 299, 372, 385
Siena 52
Silver Museum 101
Simone de Castro 220
Simonetta Pini 186
Siracusa 372
Sirni 244
Sirolo 171
Sito Archeologico di Cuma 77
skiing 290–292
Sodoma 97
Sorbillo 75
Sorgeto 199
Sorpasso 14
Sorrento 255
SoulSpace 186
Spanish Chapel 40
spas
  Bagni di Pisa 194
  Bauer Palladio Spa 187
  Fonteverde Spa 193
  Four Seasons Hotel Spa 187
  Grotta Giusti 193
  Hammam (Palermo) 205
  Hotel de Russie 185

L'Albergo della Regina
   Isabella 199
Masseria Torre Maizza 202
Mezzatorre Resort and Spa 200
Piscine Carletti 188
Poseidon Thermal Park 199
San Filippo 191
Saturnia Terme 191
Sorgeto 199
SoulSpace 186
Spazio Beauty 186
Terme dei Papi 189
Terme Manzi Hotel and Spa 200
Terme Tettuccio 192
Venezia Spa 196
Spazio Beauty 186
Spello 134
Sperlonga 167
Spiaggia di Michelino 175
Spiaggia Grande 173
Spoleto 287, 358
Stellini 262
Stresa 158
Stresa Apartments 158
Studio Cassio 329
Studio Gioielleria R.
   Quattrocolo 252

Tarot Garden–Capalbio 146
Tazza D'Oro 212
Teatro Alle Cave 172
Teatro Colla 372
Teatro Cortesi 172
Teatro dei Pupi 372
Teatro Malibran 360
Teatro Olimpico 113
Teatro Regio 360
Teatro Verde 371
Temple of Segesta 86

Temple of the Vestal Virgins 8
Terme dei Papi 189
Terme Manzi Hotel and Spa 200
Terme Tettuccio 192
Terre e Domus Enoteca della
   Provincia 11
Testaccio market 306
Tivoli 135
Tomb of the Queen of Sirolo 172
Torino 368
Torre Annunziata 124
Tower Bar 41
Tragicomica workshop 336
Tramonto Bistrot 168
Trastevere 21
Trattoria Cibreo 246
Trattoria Da Gemma 270
Trattoria dal Billy 287
Trattoria Mario 44
Trattoria Molin Vecio 116
Tropea 175, 322
Trussardi 272
Turin 120, 214, 222, 360
Tuscan Women Cook 316
Tuscany 169, 220, 229, 368

Ubaldo Grazia 249
Uffizi 31
Uliassi 378
Umbria Jazz Festival 368

Val d'Orcia 143
Venetian Dreams 255
Venetian Food Shopping Center 311
Venetia Studium 112
Veneto 249
Venezia Spa 196
Venice 59, 66, 106, 110, 187, 213,
   218, 221, 226, 241, 245, 254,

259, 263, 265, 269, 311, 336, 360, 363, 383, 395
Verona 361
Vestri 220
Via Condotti 263
Vicenza 113
Vietri Sul Mare 250
Villa Cimbrone 150, 152
Villa Comunale Antique Market 277
Villa Contarini 276
Villa d'Este 135
Villa Farnesina 96
Villa Gamberaia 143
Villa Medici 141
Villa of Mysteries 126
Villa Romana del Casale 127
Villa Rotonda 113
Villa Scarpariello 319
Villa Valmarana ai Nani 113
Vineria Le Potazzine 231
Vino Roma 225
Viterbo 188
Vivoli 217
Vizio Virtù 221
Volcano Solfatara 78

weddings 397
wine bars
  All' Arco 227
  Cantinetta dei Verrazzano 226
  Cantinone già Schiavi 109
  Cantinone Già Schiavi 227
  Casa del Vino 225
  Cul de Sac 225
  Il Goccetto 225
  Key Largo 55
  La Cantina 227
  L'Angolo Divino 224
  Le Volpi e L'Uva 226
  Sorpasso 14
  Vino Roma 225
winemaking 228
wineries 228, 378
  Casato Prime Donne 229
  Fattoria Resta 230
  Marchesi di Barolo 231
  Pira & Figli Estate 232
wine therapy 195
wine walks 227

Yamamay 261
yoga 297–299

# Acknowledgments

Why do authors so often leave husbands till the end of these sections? In my book, he's first:

With thanks to my dearest one, Jonathon Leifer, for EVERYTHING—that includes Latin translations and chocolate deliveries during this process.

Every writer should be so lucky to have such an angel-of-a-sister as Patti Sullivan, my first draft reader whose smart editing and encouragement were invaluable. Thanks to all my family, whose loving support I feel across the miles and from those in *Paradiso*. Particularly for help in the research process, I thank my father, Robert Van Benthuysen, who showed me by example what that's all about.

At the Italian Government Tourist Board in Los Angeles, Emanuela Boni has been a blessing and a joy to work with. For her assistance, along with that of the wonderful people in the L.A. office and the Italian Government Tourist Board in New York (the kind-hearted Marzia Bortolin and Riccardo Strano), I give my heartfelt thanks.

To each of you who's traveled with me somewhere along this journey to write this book, I raise a glass, with everlasting gratitude for what you've done to help make it happen: Gioia Acon, Maxine Albert, Sheila Balter, Irma Becerra, Risa Bell, Alessandra Bolzagni, Baronessa Cecilia Bellelli, Joann Biondi, Lauren Birmingham,

438

Liz Brewster, Tita Cahn, Sheryl Cancelleri, Elena Cappalini, Iris Carulli, Sara Chamberlin, Erin Champion, Maria Laura Chiacchio, Jill Clark, Paul and Suzanne Codiga, Rosanne Cofoid, Carol Coviello-Malzone, Sandy Cutrone, Cornelia Danielson, the D'Aquilas, Bruno Dascanio, Betsy deFries, Susan Engbrecht, Robin Epstein, Eurofly, Maureen B. Fant, Babs Fasano, Cydney Fowler, Elizabeth Garat, Gina Garner, Deb Gaughan, Julie Genovesi, Dorris Goodrich, Marlene Grimaldi, Valentina Grossi Orzalesi, Inge Hansen, Heather Hanson, Anne Heck, Karen Herbst, Julia Bolton Holloway, Marina Innocenzi, Barbara Kossy, Hope Levy, Maddine Insalaco, Chiara Lima, Maria Lisella, Jo Ann Locktov, Lauren Maher, Joe Maniscalco, Lori Mayfield, Megan McDonnell, Nan McElroy, Petulia Melideo, Freya Middleton, Joanne Morgante, Mario and Lexi Marmorstein, Kathy McCabe, Mona Lou McConnaughey, Yan Moati, Vittorio Muolo, Ekta Nadeau, Rachel Newman, Rachel Norman, Wendy O'Dea, Sandy and Jessica Osceola, Kristin Overn, Tom Paris, Tania Pascuzzi, Lisa Pieracini, Veronica Puleo, June Rogovin, Meredith Rolley, Phil and Monica Rosenthal, Sirpa Salenius, Voni Schaff, Jessie Sholl, Erin Shachory, Arthur Schwartz, Bryna Skuro, Jean Sondhi, Fiorella Squillante, Kristin Stasiowski, Jessica Stewart, Adrienne Storey, Bill and Patty Sutherland, Alexa Taylor, Anna Lisa Tempestini, Elfride and Bob Vaughan, Monica Vidoni, Tina Villano Chase, Joe Vinson, Margaret Vos, Wendy Walsh, Florence Welborn, and Louise Wright.

I'm thankful for the women who paved the way: Patricia Schultz with *1000 Places to See Before You Die*, and Stephanie Elizondo Griest, with *100 Places Every Woman Should Go*. And for all the writers out there who've guided me in my travels and writing about Italy.

I am especially grateful for James O'Reilly and Larry Habegger of Travelers' Tales, not only for this book, but for being editors who keep us travelers inspired with their essay series. Heartfelt thanks also to Susan Brady, the magician of production over there. And *mille grazie* to Whitney Hickey, my extraordinary intern, for wonderful assistance.

Thanks to Saint Anthony, who has helped me find words.

Always, I thank the people of Italy who have welcomed me with their open hearts.

# About the Author

Susan Van Allen has written about Italian travel for National Public Radio, *AFAR*, *Town and Country*, *Tastes of Italia*, and many other publications. She has also written for TV, on the staff of the Emmy Award winning sitcom, *Everybody Loves Raymond*. Along with writing, she designs and hosts *Golden Weeks in Italy: For Women Only Tours*. When she's not traveling off to Italy, she lives in Los Angeles with her husband. More at www.susanvanallen.com